Public Lands
and the U.S. Economy

Westview Replica Editions

The concept of Westview Replica Editions is a response to the continuing crisis in academic and informational publishing. Library budgets for books have been severely curtailed. Ever larger portions of general library budgets are being diverted from the purchase of books and used for data banks, computers, micromedia, and other methods of information retrieval. Interlibrary loan structures further reduce the edition sizes required to satisfy the needs of the scholarly community. Economic pressures on the university presses and the few private scholarly publishing companies have severely limited the capacity of the industry to properly serve the academic and research communities. As a result, many manuscripts dealing with important subjects, often representing the highest level of scholarship, are no longer economically viable publishing projects--or, if accepted for publication, are typically subject to lead times ranging from one to three years.

Westview Replica Editions are our practical solution to the problem. We accept a manuscript in camera-ready form, typed according to our specifications, and move it immediately into the production process. As always, the selection criteria include the importance of the subject, the work's contribution to scholarship, and its insight, originality of thought, and excellence of exposition. The responsibility for editing and proofreading lies with the author or sponsoring institution. We prepare chapter headings and display pages, file for copyright, and obtain Library of Congress Cataloging in Publication Data. A detailed manual contains simple instructions for preparing the final typescript, and our editorial staff is always available to answer questions.

The end result is a book printed on acid-free paper and bound in sturdy library-quality soft covers. We manufacture these books ourselves using equipment that does not require a lengthy make-ready process and that allows us to publish first editions of 300 to 600 copies and to reprint even smaller quantities as needed. Thus, we can produce Replica Editions quickly and can keep even very specialized books in print as long as there is a demand for them.

About the Book and Editors

Public Lands and the U.S. Economy:
Balancing Conservation and Development
edited by
George M. Johnston and Peter M. Emerson

Current law requires the federal government to fulfill a broad spectrum of responsibilities in managing public lands; to protect and conserve the environment; to foster the appropriate development of marketable commodities; to preserve wilderness areas, wildlife habitats, and unique historical sites; and to encourage public participation in land-use and management decisions. There is no consensus, however, on the best ways to establish a balance among these priorities when serious conflicts arise.

This book presents a wide-ranging discussion of the means by which lands and resources administered by the Forest Service and the Bureau of Land Management can better serve present and future needs for environmental preservation and resource development. The contributors consider public and private interests in the federal lands in light of political realities and uncertainties, giving particular attention to efficiency-versus-equity issues, privatization, fair market value, and the income-producing potential of publicly owned assets. Major sections of the book focus on timber, nonfuel minerals, rangelands, and energy resources. Based on a recent conference sponsored by The Wilderness Society, the book reflects the views of conservationists, scholars, industry representatives, and state and federal officials.

George M. Johnston is associate professor of natural resources at Eastern Oregon State College. Peter M. Emerson is director of the Economic Policy Department of The Wilderness Society.

Public Lands
and the U.S. Economy
Balancing Conservation and Development

edited by George M. Johnston
and Peter M. Emerson

Proceedings of a conference sponsored by
The Wilderness Society

Westview Press / Boulder, Colorado

Copyright © 1984 by Westview Press, Inc.

Published in 1984 in the United States of America by
    Westview Press, Inc.
    5500 Central Avenue
    Boulder, Colorado 80301
    Frederick A. Praeger, President and Publisher

Library of Congress Catalog Card Number: 83-051263
ISBN: 0-86531-819-0

Printed and bound in the United States of America

10 9 8 7 6 5 4 3 2 1

Contents

PART 4: RANGELAND ISSUES

Tables and Figures

Foreword

Over the past two decades, Americans have come to
expect -- in fact, to insist -- that the decisions of
their government and business leaders contribute both
to steady improvements in environmental quality and to
responsible economic growth. Governor Snelling of
Vermont aptly reflected the judgment of most Americans
when he said, "It isn't a question of balance between
environmental protection and (economic) development
being a good thing -- it's the only thing." While
final outcomes cannot be predicted, it is certain that
expanding environmental awareness has thrust the
activist environmental organizations into an important
and visible national leadership position.

Concern about the environment has become an
integral part of our everyday thinking and modern
lifestyle. Conservation activists have played a
significant role in shaping a society in which Americans are now deeply conscious of environmental
problems and the vital importance of preserving this
country's natural heritage. Now that the nation has
attained this critical threshold, we conservationists
must turn our attention to the difficult challenge of
helping to strike a balance between environmental
needs, on the one hand, and the goals of long-term
economic growth and equity, on the other hand. I
believe this challenge can be meet, but it will
require access to reliable scientific information,
interpreted and presented in a manner relevant to
solving today's problems as well as planning for the
future. In this spirit, The Wilderness Society -- the
conservation community's "specialist" on public land
issues -- is pleased to make available the proceedings
of its first national conference.

The Wilderness Society works to broaden awareness
of man's relationship with the natural environment, to
preserve America's wildlands, and to assure that all
federal lands are managed for the public good. The
fundamental philosophy of The Society is most
eloquently expressed in the writings of our
co-founder, ecologist Aldo Leopold, who called for a
"land ethic" which "simply enlarges the boundaries of
man's community to include soils, waters, plants, and
animals, or collectively, the land." Our conviction,
founded in Leopold's "ecological conscience," is that

the land is not a commodity to be carelessly used and used up, but a resource to be cherished and used wisely as an inheritance. It is important to remember that vast wildlands gave our nation life and prosperity and have profoundly influenced the character of the American people.

For a land ethic to take root, to guide our nation in the wise use of natural resources, environmentalists must fulfill a responsibility both to society and to the land. We must participate as full partners with government and industry groups in developing factual arguments, assessing the benefits and costs of land use decisions, formulating questions for future research and debate, and seeking the elusive balance among competing goals. As you investigate the many ideas presented in this volume, I ask only that you recall the succinct wisdom of Adlai Stevenson's statement, "We travel together, passengers on a little space ship, dependent on its vulnerable reserves...(and) preserved from annihilation only by the care, the work, and, I will say, the love we give our fragile craft."

William A. Turnage, Director
The Wilderness Society

Preface

Modern-day public land law requires the federal government to pursue a broad spectrum of goals -- to protect the environment and promote conservation; to allow the appropriate development of marketable commodities; to preserve wilderness, wildlife habitat, amenity values, and unique historical sites; and to seek public participation in land use and management decisions. Yet there is no consensus on the best means of establishing a balance among these goals when serious conflicts arise. Instead, there is a growing distrust of the scientific and technical expertise upon which public land management is built, a feeling that "single interest" politics is too often the deciding factor in important decisions, and, once again, a questioning of the federal government's role as landlord. In the words of Dr. Marion Clawson, a distinguished public lands scholar, "...major changes in federal land management seem likely in the future... (however) the direction and specifics of the change are less clear."

The federal government owns about one-third of the onshore land area of the country and over forty percent of the land in seven western states and Alaska. The demands placed upon these public lands have increased steadily and dramatically since World War II. The increased demand is not only for resource commodities but also for recreation, preservation, wildlife, and wilderness. Population growth, rising incomes, more leisure time, and a broadening interest in our natural heritage will certainly increase future demand for the amenity, cultural, and commodity values of the federal lands.

The contributors to this book, the proceedings of a national conference sponsored by The Wilderness Society's Economic Policy Department, provide a wide-ranging discussion of the means by which lands and resources administered by the Forest Service and Bureau of Land Management can better serve the present and future needs of all U.S. citizens. Public and private interests in the federal lands are thoroughly investigated in the context of political realities and uncertainties that will affect these lands. Particular attention is directed to efficiency versus equity considerations, privatization, fair market value, and the income-producing potential of publicly owned assets. Major sections deal with federal ownership and management of timber, nonfuel mineral, rangeland, and energy resources.

The many questions and issues addressed here are of interest to all citizens concerned with the use and management of their federal lands. For example: Does wilderness preservation "lock up" significant resources needed for the economic development of the country? What is the effect on environmental and wildlife objectives of range and timber management policies that may subsidize commodity use? How do current management practices under federal ownership affect resource trade-offs? In sum, the proceedings document an exchange of new ideas on the best means of balancing our conservation and preservation goals with our resource development needs.

This book is organized into five major parts. Part 1 explores contemporary economic and political issues affecting federal land management, including the privatization debate. Parts 2 through 5 are commodity-specific sessions on timber, nonfuel minerals, rangeland, and energy resources, respectively. Each of the five major parts includes one or more overview papers prepared by nationally-recognized public land experts. The overview papers are critiqued and supplemented by contrasting papers and discussion comments.

Part 1, entitled "Three Perspectives on the Public Lands," begins with Daniel W. Bromley's presentation of a broad conceptual framework for judging competing views on public and private interests in the federal lands. Bromley focuses especially on the analytical imprecision of the opponents of continued public administration of federal lands. In discussion, Bromley is criticized for ignoring certain practical land management problems. Also, major components of the Reagan administration's Asset Management Program are outlined. Next, John A. Baden and Dean Lueck present an alternative approach to wilderness management based on private property rights. Their premise is that the goals of conserving resources and anticipating future environmental problems are more likely to be met by assigning private property rights than by giving the responsibilities to government bureaucracies. In two subsequent papers, the privatization alternative is criticized by an economist for ignoring the consequences of imperfect information, monopoly power, and externalities. An environmentalist argues that it is essential for the government to protect the "public trust" in wilderness. Part 1 concludes with D. Michael Harvey's overview of public land politics in the 1980s and beyond. Harvey emphasizes that the changing demographics of the west are altering the traditional uses of federal lands, but that these changes can be accommodated within existing public land law. The role of the states in federal land management decisions is explored by a senior official from Montana.

Part 2, "Timber Issues," presents two major papers evaluating the economic implications of federal ownership and management of timber. William F. Hyde explores the consequences of selling federal timber land on the federal treasury, the local tax base, and environmental preservation. David H. Jackson carefully evaluates various management alternatives and concludes that federal timber management costs quite often exceed income in the west. Subsequent presentations expand the scope of the debate to include employment and community stability and to provide important historical perspectives on timber management and environmental concerns.

Part 3, "Nonfuel Mineral Issues," begins with Bruce C. Netschert's review of the Mining Law of 1872 and other issues affecting the management of nonfuel minerals on federal lands. Netschert recommends a leasing system for all nonfuel minerals and calls for the collection of reliable information on mineral resource endowments. In discussion, the views of the mining industry are presented, and specific concerns about national security and federal land withdrawals are examined.

Part 4, "Rangeland Issues," centers around William E. Martin's analysis of the economics of federal rangeland policy. Martin provides a brief description of the federal range and examines its economic role in livestock production and recreation. He concludes that the economic efficiency and equity issues are not as easily resolved as proponents of privatization or the Sagebrush Rebellion might argue.

Part 5, "Energy Resource Issues," begins with John J. Schanz's extensive taxonomy of public land management decisions related to energy resources. Included in the discussion of federal royalties, leasing practices, and efforts to achieve fair market value are estimates of the relative magnitude of onshore deposits of petroleum, natural gas, and coal. Additional papers discuss the multiple use mandate of federal lands and alternative sources of energy, an industry perspective on oil shale development, and the role of state and local governments in energy and mineral development.

Finally, we wish to express our sincere appreciation to the many individuals and institutions who contributed their time and resources to this project.

Charles M. Clusen, Rebecca Leet, and Patricia O. Attkisson of The Wilderness Society were especially helpful in planning the conference. A generous grant from The George Gund Foundation supported the conference, held in November, 1982, at Airlie House in Warrenton, Virginia. More than 130 people, including conservationists, business executives, academicians, government land managers, and public policy officials, participated in the conference. Gaylord A. Nelson, Joseph L. Fisher, Frank Gregg, Marion Clawson, Arnold W. Bolle, Charles H. Stoddard, and Robert O. Blake shared their unique knowledge of conservation issues and offered counsel throughout the conference. This proceedings volume was made possible through a grant from the American Telephone and Telegraph Company. Patricia O. Attkisson coordinated the editing and preparation of the proceedings.

George M. Johnston
Associate Professor
Eastern Oregon State College

Peter M. Emerson
Economic Policy Department
The Wilderness Society

Acronyms

ABA	American Bar Association
ACA	Angler's Cooperative Association
ACE	Allowable Cut Effect
ANILCA	Alaska National Interest Lands Conservation Act
AMC	American Mining Congress
API	American Petroleum Institute
ASCS	Agricultural Stabilization and Conservation Service
ATV	All-Terrain Vehicles
AUM	Animal Unit Month
AUY	Animal Unit Year
BLM	Bureau of Land Management
BTU	British Thermal Unit
DOE	Department of Energy
DOI	Department of the Interior
EIS	Environmental Impact Statement
EMB	Energy Mobilization Board
EPA	Environmental Protection Agency
FIP	Forest Incentives Program
FS	Forest Service
FWS	Fish and Wildlife Service
GAO	General Accounting Office
IP	International Paper company
JRP	Joint Review Process
L&WCF	Land and Water Conservation Fund
LNG	Liquified Natural Gas
MLA	Mineral Leasing Act
MOU	Memorandum of Understanding
NEPA	National Environmental Protection Act
NFMA	National Forest Management Act
NPR-A	National Petroleum Reserve - Alaska
NPS	National Parks Service
NRDC	Natural Resources Defense Council
NWPS	National Wilderness Preservation System
OCS	Outer Continental Shelf
OPEC	Organization of Petroleum Exporting Countries
OTA	Office of Technology Assessment
PILT	Payment-In-Lieu-of-Taxes
PTA	Parrent/Teachers Association
RAREII	Roadless Area Review and Evaluation II

RCT	Regional Coal Teams
RMP	Regional Management Plan
RPA	Forest and Rangeland Renewable Resources Planning Act of 1974
ROST	Regional Oil Shale Team (CO, UT, WY)
SIPI	Scientisits' Institute for Public Information
SMCRA	Surface Mining Control and Reclamation Act
SNG	Synthetic Natural Gas
TWS	The Wilderness Society
USBM	United States Bureau of Mines
USDA	United States Department of Agriculture
USDI	United States Department of the Interior
USFS	United States Forest Service
USGS	United States Geological Survey

Part 1

Three Perspectives
on the Public Lands

1
Public and Private Interests in the Federal Lands: Toward Conciliation

Daniel W. Bromley

Abstract: This paper charges opponents of public administration of the federal lands with failure to be precise in their use of the term "efficiency" and presents an alternative conceptual view of the economics of public choice. The author maintains that the use of incorrectly understood "efficiency" criteria and analysis biased towards monetary values and maximized production disregards many of the goods and services from the federal lands. He contends that concerns for distributive ends, procedural and historical principles, and nonmonetizable, discontinuous, and complex values associated with personal rights, public goods, and communitarian and ecological goals are central to federal land decisions. Furthermore, he argues that: market processes are derivative of a larger social system and do not supersede that system; there are an infinite number of output combinations from the federal lands that will qualify as being socially efficient; and traditional arguments for private enterprise are prejudiced, not soundly based on any analytic structure, and can be of little help in resolving current and future issues associated with administration of federal lands.

Key words: outcome efficiency, process efficiency, privatization, interests and rights.

INTRODUCTION

Recent political interest in the federal lands has generated a long-overdue reconsideration of the

Daniel W. Bromley is professor and chair, Department of Agricultural Economics, University of Wisconsin-Madison.

3

role of the public sector in natural resource management. In our state-capitalist economy, we should pause from time to time to assess the behavior and the performance of both the public and the private sectors. The current political discussion has tended to focus on two aspects of public sector activity: (1) the balance between what is termed preservation or conservation and those market-oriented activities that result in such tangible outputs as oil, minerals, livestock forage, and timber; and (2) the entrepreneurial agility of those public agencies responsible for managing the federal lands. The first has been referred to as a "need to restore balance" to federal land policies by swinging the pendulum away from conservation and toward production activities. The second often centers on the ostensible need to combat the "waste, fraud, and abuse" that is said to be inevitable in any decision-making organization that is not privately owned.

As an economist whose early education concentrated on natural resource management, I take more than passing interest in both the political discussion described above, and in the role of professional economists as presumed scientific arbiters. My experience in a policy analysis role in Washington, D.C. -- brief as it was -- revealed that economists are only considered useful in a debate if they can produce the "correct" numbers to substantiate a foregone conclusion. If they cannot, then economics is dismissed as witchcraft or as the equivalent of astrology -- or, worse yet, sociology.

This preoccupation with economics as outcome rather than process contributed to the rise of benefit-cost analysis as a decision aid in matters of collective choice. And, it persists today in the form of arguments that the social dividend is diminished by the continued federal administration of western lands.

Today I will present a conceptual view of the economics of collective choice over federal land issues that I hope will give you a framework within which you might judge for yourself the competing views on the public and private interest in the federal lands. A conceptual framework is needed to point up the failure of the opponents of continued public administration of the federal lands to be precise in their use of the term "efficiency" when they charge that federal lands produce an inefficient level of outputs, and that the administration of such lands is inefficient (wasteful) because of bureaucrats intent on self aggrandizement. This sloppy terminology must be clarified if we are to progress in the dialogue over social benefits of alternative institutional arrangements.

ON ECONOMIC EFFICIENCY

Outcome Efficiency

Let us start with the notion of outcome efficiency. With outcome efficiency we are interested in
securing a total product mix in society that will keep
producers and consumers of the various outputs in
equilibrium. While to a non-economist this sounds
formidable, it simply means that, if too much livestock forage is being produced relative to timber,
then market prices will upset this equilibrium. An
output reallocation away from livestock forage and
toward timber would increase outcome efficiency.

While those critical of current federal lands
administration seldom couch their arguments in such
terms, they imply as much. And, economists associated
with the privatization movement are not averse to
using such arguments to bolster their case. When
politicians talk of "balance," they imply that too
much of one output is being produced at the expense of
another, presumably more valuable, output. While such
arguments can be made as simple value judgments (such
as "when you see one redwood you've seen them all"),
it is more convincing if the argument can be couched
in economic terms to give it a gloss of objectivity.
It is then that we hear that the economy is suffering
from too much wilderness and not enough petroleum; or
from too many picnic spots and not enough timber.
This is an efficiency argument with respect to output
mix; what I have called outcome efficiency.

To make such an argument in economic terms
requires that the analyst have definitive data on the
consumption desires of the citizens for whom he or she
is speaking. Those who frequently celebrate the
"magic of the marketplace" will quickly remind us that
the market provides just that information. Overlooked, of course, is the fact that not all outputs
from federal lands are marketable commodities. Un-
daunted, those wishing to invoke market norms ask us
to imagine that they are so marketed, or to forget
about those particular outputs and to concentrate on
that subset that contributes to economic "efficiency."

Those writing about the inefficiency of federal
land administration are vague about the particular
usage of that term. At one moment we get the
impression that "special interest groups" are having
an inordinate influence on the agencies and hence
distorting the actual output mix away from some
undefined optimum. At another moment we are told that
agencies use incorrect benefit-cost procedures so as
to justify questionable projects. And then we are

told that the prices charged for various outputs do
not reflect their true social value. In each instance
there must be some norm against which the status quo
is to be compared. Though often implicit, rather than
explicit, that norm is said to be how the lands would
be managed were they under private control.

This preference for private ownership is firmly
held if not universally shared, despite widespread
evidence that private ownership of natural resources
does not guarantee that they will be wisely used.
Apparently, some have conveniently forgotten the
experience of the great Dust Bowl years when the
prairies were plowed up against the advice of a number
of agricultural experts. Were these lands under the
control of public employees or private owners?

But equally serious in these protests against
continued federal management is their failure to be
specific about which types of economic efficiency are
under consideration. There are at least three components of outcome efficiency that must be recognized
and discussed, independent of social welfare implications of production. They are: (1) technical efficiency; (2) private economic efficiency; and (3)
social efficiency.

Technical Efficiency

Imagine a piece of federally-controlled western
land that provides forage for cattle and for deer. If
it is used exclusively for cattle it has a sustained
productive capacity of, say, 300 animal unit months
(AUM)^2 annually. On the other hand, if cattle were
barred and the land was to be used exclusively for
deer it has a sustained productive capacity of, say,
250 AUMs annually. On the condition that both types
of animals could graze the same land, it is not
unreasonable to suppose that we might obtain 320 AUMs
of cattle forage, and 270 AUMs of deer forage on a
sustained basis. The complementarity between the two
different types of grazing animals results in a
greater AUM production than would be possible under a
regime of single use. It is technically inefficient
to impose single use on lands that are better suited
ecologically for multiple use. There is another
aspect of technical efficiency and that is to
determine the optimal mix of deer and cattle so as to
maximize the aggregate number of AUMs obtained from
the lands in question. Hence, technical efficiency is
concerned with the physical determinants of "ideal"
output. We could discuss similar phenomena between
grazing and watershed protection, timber production
and watershed protection, and timber production and

grazing. In each instance there is a relationship between the two (or more) outputs that gives rise to a technically efficient level of production. There is no guarantee, however, that technical efficiency will coincide with economic efficiency in either private or public terms.

Private Economic Efficiency

The private case is rather straightforward. The landowner can exercise complete control over the cattle and could select the appropriate number in accordance with market signals. It is not so easy to control deer, and even if the landowner sold hunting access, the deer cannot be prevented from ranging across a number of individual parcels of land.

When other uses -- such as watershed protection and the provision of amenities -- are admitted to the analysis, it quickly becomes obvious that any hope of determining an economically efficient mix between those outputs that pass through markets and those for which no exchange values exist must be abandoned. Those who advocate privatization of the federal lands seem unaware of these problems, or assume them to be minor compared to the "efficiency losses" arising from federal administration.

This willingness to ignore non-marketed outputs of the federal lands -- and then to complain about inefficiency in the administration of such lands -- is a common theme among those who would have us believe that salvation lies in privatization. It is indeed ironic, for the accepted view among economists is that the profit-maximizing decisions of a resource user can result in negative externalities (i.e., offsite costs for those in close proximity to the individual party making the decisions). The classic examples are the smoky factory, the odorous feedlot, or the chemical plant discharging effluent into a river. In the federal administration of western lands, we find an example of the very form of resource decision-making that is considered to be the solution to externality problems; namely the "sole owner" who will account for the implications of a number of interrelated actions that, if pursued independently, would carry substantial offsite costs for others. To be sure some economists did not quite have the public sector in mind when advocating sole ownership. But now we are arguing about the precise form of control, not the fact of a single decision-maker. A further irony is that these economists seem quite capable of ignoring the possibility of inordinate market power arising from one owner of land in sufficient scope to fully absorb the bulk of the potential offsite costs.

Social Economic Efficiency

Those who frequently celebrate market outcomes
make yet another assumption that will not stand close
scrutiny in today's crowded and technologically
complex world. They assume that the individual
maximizing decisions of independent economic agents
will lead to both private and social optima. Indeed,
their intellectual hero -- Adam Smith -- recognized
that this was not uniformly true even in the
relatively benign late eighteenth century, and
modern-day economic literature is extensive on
instances in which atomistic choice leads to
anti-social outcome.

Now I would like to draw your attention first to
an important distinction between private economic
efficiency and social economic efficiency, and then to
the distinction between social economic efficiency and
social welfare optimization. A clear understanding of
these distinctions is essential to comprehending the
arguments advanced by those opposed to federal
administration of western lands.

As indicated above, private economic efficiency
occurs when independent producers and consumers take
market signals -- that is, prices -- and adjust their
production and consumption decisions such that, at the
margin, the gain from one more unit of production (or
of consumption) is exactly offset by the added costs
of that last unit. Here market prices are taken as
given and carry great significance based on a
theoretical argument. This argument holds that in
conditions of thoroughgoing competition among a number
of buyers and sellers the social value of inputs and
outputs is correctly reflected in their respective
prices. Unfortunately, there are a number of reasons
why such prices may not reflect full social value.
The presence of uncompensated offsite costs is the
classic reason. But there are also problems arising
from market power over prices, as well as the inherent
indivisibility of certain inputs or outputs. And in
environmental problems, of course, the ability to
assign ownership to air and fugitive resources (i.e.
salmon) is missing. In these instances, prices as a
basis for choice lose their appeal. When this
happens, the calculus of the market-oriented economist
is suspect. Economists feel most comfortable with
those situations in which prices (or value) determine
choice, for the obvious reason that such prices appear
to be the happy by-product of a number of independent
and voluntary exchanges on the part of maximizing
producers or consumers. It is assumed that no
coercion was involved, and there is thought to be
little chance that price manipulation was present.

But what is to be done in those frequent instances where prices are not known? How much is a wetland area really worth to society? What value is to be placed on a magnificent sunset from Mount Rainier? In making difficult choices, two options seem possible. The first is to ignore those outputs for which no market prices exist and to conduct an economic evaluation solely on the basis of market-derived prices. This is to let prices determine choices. The second alternative is to make choices based on some other expression of demand, and to let the implicit prices thereby determined become information for future decisions. Here choices are determining prices. In the wetlands example, suppose we knew that such lands, if filled, were capable of earning $750.00 per acre into perpetuity in an agricultural use. If a collective decision is made that enough wetlands have been filled, and that the remainder should be protected, then we are determining the relative value of wetlands to be at least $750.00 per acre each year into perpetuity.

There is a continuing debate among economists concerning this matter of prices determining choices versus choices determining prices (or value). Not unexpectedly, hard-core economists are disdainful of situations in which political choices are made in the absence of market-revealed demand and prices. And yet, there can be no denial of the fact that a good number of the outputs from the federal lands are not amenable to the assignment of prices. It should also be recognized that some consider certain amenity resources to be in a class of goods that transcends normal views about commodities. To these individuals the very idea of assigning prices to a sunset, or to a unique hiking experience, is absurd. Some economists scoff at such ideas, but by doing so they discount an important aspect of social choice. Market processes are derivative of the larger social system; they do not supersede that system.

What is meant here by social efficiency is a situation in which the output mix from the federal lands is such that relative social values between any two products are equal to the rate at which one must be sacrificed for the other in production, after recognizing possible external effects (such as watershed protection, amenities, and so on). This formidable practical problem should not detract from its conceptual relevance. Moreover, stating social efficiency in these terms also reminds us of a profound aspect of public land management: efficiency calculations which ignore non-marketed outputs (and their values) seriously distort the presumed scientific basis for passing judgment on public land

10

management. Those who seem devoted to the privatization of the federal lands commit this distortion.
     In a sense, the scientific management and public
participation (limited though it is) that seems to
characterize current federal land management (Culhane)
is an attempt to determine technical and social
efficiency. To say this is not to argue that it has
succeeded. But to those who argue that it has failed,
we insist that they provide more evidence than they
have produced to date. For them to appeal to the
perfectly competitive market as a norm against which
to judge the performance of federal land management
agencies is obvious nonsense. One cannot use as a
template for the real world a scientific fiction that
has never existed in its pure form.

Social Welfare Considerations

     Let us now turn to social welfare implications of
production as distinct from social economic
efficiency. Though there are an infinite number of
output combinations from the federal lands that will
qualify as being socially efficient in an economic
sense, only one can qualify as the one to provide the
greatest social welfare.[3] The intervening variable
is, of course, the importance to be attached to the
satisfactions of the various consumers of the several
possible outputs from the federal lands.
     To make the discussion more realistic, assume
that Smith is a connoisseur of primitive wilderness,
and that Jones sells mining equipment. One
economically efficient output bundle will make Smith
happy, but Jones sad. Another efficient output bundle
will have the opposite effect. We cannot know which
of many possible bundles will maximize aggregate
welfare for all parties, including Smith and Jones,
without knowing which individuals or groups (Smith's
hiking companions or the association of mining
equipment dealers) ought to be favored. If we assume
that a society ought to be structured so that
satisfaction between the two individuals (or groups)
should be somewhat equal -- a difficult empirical
undertaking -- then only those socially efficient
outcomes with rather equal distributional aspects will
qualify as candidates for socially optimal results.
     This distinction between social efficiency and
social optimality is rarely made in economic writings
on public policy. Although we economists know better,
we habitually equate the two; perhaps because to admit
that we do not know what the social welfare function
indicates about the relative merits of Smith and Jones

would be to admit that economics does not have the
definitive answer to collective choice problems.

This extensive discussion of the various types of
efficiency and optimality is intended to clarify the
extremely complex nature of any analysis of public
land policies. It is, of course, easy to charge that
federal agencies are inefficient without specifying
the precise nature of that inefficiency. But once the
various types of efficiency are recognized, it becomes
more difficult to be quite so unequivocal in charging
that current practices are inefficient in either a
technical sense, or in terms of social economic
efficiency. Neither can it be argued with impunity
that the presumed efficiencies of privatization would
increase social welfare. While outcome efficiency
correctly can be considered a necessary condition for
social optimality, it is not sufficient. (Bromley)

ON PROCESS EFFICIENCY

Now let us consider the other major class of
efficiency pertinent to the management of federal
lands -- process efficiency, the managerial activities
that transform inputs into outputs. Those who
celebrate the efficiency of the private sector use as
their strawman the public sector bureaucrat who is
said to be driven by the desire for self
aggrandizement through larger offices, budgets, and
staffs. It is also said that since these public
bureaucrats lack the discipline of the "bottom line,"
they are slothful in management, and not sufficiently
aggressive in promoting the interests of the
"shareholders."

To listen to some of the critics of federal
administration one would conclude that the private
sector suffers from none of these problems. Yet even
casual examination of the insurance and automobile
industries indicates that this is not the case. There
is also recent evidence that economists have not been
entirely forthright in their assessment of the alleged
process efficiency of the private sector (Nelson).
Nelson addresses three issues in comparing private and
public enterprise: (1) administrative parsimony; (2)
responsiveness; and (3) innovativeness. These three
aspects comprise what I refer to as process
efficiency. Nelson summarizes the relevance of modern
economics to the debate by stating:

> Even regarding more narrowly defined
> economic performance criteria, modern
> welfare economics does not provide very
> persuasive support for private enterprise

...standard welfare economics arguments do not propose that private enterprise is better than any other organizational solution; only that if certain assumptions are met, "it can't be beat." But everyone realizes that the real conditions do not meet the assumptions needed...{p. 94}.

The argument that private enterprise is more efficient than public enterprise in a process sense is based on stylized facts and wishful thinking on the part of the current critics of the public sector. It is simply a value judgment that, with the help of economic terminology, is being passed off as objective science. To quote Nelson again: "Markets and transactions that ignore all but a few dimensions of benefits and costs are cheap compared with those that consider many. In a free enterprise regime the tradeoff is between leaving externalities and imposing a more costly market-transactional structure {p. 100}." Nelson concludes his study with the view that "much of the traditional arguments for private enterprise espoused by economists should be regarded as prejudices and not soundly based on any analytic structure {p. 109}."

ON INTERESTS AND RIGHTS

In addition to the need for a more analytical approach to the efficiency aspects of federal land administration, there are two concepts which require careful consideration if we are to understand the current disputes over the federal lands. The first is the notion of "interests;" the second concerns "rights."

The particular institutional structure that prevails over naturally occurring assets is a conscious collective decision that is predicated upon some assessment of social value and is aimed at producing benefits in excess of costs. Efforts are made to structure the institutional environment so that individual entrepreneurs can further their own lot and also contribute to the larger social good. In a sense, the entrepreneur possesses a "franchise" from the rest of us to produce something we need and for which we are willing to pay. But the private control of certain valuable assets, of course, is not an unmixed blessing. That should be obvious when we think of the deBeers diamond monopoly, feudal estates in the middle ages (as well as in many developing countries today), and other instances where private greed leads to socially unacceptable results.

The possibility of "socially unacceptable results" explains the concerns in the larger society for
how valuable assets are controlled. That is why, in
our own society, private land ownership is far from
absolute. It explains why an employer does not have
full dictatorial power over laborers. In my terminology, there is a larger social interest in the way that
individual firms order their daily business. However,
to have an interest in something is far from having a
right in something. Rights do not exist in the absence of someone else's duty. That is, rights and
duties are obvious correlates. Another set of correlates is that of privileges and no rights.

Prior to the establishment of laws to control
access to the rangelands of the west, ranchers had
privileges, but others had no rights. Once the Taylor
Grazing Act was passed, ranchers acquired duties (not
rights), and the citizenry as a whole obtained rights;
rights that "their" land (that is, the public's land)
would not be destroyed. The duties of the ranchers
involved the payment of grazing fees, the
establishment of grazing advisory boards, and the
adherence to rules formulated by those responsible for
protecting the rights of the public. We hear a great
deal about whether those who graze the public lands
have privileges or rights, and no one, certainly not
the ranchers, ever talks about their duties. But in
formal terms that is precisely what they have.

It is this notion of interest that explains the
rationale for public lands in the first instance. In
contrast to private lands, the presumption here is
that those other than the direct user have an interest
in how the asset is used. Thus, the challenge to
continued federal administration of the public lands
must rest on the premise that only the direct user has
a legitimate interest in those lands. I suspect that
this will be difficult to establish.

It is possible, of course, to argue that the
general public's interest in the federal lands will be
better protected under a regime of private ownership.
This is what the privatization movement apparently
hopes to establish by charging that federal administration of these lands is "inefficient." But, as
I've indicated above, this charge is not only poorly
substantiated but fails to address the equal concern
that efficiency (whatever that means!) may be less
crucial than having one's interests protected.

The attack against public sector (as opposed to
private sector) bureaucrats holds that the former do
not have the relentless discipline of profits and
losses to keep them alert, vigilant, and agile. All
they have, it is said, is a mandate to ensure the
long-run viability of the assets in their trust.

Many of us have interests in a number of aspects of public life, but the problem is determining which interest collective action will move to protect. The rich and the powerful are said to be quite successful in getting their interests protected. In one sense, the privatization movement seeks to take control of natural assets out of the arena where it is feared that the rich and powerful may hold inordinate sway. But to throw decision-making open to the whims of the market is to cast choice at the feet of an often fickle master.

WHAT HOPE CONCILIATION?

I submit that conciliation between the two views of the continued federal administration of public lands would be quite easy once the legitimate scope of economic science is recognized. In neither outcome efficiency, nor in process efficiency, is there a scientific standard supporting the contention that federal administration results in the wrong outputs, in the wrong proportions, and at an administrative cost that is above some legitimate norm. All such accusations -- and they are usually anecdotal -- use as their norm a scientific fiction that is not rich enough to provide guidance with respect to the complex nature of public land attributes. The existence of goods and services for which demand estimation is still primitive and inexact means that a "market test" would lead to biased results.

Simply put, those who claim that the wrong output mix emanates from the public lands are basing their conclusions on personal desires rather than on unambiguous economic evidence. Similarly, those who claim that private administration of the federal lands would be more efficient are using a fictional ideal of entrepreneurial agility that is ill-suited for the multiple outputs and multiple interests that characterize the public lands.

It is my view that there is less dissatisfaction with the public administration of the federal lands than some politicians and economists would have us to believe. Several public opinion polls seem to indicate as much. To the extent that there is some concern, I would submit that it is largely aided by the writings of a few economists who use an imprecise definition of "efficiency" to indict current practices. Irreversible changes in the natural environment are dismissed as a special case, preservation of resources for future generations and indirect users are downplayed as illusory, and multiple-use is often confined to the presumed choice between two marketable commodities. But the over-riding motivation of much of this literature is a "theological" commitment to market processes as opposed to demands and values articulated through alternative means.

I am afraid that there is no divine authority to whom we might appeal for guidance in this matter. The market clearly is a very appropriate mechanism for the allocation of certain goods and services. It is clearly inappropriate for others. On a continuum, markets work best for those commodities and services that are highly divisible, ubiquitous, mobile, self-contained (that is possess few external effects when produced or consumed), and capable of having clear entitlements (property relations) defined and enforced. At the other extreme we have some goods and services that are indivisible, unique, immobile, carry large external effects in production and consumption, and do not admit of much precision in the establishment of entitlements. Some outputs of the public lands fall at the former end of the continuum, but a good number fall at the latter end.

The current privatization movement has not been built upon an analytical base that articulates this continuum and positions the respective outputs along it. Instead, it appeals to stereotyped notions about blundering bureaucrats, vigilant private entrepre-neurs, and snickers, only partly-veiled, that public lands are really a form of welfare for the rich. It could indeed be in the general social interest if The Wilderness Society would purchase the Bob Marshall Wilderness, and all of the others for that matter. But that test would require a more careful analysis than we have seen to date. There are some obvious questions to ponder: Why should I have to join The Wilderness Society in order to be sure that a particu-lar area is preserved for the future? Why should I have to pay any group in order to use a wilderness area? And why should the citizenry as a whole be relieved of the financial responsibility for the future of these lands?

Wilderness is a small and special aspect of total federal land holdings, and surely the administration of all those lands could be improved. But with what objective in mind? Which of the several efficiencies defined earlier ought to dominate the choice process? Even if the appropriate efficiency measure could be agreed upon, there is no guarantee that social welfare would thereby be maximized. For a natural resource as varied as the public lands, it is virtually impossible to imagine how to recognize an optimal outcome when confronted with it. And getting there is equally dif-ficult.

I appreciate that this leaves us rather unfulfilled. Americans pride themselves on focusing on "problems" and then "fixing" them. The scientific revolution -- and the recent rise of decision analysis -- encourages confidence that any problem can be fixed by enough thought and analysis. Laurence Tribe has pondered this, and has written of the pressure for results-oriented analysis. He talks of the "ideology" of the policy sciences, and writes:

> ...the policy sciences' intellectual and social heritage in the classical economics of unfettered contract, consumer sovereignty and perfect markets both brings them within a paradigm of conscious choice guided by values and inclines them, within that paradigm, toward the exaltation of utilitarian and self-interested individualism, efficiency, and maximized production as against distributive ends, procedural and historical principles, and the values (often nonmonetizable, discontinuous, and of complex structure) associated with personal rights, public goods, and communitarian and ecological goals (p. 105).

I suggest that when dealing with the goods and services from the federal lands, we are precisely concerned with distributive ends, procedural and historical principles, and the nonmonetizable, discontinuous, and complex values associated with personal rights, public goods, and communitarian and ecological goals. At the risk of sounding overly negative, it seems to me that the type of analysis that traditional economics would bring to bear on the current and future administration of the federal lands will be of little help. Obviously economic analysis can be of great help in determining the degree of efficiency in both a private and a social sense. Our models also can help in determining process efficiency. But we will require considerable input from the biological sciences in assessing technical efficiency. Furthermore, unless we are prepared to accept the political articulation of the social welfare function, our preoccupation with economic efficiency will distract us from the very issues on the minds of those who make public policy.

I close with the observation that conciliation over the use and management of the federal lands is not that elusive. Several states in the west have made it clear that they do not wish to assume jurisdiction. And, we have yet to see many private parties

clamor to take over the control -- and the tax liability -- of the federal lands. As new scarcities and
new tastes and preferences appear, I suspect that
future discussions will concentrate on how to make
small improvements in the scientific management of the
public lands. The process will be slow. It will be
cumbersome. But it will also be steady, carefully
thought through, and widely discussed in the political
arena. While the public sector may disappoint a few
for its conservative pace, it will encourage others
for precisely that reason.

The nature of real estate still in the public
domain is so complex that much of it defies simple
classification as a productive asset in the sense of
land in the corn belt, or in downtown Washington, D.C.
This is not to say that it is inherently more valuable, only that it is more difficult to be sure of its
value. If we are mature enough to admit that we are
unsure of its true value to us and to those who will
follow, then it seems obvious that the subject of its
control needs more public discussion. Just as obviously, the use and control of these lands is too
important to be left to private greed.

Those inclined to celebrate market processes are
aghast at the thought that outputs from the public
lands should be the topic of continued debate,
thought, and compromise. To them the answer is
simple. Yet it is the essence of government in a
modern democratic state that the important decisions
remain in the hands of the governed. No less an
authority on conciliation than Edmund Burke was even
moved to write that "All government -- indeed, every
human benefit and enjoyment, every virtue and every
prudent act -- is founded on compromise and barter."
The political debate over the use and control of the
public lands epitomizes this process. And that is
encouraging.

NOTES

1. Technically, outcome efficiency is defined in
terms of output bundles from the federal lands that
satisfy the usual economic conditions pertaining to
relative prices and ratios of marginal utility
attaching to each possible combination of federal-land
outputs, as well as other possible goods and services.
This would be the outcome of efficiency on the
consumption side. On the product side, the rate of
transformation (or substitution) between any two out-

puts must be brought to equality with their relative prices.

2. A unit of grazing capacity; the amount of forage normally required per month for one mature cow or five adult sheep.

3. On the production side we assume efficiency in input application to produce the various outputs -- that is, relative marginal productivities of the various inputs are equated to their relative prices. On the output side we assume that consumers of the various products equate the marginal utility of each with its respective price. Finally, we assume that these relative output prices are equal to the rate at which the two outputs can be substituted for each other in production holding input levels constant.

BIBLIOGRAPHY

Bromley, Daniel W., "Land and Water Problems: An Institutional Perspective," American Journal of Agricultural Economics 64:834-844, December 1982.

Burke, Edmund, "Second Speech on Conciliation with America," The Thirteen Resolutions, March 22, 1775.

Culhane, Paul J., Public Land Politics (Baltimore: Johns Hopkins University Press, 1981).

Nelson, Richard R., "Assessing Private Enterprise: An Exegesis of Tangled Doctrine," The Bell Journal of Economics 12:93-110, Spring 1981.

Tribe, Laurence H., "Policy Sciences: Analysis or Ideology?" Philosophy and Public Affairs 2:66-110, Fall 1972.

The Public Interest in the Federal Lands and the Reagan Administration's Asset Management Program

Douglas MacCleery

Professor Bromley has provided some interesting insights on the debate over privatization of federal lands which are relevant whether or not the federal lands are sold.

Without engaging in a technical argument as to whether the privatizers have adequately supported their case, I will make several observations.

First, Professor Bromley makes several valid and perceptive points about the need to consider non-market values and the technical difficulty of doing so. Those problems must be addressed whether or not the federal lands are sold. If, as seems likely, the vast bulk of federal lands remain in federal ownership, we still must seek to determine the optimal mix of market and non-market resources which these lands should be providing. Later, I will discuss the framework under which the Department of Agriculture intends to do that.

Second, is that, while the debate over privatizing federal lands has been focused legitimately on whether public or private ownership would better serve the public interest, couching the discussion as an all-or-nothing proposition (all private or all federal, with no middle ground) has given it a distinctly unreal tone. No one can reasonably expect that all public lands will be sold. Nor can it be argued that it would be in the public interest to retain every acre now in federal ownership.

Over the years, U.S. society has concluded that both government and private ownership of land have their place. This implicitly suggests that over the

Douglas MacCleery is deputy assistant secretary of agriculture for natural resources and environment.

long term diversified ownership is superior to a
single form of ownership.

History also tells us that the balance between
public and private ownership is not static; nor should
it be. It would seem reasonable that, from time to
time, we should reexamine and reevaluate private and
federal ownership patterns, to determine whether
marginal adjustments would better serve the public
interest. Instead of debating whether all-private
ownership or all-public ownership is better, we should
focus on the specific situations and circumstances
most relevant to whether public or private ownership
will lead to superior results.

One of Professor Bromley's key points is that
those who support privatization seem to ignore
non-market and environmental values or underrate their
importance. My own observation is that the opponents
of privatization tend to go overboard in the other
direction, by claiming that transfer of any more than
a trifling acreage of federal lands to private
ownership would irreparably damage irreplaceable
non-market values.

Implicit in the arguments of those opposing sale
of federal lands is an assumption that federal lands
are public precisely because they have non-market
values which can be protected only in public
ownership. However, this is refuted by a review of
how the public lands came into federal ownership.

There is no doubt that many lands remain in
federal ownership because Congress has made an
explicit decision that they would better serve the
public interest in that ownership. The national parks
are prime examples. Also in this category are many
parts of the national forests which are components of
the Wilderness System, the Wild and Scenic Rivers
System and National Recreation Areas, or which are
otherwise specifically designated by Congress.

Many of the public lands, however, are federally
owned today only because they remained in federal
ownership after the Homestead Act and other land
transfer programs. They are in federal ownership, not
by any master design, but by omission; nobody applied
or qualified for them under the various land transfer
programs. However, times have changed.

Many federal lands are little different from
private lands. As society's needs change, and as
demands for more resources increase, it is appropriate
to ask whether the private sector may be able to
produce those resources and meet those demands more
productively and efficiently than by continuing the
lands in federal ownership.

One additional point on protecting non-market
values: we often see the implication that non-market

values on federal lands can be protected only through continuing public ownership. This is not true. Society has a variety of mechanisms, such as zoning, land use regulations, and water- or air-quality regulations that can be designed, as appropriate, to protect various non-market values on private lands.

USDA'S ASSET MANAGEMENT PROGRAM

Let's consider what the Department of Agriculture actually plans to do to implement what we call the Asset Management Program. The objectives of this program are threefold:

(1) to sell excess federal property and some public lands that would have a higher and better use in private ownership,

(2) to improve the efficiency of government by selling lands that are costly and inefficient to manage and are not necessary to serve public objectives, and

(3) to utilize sale revenues to pay off a portion of the national debt.

The Asset Management Program is not a privatization program. It is based on the premise that it is in the public interest for the vast bulk of the National Forest System to remain in federal ownership. It has never been intended that a significant portion of any national forest will be sold.

The Asset Management Program recognizes, however, that any area of land as large as the National Forest System, and which was reserved or acquired in the manner by which that system was built, will inevitably include some tracts that would better benefit the public in other ownerships. The program's purpose is to make some marginal adjustments in federal and private land ownership patterns, so that both federal and private lands can be managed with greater efficiency.

Without review or qualification land in statutorily designated areas will not be sold. This includes areas in Wilderness, National Recreation Areas, Wild and Scenic Rivers, and similar areas designated by law. These types of congressionally designated lands fall into the first of three categories under the Asset Management Program:

1. Lands to be retained in public ownership. About fifty million acres of national forest land have been placed in this category, but considerable additional acreage will be added after initial screening.

2. Lands proposed for disposal. These are lands which can be sold under existing authorities and which have met our criteria for disposal. There appear to be positive benefits from sales of this land, which initially totals only 60,000 acres. However, even some of this land will be subject to further review, including opportunity for public comment.

3. Land areas which require further screening to determine whether they should be retained in federal ownership or studied intensively for disposal. We have identified about 140 million acres of National Forest System land for this screening process, which is now under way. This review will result in most of the 140 million acres being placed in the first category -- to be retained in federal ownership.

We estimate roughly fifteen to eighteen million acres may be identified for more intensive study and considered for possible disposal. These will include isolated parcels, lands in checkerboard ownership patterns, lands needed for community expansion and certain lands under special use permit to individuals -- where there is essentially a single use of the land, and where it is unlikely that the lands will be needed for public purposes in the future. After we have identified those lands to be studied more intensively, we will invite the public to suggest which should be disposed of, which should be retained, and, perhaps, which additional lands should be considered for possible disposal.

Essential to success in the Asset Management Program is the legislative authority to dispose of national forest lands. We have not yet developed the legislative program, but expect to send a proposal to Congress early in 1983.

FRAMEWORK FOR DECISION-MAKING ON LANDS REMAINING IN FEDERAL OWNERSHIP

Many of the points Professor Bromley makes about economic efficiency, the need to consider non-market values, and the difficulties of determining the appropriate mix of market and non-market resources have relevance even if these lands remain in federal ownership.

How these issues will be dealt with in the Forest Service decision-making process is articulated in the national forest land management planning regulations which were recently published in final form. That process has a number of required steps.

Early on, the Forest Service must develop several analyses to determine how the land would be managed if only market resources were emphasized. In these analyses, each option must include meeting minimum legal requirements, such as protecting the productivity of the land and meeting minimum air and water quality standards. But other than that, land allocations and resource output levels are driven by the objective of achieving economically efficient levels of those resources to which prices are assigned -- normally the recreation, timber, grazing, and water resources. Discretionary policies, such as those relating to non-declining yield timber harvest schedules and biologically determined rotation lengths, are not imposed in these analyses.

These are analyses of what Professor Bromley calls "private economic efficiency." They are treated only as analyses, not as formal planning alternatives. They are benchmarks to assist in evaluating formal alternatives. Non-market objectives will be produced to the extent they do not reduce the economically efficient levels of the market resources. This can be a very valuable tool to illustrate compatibilities and conflicts between market and non-market resources. Many people assume that they conflict. However, we have found that on many forests there is significant compatibility between economically efficient production levels of market resources, such as timber, and producing high levels of non-market resources.

The next step is to formulate the formal planning alternatives, which are various mixes of market and non-market resources. Market resources are produced at levels which are economically efficient, given the need to produce specified levels of non-market resources. Many of these alternative mixes of market and non-market outputs are designed to respond to the issues raised by the public in the public participation sessions. It is our intent that the environmental, social, and economic effects of each of these alternative mixes be displayed for all to see. This is what Professor Bromley would term an evaluation of "social efficiency."

The last and final step is for the appropriate forest official to decide which alternative best serves the public interest. Professor Bromley refers to this as the concept of "welfare maximization." The national forest planning regulations use the term "maximization of net public benefits," but the concepts are identical. The objective is to find the particular combination of market and non-market resources which seems optimal. That is a subjective determination, for there is no single index or parameter of maximum welfare. However, the decision is aided by information about the nature of resource tradeoffs and by projections of anticipated future demands and supplies for the various natural resources.

By specifying the planning process in the regulations, we have not made the ultimate decision less subjective. But, we have made the decision-making process more systematic and better articulated. We have also required more consistent examination of the economic, social and environmental effects and tradeoffs associated with the various management options. Therefore, I hope we have improved what Professor Bromley terms "process efficiency."

Professor Bromley raises some other points. He seems to question the relevance and usefulness of economic models and the economic discipline itself in helping resolve national resource policy issues. He argues that models have many imperfections which make them unable to provide perfect analyses and solutions to resource problems. I agree completely. It is the nature of models that they will never be perfect; they are only tools to help us better understand the real world. The models themselves will not give us decisions. But models can assist in helping us make better decisions.

Professor Bromley mentioned that -- in his policymaking experience in Washington -- economics was extremely useful, but was used primarily to buttress decisions already made. That has been one of my own observations and concerns about economics. It's not a problem just in Washington. I sincerely hope we are changing this, that we are applying economic analysis prior to the decisions, and that by doing so we will be coming to better decisions.

Access and Distributional Impacts
of Public and Private Land Ownership

Sterling Brubaker

I hope most of you are economists because well over half of Bromley's paper consists of a quarrel with those economists who have a theological commitment to the market, particularly with market-mediated outcomes of economic efficiency. I think Bromley treated this subject quite well.

He was, however, unfair in suggesting that economists ignore externalities in public goods. I think nearly all economists make room in their analysis for them. They may disagree on the extent of such qualifications and they disagree quite strongly on the capacity of the market to incorporate externalities. After all, you can regulate, you can provide incentives, and you can subsidize the production of public goods on private lands so that you do not necessarily forego these benefits, if you have a private ownership regime.

The fact that the social optimum is elusive is not really a novel suggestion. The outcome very much depends on the prior distribution of wealth and income. But again, what's the significance of that for the question of land tenure? How does federal government holding land affect that income distribution? And does it do so in a way that is favorable to the more egalitarian outcome that Bromley seems to favor? Many who have studied the public lands would suggest that federal tenure involves a redistribution of income toward the west, toward ranchers and outdoorsmen, at the expense of those who are not in those categories. Is that fair or not?

Bromley gives process efficiency equal rank with outcome efficiency though he didn't treat it in great

Sterling Brubaker is a senior fellow at Resources for the Future.

length. He defines process efficiency as essentially
the cost-minimizing and innovation roles of an
entrepreneur and any private firm must obtain some
degree of process efficiency -- under the discipline
of the market -- if it's going to survive. Now, how
does that translate into the public arena when we're
speaking of public managers? Here, the concept becomes
much more vague. We start with some kind of political
decision. We implement it through an administrative,
bureaucratic process. And in many instances, it's
subject to participatory process. By what criterion
do you then judge the outcome? How can you say that
what emerges is efficient or not? What we end up
doing in most instances is saying that the outcome is
self-validating.

Bromley is marching out a platoon of economists
who have been committed to the usual economic
efficiency criteria and marching in a platoon of
lawyers and politicians. Instead of economics in
command we will have politics in command and, perhaps,
even special interests in command.

References to the market guarantee of social
optimum -- that is, ignoring the failure of a free
market system to achieve a social optimum because
certain conditions are not met in practice, because
externalities and public goods exist and so forth --
are unreal premises. It is entirely appropriate that
Bromley has challenged this. If you then want to
argue about efficiency with regard to the management
of public lands, you have to make the argument at a
more micro level, that is, the kind of process-type of
efficiency that was alluded to.

Richard Nelson (1981) has observed that welfare
economics criteria do not apply in this situation, and
that at the micro level the superiority of private
management is largely undocumented. But that's as far
as he goes. In fact, he would say that he finds it
plausible that private management could be more
efficient; it simply has not been proven that it is.
I think that those who would argue for private
management would respond that, while it is true that
there are bureaucrats in private organizations, they
have a stronger accountability and a stronger
motivation to perform efficiently than bureaucrats in
public management. Again, it's a question of what
kind of criteria apply to the two spheres. Let's
grant, however, that this is not fully documented.

Bromley argues that the existence of a public
interest in how land is used provides the rationale
for public ownership. Elsewhere, he has recognized
that private ownership is also constrained, and,
indeed should be constrained by a public interest in
the outcome. Could the public interest in the way the

land is used be sought in ways other than through ownership, that is, through regulation or other devices? In a recent paper, Joe Sax (1982) defended public ownership but recognized at the outset that those things which he sought through public ownership could be attained equally well through private ownership and public regulation.

So is there any kind of product peculiar to the public lands that requires public ownership? Well, certainly it's not grass or timber. Is it watershed? Is it game? Is it fuels? Is it recreation? Is it sunsets? All of these are found on private land and many of them, with the exception of sunsets, can be regulated. It seems to me the issue between public and private tenure really is a question of access and of distributional impacts, not whether the outputs can be produced under one situation but not under the other. Where would Bromley then draw the line? Externalities occur both on public land and on private land, and both public and private lands have the potential to produce public goods.

Much of the argument concerning efficiency was at a very theoretical and abstract level. Bob Nelson (1982) of the Interior Department has studied the relationship between the expenses of administering public lands and the revenues from those lands. Looking only at the surface estate of grazing lands, he finds that revenues amount to about one-fifth of the cost of administering that land. He found the cost of administering the land to be considerably in excess of the value of the product from the land. The Forest Service, which holds some very good timber land and -- like BLM -- pays no capital charges on it, spends about twice as much as it gains in revenues. Are these discrepancies due to the production of non-market goods which are equal to the value of the discrepancy between revenue and costs, or are they the result of undercharging those users of the public lands?

Bromley does acknowledge that markets are superior at some range of the spectrum of products, while public ownership is superior at another range, and that is a useful insight. Bob Nelson suggests that one might classify the land according to its principal use. Those lands used mainly for commodity production, where there is a direct and very comparable commercial analog, might then be turned into private lands (that would be primarily timber and grazing); those lands which are used largely for recreation (and that would include most of the acreage of the public lands) might be considered for operation by the states where the recreation occurs for the most part; and areas that have scenic uniqueness or wilderness characteristics of national significance would be reserved for federal ownership. Marion Clawson has proposed an alternate scheme which would retain title but allow for long-term leasing of most lands.

Some of these ideas might be tested. Almost everyone would agree that some shifts of ownership of public lands would be justifiable purely from an administrative standpoint, though there will be argument about how much land might be involved.

Explicit political decisions on preserving wilderness or scenic areas, ought to be based on the best available knowledge of opportunity costs. We don't have to engage in slavish pursuit of theology of the market in these instances. But we can still make use of economic analysis for a broad range of decisions. This might suggest that some changes of tenure on the non-unique, ordinary federal lands should be considered.

BIBLIOGRAPHY

Nelson, Richard R., "Assessing Private Enterprise: An Exegesis of Tangled Doctrine," The Bell Journal of Economics 12:93-110, Spring, 1981.

Nelson, Robert H. and Gabriel Joseph, "An Analysis of Revenues and Costs of Public Land Management by the Interior Department in 13 Western States - Update to 1981," Office of Policy Analysis, U.S. Department of the Interior, September, 1982.

Sax, Joseph, "For Sale: A Sign of the Times on the Public Domain," A National Workshop on Rethinking the Federal Lands, Resources for the Future, Portland, Oregon, September, 1982.

2
A Property Rights Approach to Wilderness Management

John Baden and Dean Lueck

Abstract: Goals of conserving resources and anticipating future environmental problems are more likely to be met by private means than by assigning these responsibilities to governmental bureaucracies. The most important role for government is to define and enforce property rights, which will lessen the tragedy of the commons and other negative spillovers and encourage effective responses to changing relative scarcities.   When private property rights to resources, including wilderness lands, are well-defined, enforced, and transferable, owners tend to allocate those resources efficiently. When decisions are made by bureaucrats who are seeking budgetary increases, workplace amenities, discretionary power, career advancement, and minimal tension, we can expect resources to be allocated inefficiently.

Profit-motivated individuals and groups are already providing some "environmental goods" in the marketplace. "Wilderness homesteading" by conservation groups who would build trails, provide campgrounds, and so forth is proposed. Under this scheme, the wilderness owner would have every incentive to use his resources efficiently and to promote environmentally sensitive development. The alternative of politicized decision-making, especially in the face of increased resource scarcity, offers little long-term security for wilderness enthusiasts.

Key words: privatization, common property, environmental destruction, wilderness homesteading.

John Baden is director, Center for Political Economy and Natural Resources, Montana State University, and Dean Lueck was a research assistant. Dean Lueck's research was sponsored by the Earhardt Foundation.

INTRODUCTION

We conservationists would like to keep the
Forest Service out of the wilderness, and,
for that matter, the National Park Service
too.

David Brower[1]

Environmentalists are concerned with the question of why natural resources, especially amenity
resources, are becoming more scarce. They deny that
there is any substance to the claim made by some
resource economists, such as Julian Simon in The
Ultimate Resource, that resources are becoming less
scarce.[2] Thus, it is no surprise that prominent environmentalists, including Garrett Hardin who first
made us aware of the "tragedy of the commons," have
attacked Simon's work. While environmentalists may be
able to tolerate some optimism, Simon clearly went too
far in predicting a rosy future.

Along with a concern for resource scarcity,
conservationists insist that more emphasis be placed
on conserving resources for future generations. A
good case can be made, however, for transferring
resources, especially much of the public land, to the
private sector in order to realize more fully the
goals of mediating resource scarcity and providing for
future generations. We believe that the goals of
conserving resources and anticipating future
environmental problems are more likely to be met by
private means than through governmental bureaucracies.
The most important role for government is to define
and enforce property rights, which would lessen the
tragedy of the commons and other negative spillovers,
promote positive externalities, and encourage
effective responses to changing relative scarcities.

Wilderness has become an important form of land
use, and rising incomes, higher marginal tax rates,
and changing preferences have caused the value of
wilderness to grow rapidly. The overwhelming majority
of currently designated wilderness areas provide their
highest value by being maintained as such and by
providing recreation, grazing, wildlife habitat, and
environmental buffering. Thus, the opportunity cost
of preserving most of our wilderness land is zero.

While it is true that wilderness is a valuable
good, that value is not infinitely high. There are
small areas that overlay valuable energy or mineral
deposits or that contain valuable timber inventories.
In such areas, the opportunity costs of maintaining
wilderness in its pristine condition may be quite
high. Intense political conflict has surrounded the

management practices in these areas; and if Simon is
wrong and resources do become more scarce, the conflict will be more inflamed by increased competition.
The high costs and the probability of unsatisfactory
outcomes suggest that decision making on wilderness
land would be improved if decisions were made in the
private sector.

CONSERVATIVES AND CONSERVATIONISTS

While some environmentalists have recognized the
imperfections inherent in the governmental management
of natural resource management, few have recognized
the common ground they share with fiscal conservatives. Environmentalists often forget how much of
their time has been spent fighting the Forest Service,
the Bureau of Land Management, the Bureau of Reclamation, and the Army Corps of Engineers.³ These agencies have done much to reduce environmental quality
while actively transferring wealth from taxpayers to
special interest groups and bureaucratic entrepreneurs.
The potential for conservatives and conservationists to join together to curb governmental waste is
substantial and is only now beginning to gain general
recognition. A growing number of well-known environmentalists are coming to recognize the importance of
property rights and markets in fostering environmental
quality. For example, Thomas Barlow of the Natural
Resources Defense Council (NRDC) made the following
comments on governmental timber practices:

> The best way to leave the greatest
> number of trees to nature is to intensify
> the farming of the rest....Overly generous
> Forest Service timber-sale pricing and
> management practices are acting as a
> magnet, needlessly drawing logging demand
> to the national forests and ensuring that
> it stays there. Analysis in recent years
> has disclosed that the Forest Service
> sells tremendous quantities of timber at
> less than the cost of managing the for-
> ests, and therefore at a loss to the
> United States Treasury....The number of
> sales below costs in the national forests
> is huge....As the lure of below cost sales
> pulls timber companies to the national
> forests private forest owners are the
> losers....The present sale process also
> brings the Forest Service into direct
> conflict with wilderness advocates intent

on saving remote roadless areas from the
chainsaw.[4]

Thomas J. Graff of the Environmental Defense Fund
commented on the defeat of the California Peripheral
Canal proposition:

> What now? Will it be development without
> environmental protection as some have
> threatened? Or has all future water-
> project development been choked off by the
> new conservationist-conservative alliance,
> leading to economic stagnation and possi-
> bly even water rationing?...To make a
> significant difference in California's
> water budget a comprehensive water-effi-
> ciency program should contain at least
> three elements:
>   First, there must be an infusion of
> free-market principles into the state-run
> water allocation system. Legal and insti-
> tutional barriers to the voluntary sale
> and purchase of water rights ought to be
> eliminated.
>   Next, there ought to be a commitment
> to least-cost public investment....
>   Finally, there must be pricing
> reform....The subsidy must be discontin-
> ued....
>   Conservationists believe that the
> water development sector of government can
> shrink without harming anyone...and that
> more efficiency would benefit the govern-
> ment as well....(Their) next challenge is
> to persuade California's decision makers
> to pursue a new politics of efficiency
> rather than the old politics of pork
> barrel.[5]

Ernst R. Habicht Jr., formerly with NRDC, wrote:

> Any governmental policy dealing with
> a commodity like energy must...be a pri-
> cing policy. Prices have incentive ef-
> fects; that is, they determine the demand
> for and supply of goods and services.
> High prices inhibit demand and encourage
> investments in more supplies or they coax
> forth innovative alternatives to tradi-
> tional supplies. Low prices have precise-
> ly the reverse effect....
>   The true costs of SNG (synthetic
> natural gas), LNG (liquified natural gas),

and other uneconomic energy ventures
appear in the form of inflation, unemployment, trade deficits, and environmental
devastation....
      The energy situation that has
attracted so much attention will soon
appear in other sectors of our economy,
most notably, raw materials and water.
Thus, the policies accepted for energy
will probably provide the keystone for
reforms in other areas. In a very real
sense, a mistaken energy policy is a
prescription for national disaster, not
only for energy, but also for other
natural resources.[6]

Phillip A. House of The Nature Conservancy made
the following statements about water:

      Because water from numerous federal
water projects is so cheap (to the users),
there is as yet little incentive to
actually conserve water. To the contrary,
many western commentators have observed a
"water grab," a rush to get projects built
before the water runs out. In the clamor,
voices calling for protection of plants
and animals are barely audible....[7]

Amory Lovins of Friends of the Earth stated:

      Economics is a handy way to focus on
the gaps between rhetoric and action.
Where given a chance, what semblance of a
free market we have has done remarkably
well at solving the energy problem very
quickly....
      It's faster as well as cheaper to do
a lot of little simple things than a few
big complicated things. This is the market
in action, and it has all worked a lot
better and faster than any of us thought
possible....
      Imperfect though (the market) is, it
can't be all that stupid. Look, for
example, at how it has killed nuclear
power; how it is clearly starting to favor
efficiency and renewables.[8]

Jon R. Luoma of the National Audubon Society has
commented on the Garrison Diversion Unit in North
Dakota:

...to irrigate those 250,000 acres, the
bureau (of Reclamation) would have to
acquire 220,000 acres -- most of which is
productive farmland. Some farms would be
wiped out, others sliced in two. And, by
any reasonable evaluation, the project was
a blue-ribbon economic horror. True, some
eastern North Dakota farmers would be able
to boost productivity and diversify crops,
but by 1981 calculations at a whopping
$800,000-per-farm subsidy from American
taxpayers....[9]

Christopher Palmer of the National Audubon
Society made the following comments on the free
market:

Too often environmentalists think of
profit as dirty. We don't always appreciate the effectiveness of the free market.
Too few of us have ever worked as entrepreneurs and consequently, lack an appreciation of just how hard it is to succeed
in business. We are much more expert at
grantsmanship....
But economic growth and increased
productivity are needed to create new
jobs, to increase our investments in
energy efficient housing, and our investments in new less polluting industrial
processes...environmentalists could form
alliances with business (by entering) into
business partnerships. Is there any reason why environmental groups have to be
limited to writing and lobbying? Why
shouldn't they help to market pro-environ-
mental products.[10]

William Reilly of the Conservation Foundation
criticized President Carter's energy program:

The President's energy proposals
should be opposed vigorously by both
environmentalists and business leaders.
This may seem an "unholy alliance" --
unrealistic and unworkable. But I ask
both the business and environmental
communities to consider the following.
...(Under Carter's energy program) we
would have the dubious distinction of
buying heavily subsidized synthetic oil
at a price higher than OPEC would likely
charge for the natural product....

> Accept for a moment...that a massive
> synfuels program is bad for the environ-
> ment...and let us concentrate on how it is
> bad for business and industry. The
> President has suggested a program that
> removes a vital part of the American
> economy from the normal controls of com-
> petitive free-market tests....Pricing that
> reflects the full costs of energy consumed
> is fully consistent with environmental-
> ists' view of the world; that we can have
> economic growth and improved productivity
> with fewer investments of natural re-
> sources....Cost effectiveness is the test,
> not some predetermined "synfuels or bust"
> strategy.[11]

These comments indicate a growing awareness by
the environmental community of the potential for
property rights and markets to enhance environmental
quality. Perhaps no one has understood this better
than Lawrence Burke, editor-in-chief of Outside
magazine. In the June/July 1982 issue of his
outdoorsman-conservationist journal, Burke hailed the
return of the price system to the energy market as an
environmental blessing.[12] In an editorial entitled
"Free Market Environmentalism," Burke recognized that
(a) governmental action has been responsible for many
of our environmental problems and (b) the potential
for market oriented solutions to environmental problems has been largely overlooked.

RECOGNIZING PROPERTY RIGHTS AND FREE MARKETS

> Therein is the tragedy. (In a
> commons) each man is locked into a system
> that compels him to increase his herd
> without limit--in a world that is limited.
> Ruin is the destination toward which all
> men rush, each pursuing his own best
> interest in a society that believes in the
> freedom of the commons. Freedom in a
> commons brings ruin to all.[13]

In his classic essay, "The Tragedy of the
Commons," ecologist-environmentalist Garrett Hardin
revealed the root cause of environmental degradation
from an economic perspective. Resources will be
overused (misallocated) when they are owned in common.
Common ownership often separates authority from
responsibility and thus skews the information and
incentives faced by individuals in socially expensive

ways.   Hardin's   powerful logic offers a broader explanation of environmental problems than is offered by
those who have blamed capitalism and Christianity.[14]

The logic of the commons prevails in capitalistic
or socialistic systems, in 1700 or 1982, for Buddhists
or for Christians.[15]   The United States' "tragedy" is
evident   in   its   air, its ocean fisheries, its bison,
and, most recently, its public lands. Hardin pointed
out   how   "the National Parks present another instance
of the working out of the tragedy of   the   commons."[16]
The   tragedy   is also being manifest in our wilderness
areas.   Prime   camping   areas have been trampled,
popular   trails   have   become   waist-deep ruts,   and
special interests have converged on the political
system.

In economic terms, the commons produces   problems
precisely because property rights to resources are not
well defined and enforced.   Where all such rights are
well   defined   and   defended, economic theory predicts
that resources will at the minimum tend to be used
efficiently.   A comparison of domestic cattle and wild
bison teaches the importance of property rights.   No
one was able to establish rights to the bison because
of its fugitive nature; hence, the species was almost
wiped out as hunters pursued their own interests.   The
exploitation   did   not   end   until   the government
established   rights   to the bison (or perhaps when the
resource became so rare that it was costly to pursue).
Domestic cattle, however, never have been threatened
with extinction (and probably never will be), because
rights to cattle are easy to define and enforce.[17]

The commons is   a   self-destructing system that
must be replaced by established rights to the common
property resource. Only in this way will wise use
prevail.   The relevant question is whether rights
should be held collectively or privately.   In 1949,
Aldo Leopold gave us an inkling of what can be
expected when the government tries to manage natural
resources:

At   what   point will governmental
conservation, like   the   mastadon,   be
handicapped by its own dimensions....
In 1909, when I first saw the West,
there   were   grizzlies in every major
mountain   area, but you could travel for
months   without   meeting a conservation
officer.   Today there is a conservation
officer "behind every bush" yet as wildlife bureaus grow, our most magnificent
mammal retreats steadily toward the Canadian border.[18]

Economic theory states that when property rights to resources are well defined, enforced, transferable, and privately held, owners will tend to allocate the resources efficiently; that is, there will be a tendency to allocate resources to their highest valued uses. When property rights are adequately arranged, private costs align with social costs. This is Adam Smith's "invisible hand" at work. With property rights firmly in place, people are led to do good while doing well. Unfortunately, private and social costs diverge when the property rights system breaks down or is not allowed to evolve. Where rights are collectively held, the predictable consequence is a movement away from the socially optimal point of resource allocation. Evidence suggests that the cost to society of having the government own and allocate natural resources has been high in terms of environmental quality and economic efficiency.

Since decisions are made on the basis of information and incentives, the institutions that shape them have a great deal of influence on results. When resources are held by collective bodies and allocated by bureaucrats, we can expect poor information in the absence of prices and perverse incentives in the absence of the profit motive. Thus, bureaucratic decision-makers, who are seeking budgetary increases, workplace amenities, discretionary power, career advancement, and minimal tension, can be expected to allocate resources inefficiently. When natural resources are allocated by such a system, lower environmental quality is often a byproduct.

Most environmentalists and a growing number of studies on natural resource bureaucracies support this indictment.[19] There is substantial evidence that the U.S. Forest Service has degraded pristine areas by selling timber below cost.[20] The Bureau of Land Management (BLM) has chained vast acres of woodland at an economic loss and has initiated questionable grazing practices on much of its land.[21] Nearly twenty different federal agencies are involved in subsidizing the development and redevelopment of the fragile barrier islands.[22] For over three generations, the Bureau of Reclamation and the Army Corps of Engineers have been building dams that have no net economic justification and generate severe environmental impacts.[23] Federal energy policy has artificially induced increases in demand, subsidized environmentally costly development, and stifled the development of alternative energy.[24] Even wildlife has suffered at the hands of competent, well-intended bureaucrats.[25]

The government's conservation record is less than admirable, but quite predictable. The actions in the private sector can also be predicted, but when actions are internalized they have far better consequences. Consider, for example, the policies of the International Paper Company:

> In recent years income from outdoor recreation has become significant. Improved public relations have been gained from wildlife/recreation programs, management of endangered species, and other aspects of multiple use. As forest management intensifies, provisions for wildlife must be better planned in all stages of management if we are to maintain our programs, realize their full benefits, and further increase returns from investments in wildlife resources. Professional judgment is required by foresters on the ground, for they are the wildlife managers of our forests.
> International Paper today practices intensive wildlife management on much of its land, committing more acreage to managed wildlife production than any other private landowner or any state game agency in the United States. Application of IP's research is doubling and, in some cases, tripling game populations on these lands.[26]

While bureaucracies are being cited for failures in environmental quality and economic efficiency, private individuals and groups operating within the market system increasingly are being commended for their conservation efforts. This is not surprising, for there is a growing demand for environmental amenities, and publicly provided and underpriced resources are being overused. Since well-defined, well-enforced, and easily transferable private property rights lead individuals to use resources responsibly and efficiently, we find that markets are emerging for environmental goods.

Led by The Nature Conservancy, the National Audubon Society, and Ducks Unlimited, many other private conservation groups are concentrating on directly protecting natural areas rather than lobbying for protective legislation. Some land is protected by ownership and some by easement or lease arrangements. In addition, numerous local "land trust" groups have been established to protect local resources.[27] Groups are also attempting to acquire instream water rights

for preservation in much the same way that instream
uses have been traditionally protected and preserved
in Great Britain.[28]

J.H. Dales illustrated the ability of property
rights to foster a quality environment:

> The island of Great Britain is moist
> and verdant, and blessed with innumerable
> cool streams that once were all haunts of
> trout and salmon. Most of them still are,
> even though they now flow through an
> industrial countryside. The total
> poundage of fine game fish taken would put
> any accessible part of Canada to shame.
> (Canadians) are so used to the idea that
> the waters of any industrial area are a
> write-off, so far as quality angling is
> concerned, that one cannot help but be
> curious as to how all that fishing is
> maintained.
>
> It is not because they do not have to
> watch out for pollution...an organization
> called the Angler's Cooperative Associa-
> tion...has taken over the watchdog func-
> tions formerly left to individuals....It
> has a fluctuating and rather small list of
> members and subscribers,...but it is able
> to call on some powerful help, especially
> legal. It has investigated nearly 700
> pollution cases since it started and very
> rarely does it fail to get statement or
> damages, as the case requires. These
> anglers have behind them a simple fact.
> Every fishery in Britain, except for those
> in public reservoirs, belongs to some
> private owner. Many of them have changed
> hands at high prices and action is always
> entered on behalf of somebody who has
> suffered real damage....(In Canada) the
> fishing belongs to everybody -- and thus
> to nobody. The A.C.A. exists merely to
> take action where individuals many not act
> themselves.[29]

Increasingly, profit-motivated individuals and
groups are providing environmental goods in the marketplace. The Diamond-A Cattle Company, for example,
manages for and profits from hiking and hunting on its[30]
rugged and remote lands in western Texas. In
Montana, ranchers are earning revenue on their wild-[31]
life stocks by charging hunters for access. Some
companies are profiting by reclaiming streams in order
to increase fish productivity.[32] Ed Zern, fishing

editor for Field and Stream, reported that "it seems
likely there's now a permanent industry devoted to
improving the fish supporting capacity of streams that
have deteriorated badly."[33]

The list of privately produced environmental
amenities is likely to grow as more entrepreneurs
discover the opportunities that exist and as public
resources suffer the consequences of the tragedy of
the commons. The marginal value of privately held
resources will increase as their public counterparts
are degraded and mismanaged. In terms of conservation
efforts, entrepreneurship is our most precious -- and
most scarce -- resource. Entrepreneurs provide the
only free lunch available to society, and only through
a system of private property rights can their efforts
be effectively channeled into productive activities.

ESTABLISHING PRIVATE PROPERTY RIGHTS IN FEDERAL LANDS

Contrary to the beliefs held by many conservationists, sound economics does not conflict with
environmental quality. It is, rather, the inefficient
resource allocation by bureaucracies that is often the
cause of environmental degradation. When rights to
resources are held in common or are determined by
governmental agencies, inefficiency and environmental
disturbances are predictable consequences. Inefficient resource allocation and reduced environmental
quality are inexorably linked when authority is
divorced from responsibility.

The establishment of private property rights in
publicly owned natural resources would foster
environmental quality in several ways. First, a
system of private property rights would largely reduce
the bureaucracy's ability to lower environmental
quality by inefficiently using taxpayer dollars. In
his study of timber policy on the San Juan National
Forest, Colorado, William F. Hyde concluded that
"wilderness values would be better preserved on this
land if it were privately owned, because no
profit-oriented owner would bother to cut down the
trees. This is a somewhat paradoxical conclusion,
since profit-seeking is frequently thought of as
leading to environmental degradation, which must in
turn be mitigated by government regulation."[34]

The list of bureaucratic projects that have
threatened pristine environments is widely known among
those in the conservation movement. (One need look
only so far as The Living Wilderness or Audubon to
read about the government's plans for wilderness and
park lands.) Thus, the benefits accruing to those who
value the pristine are likely to be quite significant

in the absence of bureaucratic projects. One benefit
of wilderness designation that environmentalists often
fail to talk about is that the law requires passive
management, which effectively keeps bureaucracies from
expanding uneconomical programs into pristine areas.
Wilderness areas (and environmentalists) would benefit
even more if private property rights were established
in these areas. Since this would largely remove
natural resource management decisions from the political arena.

The political process is incredibly whimsical and
fickle. Witness the policy shifts since James Watt
succeeded Cecil Andrus as secretary of the interior.
Even if Julian Simon is correct and natural resources
are becoming less scarce, it is difficult to believe
that conservationists will be the long-term winners in
such an unstable environment.

The recent "energy crisis" provides a clear
example of how environmental concerns can be tossed
aside in the midst of political hysteria. Oil
shortages, largely caused by perverse governmental
pricing schemes, brought the situation to crisis level
and beyond. The Alaskan pipeline was built with the
blessing of the U.S. Congress, which overruled its own
National Environmental Policy Act in the process.
Energy policy soon became the "moral equivalent of
war" and the U.S. Synfuels Corporation became a highly
touted weapon. Environmentalists wondered what had
happened to the government's responsibility to protect
the environment.

There are good reasons to expect this kind of
political railroading to threaten environmental values
again. James Watt's mineral leasing plans may be an
indication of the inherently unstable base upon which
our environmental policy rests. A significant potential threat to the wilderness comes from the demand
for strategic minerals, including chromium, cobalt,
manganese, nickel, and titanium. These minerals have
been labeled "strategic" by the U.S. Congress because
they are "essential in the event of a national emergency."[35] The United States is almost totally dependent on foreign sources for at least a dozen of these
minerals.[36] Over ninety percent of our columbite,
strontium, titanium, manganese, chromite, and cobalt
requirements come from countries that are politically
unstable or potentially hostile. Given the limited
short-run potentials for substitution, our high technology society is extremely dependent on these minerals.[37] Appendix Tables 2.1, 2.2 and 2.3 illustrate
the nature of the problem.

Because wilderness areas have never been fully
explored for mineral resources, the United States'
actual mineral wealth is largely unknown. The real

threat to the wilderness could come from governmentally mandated exploration and mining in the event of politically induced constraints on the supply of strategic minerals. Comments by congressmen and governmental officials suggest that some people feel uneasy about the country's strategic mineral situation. Representative James Santini (D-Nev.), chairman of the House Committee on Mines and Minerals, believes that "a chrome embargo by the Soviet Union would bring the entire industrial world to its knees in just six months."[38] William Dresher, former chairman of the National Academy of Sciences Committee on Nonrenewable Resources[39] has documented and amplified Santini's concerns.[39] Yet John P. Morgan Jr., chief staff officer of the United States Bureau of Mines, has maintained that "the U.S. could be virtually self-sufficient in all but a few minerals."[40] His view is shared by former Senator Harrison Schmitt, a geologist and one-time astronaut, who said that "nature endowed us with unbelievably vast resources, most of which have not been tapped."[41]

The current political system leaves the future of the wilderness on very shaky ground. Conservationists who are concerned about future generations should question the ability of political decision makers to provide adequately for the future. The political process offers little room for trade-offs across generations or across contending inconsistent uses. Conservationists insist on no development while developers want open access. Since the property rights to the wilderness are managed by bureaucracies, neither conservationists nor developers have to face the true opportunity costs of their actions.

Anderson and Hill have called attempts by individuals and groups to use the political process to increase their wealth "transfer activity."[42] Such activity transfers wealth among parties. Unlike market activities, it does not create wealth through voluntary exchange. Just as pork barrel water projects involve transferring wealth from taxpayers to a small group of water users, wilderness designation transfers wealth from the taxpayer to a small group of outdoorsmen, most of whom are neither underprivileged nor undereducated.

When property rights to resources are well-defined, well-enforced, and easily transferable, the private owner receives accurate price information on the value of his resource relative to other resources. Further, when he can capture the benefits he will be confronted with incentives to use those resources in socially efficient ways. The National Audubon Society holds private property rights to 26,800 acres of marshland in Louisiana. While Audubon's primary goal

in managing the Rainey Wildlife Sanctuary is to provide habitat for migratory waterfowl, ownership of the
land has forced the society to face the opportunity
costs of its actions.

Rather than condemn development as incompatible
with preservation values, as they have done regarding
the public lands, the Audubon Society has allowed
carefully monitored development to occur on the Rainey
preserve.[43] Natural gas is pumped out of the sanctuary, providing close to a million dollars of revenue
in annual royalties. Cattle graze in some of the
drier areas for a per-head fee to the owners. From
1927 to 1932, the Audubon Society used steel traps to
capture nearly a quarter-million muskrats who were
competing with snow geese for three-corned grass,
bringing in over $100,000 in revenue from the
pelts.[44] The Rainey Sanctuary illustrates how private
property rights can encourage cooperation instead of
rhetoric.

Along with the gains in environmental quality
that result from private ownership, we would expect to
see significant gains in economic efficiency. Most
people do not appreciate the social value of attaining
economic efficiency, perhaps because the concept is
often misunderstood. In simple terms, an economic
system is efficient if resources are allocated so that
no one can be made better off without making a least
one person worse off. It is difficult to think of a
more worthy goal. Too often, people perceive efficiency as "making the most money," "maximizing profit," or conserving BTUs; but efficient resource
allocation is simply using our scarce resources so
that they produce their maximum value.

While the case for establishing private property
rights to federal lands is largely based on predicted
gains in environmental quality and economic
efficiency, other benefits would derive from taking
natural resources out of the public sector. On purely
ethical grounds, it is difficult to justify putting
control of vast areas of land in the hands of
political appointees like Cecil Andrus or James Watt.
Likewise, it is difficult to justify the transfers of
wealth that have taken place as a result of the
governmental allocation of natural resources. Wealthy
farmers have received subsidized water, large timber
corporations have received subsidized logs, and
outdoorsmen have received subsidized wilderness.

In the case of wilderness users, it is difficult
to justify the provision of a zero-priced good. Many
studies have shown that the average wilderness user is
significantly above average with regard to personal
income and level of education.[45] This is true despite
the high number of students who use wilderness.

Students, however, are not equivalent to the inner city poor; they are generally living through a period of voluntary poverty while they invest in their human capital. A close examination of the governing body of one influential environmental group gives one a feeling for the segment of society that values the wilderness the most. The board of directors of the Sierra Club during the late 1960s included two writers, two lawyers, two medical doctors, one Superior Court judge, one biochemist, one nuclear engineer, one journalist, one biophysicist, one physicist, one realtor, one photographer, and one hydrologist,[46] hardly the kind of group you would expect to find at a PTA meeting for a downtown Chicago public school. As Milton Friedman has stated, the poor and the disadvantaged have rarely been the recipients of governmental subsidies.[47] Given that wealth and political power are positively related in all societies, this is the expected outcome.

It can also be argued that the government has some responsibility to adhere to the U.S. culture, partially and elegantly expressed in the wishes of the Founding Fathers. Those who provided the intellectual foundations for the U.S. Constitution, made it clear that government was most useful when kept to a minimum.[48] Adam Smith, Thomas Jefferson, and others held that land was most productive and society most just when resources are placed in the hands of private individuals. Alexander Hamilton recognized the power of individual self-interest and the need for structuring institutions in such a way that private actions promoted increased social welfare. It is obvious that a government involved in growing trees and grass, building dams, and managing parks is far different from one that is designed primarily to define and defend property rights and "provide for a common defense."

The case for establishing private property rights is quite persuasive. Improvements in environmental quality would result, wasteful lobbying efforts by environmentalists and developers would no longer be as profitable as they are now, resources would be channeled toward compromising and mutually beneficial activities, and natural resources would be extracted only when they could pay their way out of pristine environments. Beyond these gains, ethical and equity considerations would be more significant. We would reduce the mining of moral capital of our nation. Individuals would have to pay for the goods and services they desire, be they pristine lakes or acre-feet of irrigation water, instead of relying on the political apparatus to allocate them. All parties would be forced to consider the true opportunity costs

of their actions. Finally, the establishment of
private property rights in federal lands would bring
us back to the constitutional contract that has done
so much to advance the cause of individual freedom and
economic well-being.

PRIVATIZATION: CONFRONTING THE CRITICS

The Reagan administration has initiated an asset
management program that includes plans to sell small
scattered parcels of little-used federal lands. This
program has been under attack by environmentalists and
others who use "privatization" and "divestiture" as
catch words for environmental destruction. The following comments illustrate the emotional reaction to
this rather small land sales program.
Jack Anderson, the syndicated columnist, wrote:

> It's time someone blew the whistle on
> a Reagan Administration scheme that could
> lead to one of the biggest land grabs by
> greedy private interests in the nation's
> history.[49]

Caroline Adams wrote in the Wall Street Journal:

> Conservationists fear a wholesale
> disposal of public lands that disregards
> the tract's beauty or economic value for
> the sake of budget cutting. Some federal
> officials and conservationists are also
> skeptical about the amount of revenue the
> sale can generate.[50]

Charles H. Callison warned in Audubon Action:

> The nation's environmental organi-
> zations were unanimous in opposing the
> massive land sale program at Senator
> Percy's hearing and at subsequent over-
> sight hearings conducted by the Senate
> Energy Committee and the House Subcommit-
> tee on Public Lands and National Parks.
> Alison Horton of National Audubon's Wash-
> ington staff presented discerning testi-
> mony. She concluded: "Once again the
> Reagan Administration has launched an
> attack on the publicly-owned natural re-
> sources and lands of the country....The
> course which the Administration is taking
> must be altered."[51]

Bill Cunningham of The Wilderness Society predicted that the land sale program is

>...starting out small and appears benign,
>but could be a cancerous growth that
>denies access of Americans to part of
>their birthright....The Wilderness Society
>is concerned that the administration's
>property review board and land sales
>program could go too far too fast. A
>wholesale transfer of land to the private
>sector would eliminate multiple-use pro-
>tection of the land and destroy free
>public access to the lands.[52]

John Hooper of the Sierra Club wrote:

>Since the beginning of the Reagan admin-
>istration, environmentalists have objected
>to appointment after appointment and poli-
>cy after policy. In recent months, how-
>ever, many of the specific proposals and
>attitudes environmentalists protested have
>coalesced into one general and pervasive
>threat. It's called "privatization" and
>it sounds innocent and simple: the gov-
>ernment sells off "excess" federal proper-
>ty and uses the proceeds to balance the
>budget. An important variation of the
>theme calls for long-term leasing of
>energy and mineral resources to private
>corporations at minute fractions of their
>true value....Both privatization and give-
>away leases transfer publicly owned wealth
>to a few large companies.[53]

Joan Nice wrote in Audubon:

>To environmentalists "privatization"
>-- the Reagan Administration's buzz word
>for shifting federal land into private
>lands -- is "piratization" of valuable
>public assets....Privatization sounds good
>to some ranchers, until they think about
>who might get the land. If it were to be
>auctioned off to the highest bidder, as
>the budget scheme implies, most ranchers
>would lose the federal grazing leases upon
>which their livelihood depends....But even
>where land sales seemed prudent, the
>plan's emphasis on making as much money as
>possible to reduce the debt was controver-
>sial. If the politicians were determined

to get top dollar, it meant many public projects were out of the question. What is now open space on Waikiki Beach[54] might be lost to condominium development.

Ted Trueblood wrote in Field and Stream:

> It started as the Sagebrush Rebellion and it has now grown into what will be the biggest ripoff in American history--if it succeeds. And it will succeed unless the victims, the American people, raise such a hue and cry as never has been raised before. It is the proposed sell off or "privatization" of the public lands, both the national forests and the range lands now under the jurisdiction of the Bureau of Land Management.
> All these lands belong to all of us, to you and me, and if they were divided up each of us would receive a little more than 2-1/2 acres. They hold incredible wealth in timber, grazing, and minerals. That's the reason why the sharpies want them, of course, and it explains the repeated attempts to steal them in the past....What can we do? The only thing I can suggest is to elect Congressmen and Senators whose first concern is the public they're supposed to represent, not the special interests.[55]

William Turnage of The Wilderness Society said:

> It is ludicrous to sell land when the U.S. real estate market is going through one of its most depressed periods in history.[56]

Geoffrey Webb spoke for Friends of the Earth:

> We believe in the public lands. We strongly believe that they should remain public and should be maintained and managed for the public, not for the narrow interests of those who might want to mine coal or explore for oil, gas, or minerals. ...What the Administration is doing is trying to transfer as much of the publicly owned land and resources as possible to the private sector in as short a time as possible. But none of this is being debated in a public forum. It is simply being done.[57]

The Wilderness Society itself officially declared
that:

> American history has demonstrated that the
> public is not well served, in the long
> run, by turning over commodity lands to
> private interests. The aim of business is
> short-run profits, not long-run preserva-
> tion -- and experience has shown that
> conservation of resources is critical to
> sustaining a high standard of living -- of
> living at all.[58]

Several themes run through these attacks on the
establishment of private property rights in federal
lands. Perhaps the most common is that federal lands
are a citizen's birthright and as such must be
provided free to the public. Another theme is that
public managers will act in the long-run interests of
the public and that private owners cannot be trusted
to see beyond short-run profits. It is assumed that a
land sales program will yield a world in which large
corporations own everything. Many critics also
contend that the program is merely a last ditch
attempt to balance a runaway budget. Others have
complained that the land sales program is being forced
through without any appropriate public comments.
These criticisms deserve to be addressed, and perhaps
the best way to do so is to first separate ideology
from economics.
Though the problems of common ownership were
first illustrated by Garrett Hardin, an environmentalist, most environmentalists fail to realize the
common pool nature of the public lands. Just as the
air is overused as a garbage dump because it is free,
the public lands are overused because access is free
or grossly underpriced. National parks are crowded
and abused, prime hunting areas in the national
forests are overhunted, and popular wilderness areas
are overrun by enthusiastic hikers. It is ironic that
conservationists who talk in terms of a finite world
insist that the public lands provide infinite
opportunities for multiple-use management. While free
access to the natural environment may be an appealing
philosophy, it is a philosophy far less effective than
property rights in conserving resources.[59]
The widely held fear that privatization plans
would ensure that all land ends up in the hands of
giant development corporations is without foundation.
Even corporations have limited resources, and they go
to where the expected marginal payoff is highest. It
is doubtful that they would squander their resources
on low-valued land. On land where the opportunity

cost of development is high and the opportunity cost
of preservation is accordingly low, conservation
groups could compete for ownership with wealthy
corporations. We cannot predict what kind of novel
institutional arrangements would be developed by
entrepreneurs who want to capture the benefits of
providing natural amenities. But these amenities are
highly superior goods, so we would expect the action
to be intense.

Criticism of privatization also suggests that the
legitimate rights of those who have been long-term
public land users would be ignored. A politically and
economically sound privatization program would
recognize these rights and consider them either by
compensation, preemption, or accommodation to existing
rights. There is no reason to believe that the Exxons
of the world would force all western ranchers off the
land they have been using for generations.[60]   Nor is
there any reason to believe that environmentalists
would not be able to secure rights to ecologically
significant areas through ownership, lease, or
easement.

Most conservationists still cling to an economic
mythology born during the progressive era. By ob-
serving the "exploitation" of relatively abundant resources on the commons of the U.S. frontier, progressive conservationists concluded that without governmental intervention private enterprise would ravish
the earth. They came to believe that only scientific
management by bureaucrats isolated from the profit
motive could ensure the efficient utilization of our
natural resources.[61]

Not only did the progressives overlook the common
property nature of the frontier, they also misunderstood the role of wealth, prices, scarcity, and private property in promoting environmental quality. The
average citizen of 1882 lived in relative poverty. It
is hard to believe that he placed much value on wilderness when he was continually trying to scratch out
a living in it. It is not surprising, then, that the
conservation movement had its roots in New England
where income was relatively high and civilization
well-established.

As pioneers moved westward, huge inventories of
timber hindered their ability to cultivate the land.
The value (price) of this timber was very low, in some
cases even negative. From both a private and a social
perspective, it made little sense to conserve such an
abundant resource. As the resources became more
valuable, however, parties began to establish property
rights.[62]   In many cases, governmental actions
restricted the establishment of property rights and
prolonged the exploitation of the commons.[63]   Never-

theless, policy makers perceived the market system to be flawed and began to involve the government directly in natural resource management and to ensure that the commons would remain common. The action was predicated on the notion that governmental agents would divorce themselves from self-interest and act in the best interest of the public.

Much modern environmental rhetoric has its roots in the progressive era, but environmentalism also has taken on a "religious" tone by purporting to be concerned with the public interest while accusing others of pursuing narrow self-interests. In addition, the movement is plagued by a doomsday, no-growth view of the modern economy, which by its nature rules out reasonable solutions to many problems. Instead of attempting to design institutions that encourage individuals to make the world a better place, environmentalists too often are preoccupied with saving the world from the reality of changing factor prices.

We do not want to defend the Reagan administration's proposed land sales program, because that program is seriously flawed in both presentation and attempted execution. As critics have noted, the administration has said that the primary reason for the program is the deficit-reducing revenues to be realized from it. The best reason for the asset management program is to place the land into private hands in order to realize gains in environmental quality, economic efficiency, and reduced governmental operations. Unfortunately, the administration has lost support by appearing to sneak the program past the public. A better approach would be to promote the program openly and actively by outlining the gains to society of reduced government and increased efficiency. Such a positive approach would present a golden opportunity for wilderness enthusiasts to move beyond rhetoric to action.

PRIVATE PROPERTY RIGHTS IN WILDERNESS AREAS

I don't think The Wilderness Society would want to own a wilderness. We think of it as a national legacy that should be owned by no one and enjoyed by everyone. We're not in the business of owning land to exclude other people from it. We want to see it protected and managed as public lands, by public agencies and available to the public.[64]

In this country, one of the first suggestions for preserving nature in its wild state came from frontier

artist George Catlin. Writing in 1839, Catlin proposed the establishment of "a nation's park, containing man and beast, in all the wild and freshness of
their nature's beauty!"[65] Soon after, in the 1840s,
the U.S. Congress designated the Hot Springs area in
Arkansas as a national preserve.[66] Californians set
aside the Yosemite Valley in 1864 for use as a public
park, and in 1872 Yellowstone National Park was established. These actions signaled the beginning of new
forms of land use and, more importantly, a new role
for government.

Wilderness did not become an official use of
federal lands until 1924, when a young forester named
Aldo Leopold persuaded the Forest Service to establish
the Gila Wilderness in southwest New Mexico. During
the 1920s, the Forest Service established its
L-regulations, which permitted the Forest Service
chief to set aside "primitive areas."[67] By 1933,
sixty-three such areas had been designated within the
national forest system.[68] During the 1930s, another
Forest Service employee, Robert Marshall, one of the
founders of The Wilderness Society, wrote the
U-regulations, authorizing the establishment of
wilderness areas through administrative discretion.[69]

Wilderness designation continued to be handled by
governmental administrators until 1964, when Congress
passed the Wilderness Act. The act formed a National
Wilderness Preservation System (NWPS), comprised of
9.1 million acres of land previously managed under the
U and L regulations.[70] Because of the strict wording
in the original act regarding minimum acreage and
roadless characteristics, relatively few areas in the
eastern United States were included in the NWPS.
Eventually, however, the criteria for wilderness
became less demanding when the Eastern Wilderness Act
of 1974 was passed.[71] Since then, a significant
amount of land has been added to the NWPS (see
Appendix Table 2.4).

Often omitted from preservation history is the
important role played by private parties. Since the
bulk of this country's scenic lands were withdrawn
from private entry via the Forest Reserve Act of 1891,
there was little opportunity for private landowners to
meet preservation demands. There have been, however,
interesting exceptions. The Rockefeller family
provided the core lands for Grand Teton, the Great
Smokies, and Acadia National Parks.[72] Percival P.
Baxter, one-time governor of Maine, donated a
200,000-acre preserve containing Maine's tallest peak,
Mt. Katahdin.[73] The Save-the-Redwoods League, a
private conservation group, helped provide land for
the Redwoods National Park. In addition, there are
significant holdings of private land within designated
wilderness areas.

Until the last decade or so, competition for the wilderness was trivial. Backcountry enthusiasts were relatively few in number, and resource developers had no desire to explore relatively inaccessable wilderness areas. As population and wealth have grown and as preferences have changed, however, demands on the wilderness and on all public lands have increased dramatically. Competition not only heightened between wilderness users and resource developers, but also between wilderness users themselves --between nordic skiers and snowmobilers, for example.[74] These demands have led to calls for more wilderness preservation and for more development access.

The provisions of the Wilderness Act preclude exploration and removal of developable resources except in special cases,[75] and until the Reagan administration came to power few exploration permits had been approved. With the recent change in policy promoted by Secretary of Interior James Watt and with the nearing of the December 31, 1983, deadline for mining entry, there has been a rush to explore the wilderness. To compound the problem, there is little knowledge on the extent of the valuable commodity resources that might lie within wilderness boundaries. As a result, the issue has become polarized; developers want to access everywhere, and conservationists want everything locked up. The current institutional framework offers only a negative-sum solution, and society will be the ultimate loser.

Although there is relatively little solid information on resource values within wilderness areas, those areas where values are known have been the scene of intense conflict. Perhaps the most notable confrontation was over oil exploration in the Bob Marshall Wilderness in Montana. After months of heated debate, the issue was settled when a congressional subcommittee declared the Bob Marshall off-limits. The legislative tactics used by the subcommittee are of questionable legality and have been challenged in court. Other conflicts include copper in the Glacier Peaks Wilderness in Washington;[76] coal in Bryce Canyon National Park in Utah;[77] molybdenum in Misty Fjords National Monument in Alaska;[78] and copper and silver in the Cabinet Mountains Wilderness Area in Montana.[79]

Given the complexity of the issues and their emotional nature, it is unlikely that the political process will yield a solution that will satisfy many. The political process is significantly different from the one portrayed on the television series "Dallas," where Senator Bobby Ewing finds a positive-sum solution to the conflict between Jock, his developer-father, and Miss Elly, his conservationist-mother.[80]

It is safe to assume that the Sierra Club and Mobil Oil are not as close as Jock and Miss Elly. We can only be skeptical of the possibility that good public decisions will be made on wilderness areas. Private rights and the rule of willing consent provide powerful incentives to reach agreement, but political decision making fosters protracted, vitriolic conflict.

Wilderness has long been considered a "public good."[81] According to economists, public goods are characterized by jointness of consumption and nonexcludability. In other words, use of a public good does not diminish the quality of the good for the next user, and the nature of the good is such that it is difficult for a private owner to establish property rights to it. National defense is the economists' favorite example of a public good, but wilderness is also used.

In his 1967 article, John Krutilla expanded the definition of a public good with regard to wilderness preservation to include indivisibility, irreversibility, and the existence of nonmarket demands.[82] The concept of indivisibility suggests that certain goods must remain intact for them to maintain their value; that is, the Grand Canyon would not be the same if half of it were gone. Because of indivisibility, a private owner supposedly could not afford to own such a resource. The irreversibility argument suggests that the nature of some resources is such that any development would destroy the resource for all time. Once Old Faithful has been developed for geothermal energy, its ecological value would likely be destroyed. Regarding nonmarket demands, economists have argued that many people value goods like wilderness simply because they exist, because they would like to have the option of visiting a wilderness, and because they would like to pass on wilderness to their children. It is argued that a private owner will not be able to capture these values with a market price for entry.

Natural resource economists typically have nodded their heads in approval when the public good criteria have been applied to wilderness. Yet all of these criteria can be criticized. It is clear that after some point of use the wilderness good is reduced in quality, and there is an incentive for a private owner to control use so the resource retains its integrity, that is, its value. There is no reason to assume that individuals cannot be excluded from a wilderness area. Simple checkpoints at trailheads would keep track of those who paid. It is true that some people would attempt to be free riders, bushwhacking their way into the backcountry in order to avoid checkpoints; but it

is also true that free riders sneak into drive-in
theaters by arriving in the trunk of the car.
Monitoring systems would develop to minimize the free
rider problem in the wilderness, just as in a drive-in
theater.

While it is true that certain areas lose their
wilderness character if they are divided, it does not
follow that private parties cannot muster the
resources necessary to own large tracts of land. The
ability of the private sector to acquire a large
amount of capital is almost limitless; witness the
private funding of the enormously expensive Alaskan
pipeline. The irreversibility argument is strong in
certain cases and not so strong in others. Biological
species, once lost, are gone forever; so are unique
geological formations like Old Faithful and the Grand
Canyon. In these instances, the public good argument
is strongest. In most wilderness settings, however,
irreversibility need not be a major concern, especially if the institutions provide incentives to maximize
long-run values. Gas development in Audubon's Rainy
Preserve has not ruined the wilderness character of
the marsh, nor has logging on Baxter State Park, the
Great Smokey Mountains National Park, and many of our
eastern wilderness areas. Nature sometimes can, and
does, heal itself. Under incentives of private ownership, man can hasten the healing process significantly.

Meadowlark Farms Inc. provides an excellent
example of how incentives can shape sensitive development and how development need not cause irreversible
change. Meadowlark was a subsidiary of Ayrshire
Collaries Corporation, a coal mining company. It was
established in 1946 to reclaim and ultimately put to
agricultural and recreational use thousands of acres
of stripmined land. The Meadowlark program has been
enormously successful; the farming operations involve
varied livestock (hogs, cattle, and sheep) and small
grains as well as amenity areas.[83] Similar reclamation projects have also improved wildlife habitat.[84]

With regard to nonmarket demands for wilderness
and other environmental amenities, it should be noted
that this is precisely one of the economic roles of
private conservation organizations, especially those
who spend their dollars in the market rather than in
the political sector. When an individual gives money
to The Nature Conservancy, he is expressing his value
for those resources he might use some day (option
demand), for those resources he enjoys simply because
they exist (existence demand), and for those resources
he wishes to provide for future generations (bequest
demand). Obviously, not all demands are captured in a
market setting, but it is foolish to write off market

possibilities by blindly following well-publicized myths.

The preceding arguments suggest that private ownership of wilderness is not an economic impossibility. Coupled with the argument that the current political-bureaucratic institutional arrangement is hazardous to the welfare of the wilderness, the rationale for establishing private property rights to wilderness becomes quite strong. Some have suggested that wilderness areas be given in fee simple title to environmental groups,[85] that wilderness endowment areas be established and administered by a board staffed by environmental leaders,[86] or that wilderness be sold at auction to the high bidder.

We propose that designated wilderness areas be opened to a type of homesteading modeled after the Homesteading Act of 1865. Instead of cultivating the land to establish a legitimate claim, the wilderness homesteader would have to maintain or build trails, provide campgrounds, establish visitor centers, or reclaim land. The list of possible activities that might qualify a group for wilderness ownership is almost limitless and wide open to entrepreneurial talents. The parcel size would be determined by the current legal boundaries of each wilderness area, and only nonprofit tax-exempt conservation organizations would be eligible to homestead. Once title to the wilderness is in private hands, the management decisions would be up to the owner, subject to the constraint that the owner remain a nonprofit conservation organization. Development could take place only with the owner's approval.

Since many individuals have been using certain wilderness areas for long periods of time and have essentially established property rights to certain uses and areas, it would be important to allow them to retain their rights. Using the precedent set by the Preemption Act of 1841, our proposal would legally establish all legitimate rights of past use prior to any actual homesteading. Uses that would fall under this preemption clause would include outfitting, guiding, and grazing. For example, if a guide had previously used a Forest Service wilderness area to set up his hunting camps, he would be able to retain that right to the exclusion of any future homestead. An administrative court could be established to handle preemption claims over a one- or two-year period, after which time no more preemption claims could be made and homesteading could begin.

In certain cases, it may be desirable to establish publicly held covenants to protect an irreplaceable resource. Such covenants might be used to protect endangered species or unique geologic, archeologic, and historic sites, but we would not expect them to be used extensively. This proposal would make significant gains over an existing system that is subject to political whims. The wilderness owner would have to face the full opportunity costs of his decisions and would have every incentive to use his resources efficiently. If a significant mineral resource was sought after by developers, the owner could either forego development or allow it on his own terms subject to a specific contract. This arrangement would not inhibit development but would contribute to orderly and environmentally sensitive development. In some cases, the wilderness owner might disallow development of a valuable resource if he did not believe the revenues would exceed the costs in terms of wilderness quality.

A real world example supports this contention. In Montana's Cabinet Mountains Wilderness, Billo Comola and Cesar Hernandez, wilderness advocates and "pick and shovel" miners, hold mining claims to an area sought by major mining companies. As of this past September, Comola and Hernandez had refused offers of as high as $3 million for their mining claims. Will they sell out at $3.5 million or at $3 million with an exploration contract specifying tough reclamation? Not even the scientific manager knows. Currently, they are attempting to negotiate a contract that would require Chevron Oil to establish a wildlife research fund (along with paying the $3 million).[87] This case, unique under existing institutions, provides a clear example of how private property rights to wilderness can foster efficient and environmentally sensitive development. For wilderness enthusiasts, the alternative of politicized decision-making offers little long-term security.

SUMMARY

The arguments developed in this paper point to the perilous nature of our present wilderness system under existing institutions. These arguments also point to a growing awareness by conservationists of the environmental benefits of private property rights and free markets. The proposal we have developed is an attempt to redirect environmental policy so that resource decision making becomes a positive-sum game. Wilderness enthusiasts who tend to fear pending resource shortages would do well to consider how the wilderness will fare if politicians and bureaucrats become convinced that resources are scarce. A system of privately owned wilderness may be the best way to ensure a wilderness heritage for our descendants.

NOTES

1. John McPhee, Encounters with the Archdruid (New York: Farrar, Straus, Giroux, 1971), p. 71.

2. Julian L. Simon, The Ultimate Resource (Princeton, N.J.: Princeton University Press, 1981). Simon criticizes The Global 2000 Report and the National Agricultural Lands Study for using questionable data and for not recognizing price-induced conservation, exploration, and substitution. Simon's data show that prices for the vast majority of goods and services, including natural resources, have exhibited long-run declining trends.

3. John Baden and Richard Stroup, eds., Bureaucracy vs. Environment (Ann Arbor: University of Michigan Press, 1981).

4. Thomas Barlow, "The Giveaway in the National Forests," Living Wilderness (October-December 1979), pp. 29-32.

5. Thomas J. Graff, "Water Development Takes Beating," Bozeman (MT) Daily Chronicle, June 14, 1982.

6. Ernst R. Habicht Jr., "U.S. Natural Gas Policy: An Autopsy," in Bureaucracy vs. Environment, Baden and Stroup, eds., pp. 64-76.

7. Phillip A. House, "Leaving Water in Western Streams," The Nature Conservancy News (January-February 1979), pp. 25-30.

8. Quoted in an interview by Rob Eshman, "The Lovinses and the Soft-Energy Path," Dartmouth (June 1982), pp. 36-40.

9. Jon R. Luoma, "Water: Grass-Roots Opposition Stymies Garrison Diversion," Audubon (March 1982), pp. 115-17.

10. Christopher Palmer, "Environmentalists Can Be Friends," Bozeman (MT) Daily Chronicle, August 12, 1982.

11. Quoted in Baden and Stroup, eds., Bureaucracy vs. Environment, pp. 7-8.

12. Lawrence Burke, "Free Market Environmentalism," Outside (June-July 1982), p. 6.

13. Garrett Hardin, "The Tragedy of the Commons," in Managing the Commons, Garrett Hardin and John Baden, eds., (San Francisco: W.H. Freeman, 1977), pp. 16-30.

14. For an attack on Christianity, see Lynn White Jr., "The Historical Roots of Our Ecologic Crisis," Science (March 10, 1967), pp. 1203-07. One of the early attacks on capitalism with regard to natural resources can be found in Gifford Pinchot, The Fight for Conservation (New York: Doubleday, Page, 1910).

58

15. For an examination of the way two different religious groups managed the commons, see Kari Bullock and John Baden, "Communes and the Logic of the Commons," in Managing the Commons, Hardin and Baden, eds., pp. 182-99.

16. Hardin, "The Tragedy of the Commons," p. 21.

17. See Terry L. Anderson and Peter J. Hill, "The Evolution of Property Rights: A Study of the American West," Journal of Law and Economics (April 1975), pp. 163-79.

18. Aldo Leopold, A Sand County Almanac (New York: Ballantine Books, 1971), pp. 250-77. The careful reader will find many examples of Leopold's skepticism of governmental conservation. Leopold's "land ethic" can be appropriately seen as a call for private sector conservation.

19. For a collection of essays examining this problem, see Baden and Stroup, eds., Bureaucracy vs. Environment.

20. Thomas Barlow et al., Giving Away the National Forests (Washington D.C.: Natural Resources Defense Council, 1980); Barney Dowdle, "An Institutional Dinosaur With an Ace," in Bureaucracy vs. Environment, Baden and Stroup, eds., pp. 170-85; William F. Hyde, Timber Supply, Land Allocation, and Economic Efficiency (Baltimore: Johns Hopkins University Press, 1980); and idem, "Timber Economics in the Rockies: Efficiency and Management Options," Land Economics (November 1981), pp. 630-36.

21. Sabine Kemp, "A Perspective on BLM Grazing Policy," in Bureaucracy vs. Environment, Baden and Stroup, eds., pp. 124-53; and Ronald M. Lanner, "Chained to the Bottom," in ibid., pp. 154-69. For the problems arising from a system of uncertain property rights arrangements, see Gary D. Libecap, Locking Up the Range (San Francisco: Pacific Institute, 1981).

22. William J. Siffin, "Bureaucracy, Entrepreneurship, and Natural Resources: Witless Policy and the Barrier Islands," Cato Journal (Spring 1981), pp. 293-311.

23. Steve H. Hanke, "The Political Economy of Water Resources Development," Transactions of the 38th North American Wildlife and Natural Resources Conference (Washington DC: Wildlife Management Institute, 1973), pp. 377-89; and Bernard Shanks, "Dams and Disasters: The Social Problems of Water Development Policies," in Bureaucracy vs. Environment, Baden and Stroup, eds., pp. 108-23.

24. John Baden, "The Subsidized Destruction of Alternative Energy Generation in the United States," SPEA Review (Spring 1980), pp. 4-8; Burke, "Free Market Environmentalism;" Habicht, "U.S. Natural Gas

Policy;" and Richard L. Stroup, "The Policy-Induced Demand for Coal Gasification," in Bureaucracy vs. Environment, Baden and Stroup, eds.

25. Frank C. Craighead, Track of the Grizzly (San Francisco: Sierra Club, 1979), especially "Bureaucracy and the Bear"; Robert K. Davis, Steve Hanke, and Frank Mitchell, "Conventional and Unconventional Approaches to Wildlife Exploitation," Transactions of the 38th North American Wildlife Conference, pp. 75-89; William C. Dennis, "The Public and Private Interest in Wilderness Protection," Cato Journal (Fall 1981), pp. 373-90; and Robert J. Smith, "Resolving the Tragedy of the Commons by Creating Private Property Rights in Wildlife," ibid., pp. 439-68.

26. William C. Dennis, "Private Land and Public Amenities," unpublished, 1982.

27. Allan D. Spader, A Prospectus: Land Trust Exchange (Boston, Mass.: Land Trust Exchange, 1981).

28. House, "Leaving Water in Western Streams." The main barrier to entry into water markets by conservationists is a legal one. Most courts have declined to allow instream water use to be considered a "beneficial" use.

29. Quoted in J.H. Dales, Pollution, Property, and Prices (Toronto: University of Toronto Press, 1968), pp. 68-70.

30. Dennis, "Private Lands and Public Amenities."

31. For example, the Eastern Slope Landowners Association, Great Falls, Montana, and H and H Hunting Unlimited, Grass Range, Montana. Both firms began operations this year.

32. Ed Zern, "Rx for Ailing Waters," Field and Stream (November 1982), pp. 87-89. Timberline Reclamation of Bozeman, Montana, is the company described in the article.

33. Ibid.

34. William F. Hyde, "National Forest Logs Red Ink for Treasury," Wharton Magazine (Fall 1981), pp. 66-71.

35. Strategic Minerals: A Resource Crisis (Washington DC: Council on Economics and National Security, 1981), p. 8.

36. U.S. News and World Report, November 12, 1979, p. 75.

37. Wall Street Journal, February 26, 1979, p. 4.

38. Quoted in Tony Velocci, "Minerals: The Resource Gap," Nation's Business (October 1980), p. 36.

39. Ibid., p. 34.

40. Ibid., p. 36.

41. Ibid.

42. Terry L. Anderson and Peter J. Hill, The Birth of a Transfer Society (Stanford: Hoover Institution Press, 1980). Anderson and Hill distinguish

60

negative-sum games (transfer activity) from positive-sum games (voluntary exchange) and note that increased governmental control of resources tends to foster transfer activity at the expense of productive activity.

43. John Baden and Richard Stroup, "Saving the Wilderness: A Radical Proposal," Reason (July 1981), pp. 26-36; and Donald G. Schueller, "Land of Snow Geese, Three-Cornered Grass -- and Lonnie Lege," Audubon (July 1978), pp. 18-37.

44. John G. Mitchell, "The Trapping Question: Soft Skins and Spring Steel," Audubon (July 1982), p. 81.

45. Lloyd C. Irland, Wilderness Economics and Policy (Lexington, Mass.: D.C. Heath, 1979), pp. 107-13. Irland states that "wildland recreationists tend to be more highly educated, and to earn more than the average for the U.S. population."

46. McPhee, Encounters with the Archdruid, pp. 213-18.

47. Milton Friedman, Capitalism and Freedom (Chicago: University of Chicago Press, 1962); idem, An Economist's Protest (Glen Ridge, N.J.: Thomas Horton, 1972); and idem and Rose D. Friedman, Free to Choose (New York: Harcourt, Brace, and Jovanovich, 1980).

48. Alexander Hamilton, John Jay, and James Madison, The Federalist (New York: G.P. Putnam's, 1895); and Adam Smith, The Wealth of Nations (London: George Bell, 1892).

49. Quoted in "Privatizing Public Lands: The Ecological and Economic Case for Private Ownership of Federal Lands," Manhattan Report (May 1982), p. 1.

50. Caroline R. Adams, "Federal Sale of Extra Land Stirs Dispute," The Wall Street Journal, July 26, 1982.

51. Charles H. Callison, "The Scheme to 'Privatize' the Public Lands," Audubon Action, October 1982, p. 3.

52. Quoted in JoAn Mengel, "Public Land Sales," Bozeman (MT) Daily Chronicle, June 6, 1982, pp. 1, 3.

53. John Hooper, "Privatization: The Reagan Administration's Master Plan for Government Give-aways," Sierra (November-December 1982), pp. 32-37.

54. Joan Nice, "Public Lands: Reagan Sell-Off of Federal Real Estate Fizzles," Audubon (September 1982), pp. 118-22.

55. Ted Trueblood, "The Biggest Ripoff," Field and Stream (November 1982), pp. 33-45.

56. Quoted in Peter Stoler, "The Land Sale of the Century," Time, August 23, 1982, p. 21.

57. Quoted in ibid., pp. 17, 20.

58. Quoted in ibid., p. 21.

59. For a study of the impacts of ethics and institutions on resource management, see John Baden, Richard Stroup, and Walter Thurman, "Myths, Admonitions, and Rationality: The American Indian As a Resource Manager," Economic Inquiry (January 1981), pp. 132-43. See also Harold Demsetz, "Toward Theory of Property Rights," American Economic Review (May 1967), pp. 347-59.

60. John Baden, "Property Rights, Cowboys, and Bureaucrats: A Modest Proposal," in Earth Day Reconsidered, John Baden, ed. (Washington DC: Heritage Foundation, 1980), pp. 83-94.

61. Richard Stroup and John Baden, Natural Resources: Myths and Management (Cambridge, Mass.: Ballinger, 1983).

62. See Anderson and Hill, "The Evolution of Property Rights."

63. Gary D. Libecap and Ronald N. Johnson, "Property Rights, Nineteenth-Century Federal Timber Policy and the Conservation Movement," Journal of Economic History (March 1979), pp. 129-42. The authors show how governmental policy encouraged fraud and waste in the timber industry by prohibiting the establishment of private property rights to parcels greater than 640 acres and by requiring development of the land before an individual could receive title to it.

64. Quoted in Mengel, "Public Land Sales," p. 3.

65. George Catlin, "An Artist Proposes a Park," in The American Environment, Roderick Nash, ed. (Menlo Park, Calif,: Addison-Wesley, 1976), p. 9.

66. Irland, Wilderness Economics, p. 19.

67. Ibid., pp. 22, 23.

68. Ibid., p. 23.

69. Ibid.

70. Ibid., pp. 32, 33.

71. Ibid., pp. 36-38. The fact that the Eastern Wilderness Act passed illustrates how "wilderness" can have different meanings in different settings.

72. Ibid., pp. 26, 27.

73. Ibid., pp. 172-74.

74. John Baden, "Neospartan Hedonists, Adult Toy Aficionados, and the Rationing of Public Lands," in Managing the Commons, Hardin and Baden, eds., pp. 241-51.

75. Irland, Wilderness Economics, pp. 195, 196.

76. See "Book I" in McPhee, Encounters with the Archdruid.

77. Gordon Anderson, "Threat to the Canyonlands," The Living Wilderness (December 1980), pp. 4-11.

78. Rollo Pool, "Quartz Hill: Mine Within a Wilderness," Alaska (March 1982), pp. 20-49.

79. Hank Fischer, "The Fight of the Cabinet Mountains Grizzlies," Sierra (January-February 1982), pp. 109-13.

80. In this classic conservationists vs. developer conflict, the solution was far from typical. Miss Ellie and her preservationist friends sought to preserve a coastal marsh as a state park, while Jock and his developer friends sought to make something "valuable" out of the swamp by building a resort complex. Senator Bobby Ewing, carrying the swing vote on the senate committee, had no problem in finding a solution in which everyone wins. He simply relocated the development to a less ecologically sensitive area that also happens to have lower development costs. The rest of the marsh-swamp becomes a state park. Both sides naturally agreed to this compromise. The absence of J.R., of course, made things all the more workable.

81. For the original economic description of a public good, see Paul A. Samuelson, "The Pure Theory of Public Expenditure," The Review of Economics and Statistics (May 1954), pp. 387-89.

82. John V. Krutilla, "Conservation Reconsidered," American Economic Review (September 1967), pp. 777-86. Krutilla also addresses the issue of asymmetrical technological change regarding commodity and amenity goods. The concept is closely linked to the irreversibility argument.

83. Carol L. Cornforth, "Reclamation Commitment Proves Rewarding," Coal Mining and Processing (March 1973).

84. See Russell Stuart, "Surface Mining and Wildlife," North Dakota Outdoors (November 1974), pp. 2-7. Stuart, North Dakota Fish and Game Commissioner, states that some "reclamation attempts have actually resulted in greater production of certain species of wildlife than is found on the surrounding intensively farmed areas." See also Larry Kruckenberg, "Lessen in Variety," North Dakota Outdoors (May 1975), pp. 15-19.

85. Baden and Stroup, "Saving the Wilderness," and idem, "Political Economy Perspectives on the Sagebrush Rebellion," Public Land Law Review (Spring 1982), pp. 103-18.

86. Richard L. Stroup and John Baden, "Endowment Areas: A Clearing in the Policy Wilderness?" Cato Journal (Winter 1982), pp. 691-708.

87. Jim Robbins, "Mining: Wilderness Advocates Hold Trump Card at Scothman's Peak," Audubon (September 1982), pp. 124-27. In this case, the "trump card" happens to be well-defined, well-enforced, and easily transferable private property rights.

APPENDIX

Table 2.1: What Does it Take to Build an F100 Jet
            Engine?

Input Requirement[1]	Pounds
Aluminum	670
Chromium	1485
Cobalt	885
Columbium	145
Manganese	23
Nickel	4504
Tantalum	3
Titanium	5440

SOURCE: Strategic Minerals: A Resource Crisis
           (Washington, DC: Council on Economics
           and National Security, 1981), p. 1.

[1] U.S. dependence on imports of above minerals ranges
     between 77 and 100 percent.

Table 2.2: U.S. Net Import Reliance for Selected
Minerals and Metals as a Percentage of
Consumption in 1978

| | NET IMPORT RELIANCE | |
MINERALS AND METAL	NET IMPORT RELIANCE AS A PERCENTAGE OF APPARENT CONSUMPTION	MAJOR FOREIGN SOURCES (1974-1977)
Columbium	100	Brazil, Thailand, Canada
Mica (Sheet)	100	India, Brazil, Malagasy Republic
Strontium	100	Mexico, Spain
Manganese	98	Gabon, Brazil, South Africa
Cobalt	97	Belg.-Lux., Zambia, Finland
Chromium	92	South Africa, USSR, Southern Rhodesia, Turkey
Platinum-Group Metals	91	South Africa, USSR, United Kingdom
Tantalum	97	Thailand, Canada, Malaysia, Brazil
Bauxite & Alumina	93	Jamaica, Australia, Surinam
Asbestos	84	Canada, South Africa
Fluorine	82	Mexico, Spain, South Africa
Tin	81	Malaysia, Bolivia, Thailand, Indonesia

Table 2.2: Continued

| MINERALS AND METAL | NET IMPORT RELIANCE | |
	NET IMPORT RELIANCE AS A PERCENTAGE OF APPARENT CONSUMPTION	MAJOR FOREIGN SOURCES (1974-1977)
Nickel	77	Canada, Norway, New Caledonia, Domin. Rep.
Cadmium	66	Canada, Australia, Belg.-Lux., Mexico
Zinc	62	Canada, Mexico, Australia, Belg.-Lux.
Potassium	61	Canada, Israel, W. Germany
Selenium	61	Canada, Japan, Yugoslavia, Mexico

SOURCE: Strategic Minerals: A Resource Crisis, (Washington, D.C.: Council on Economics and National Security, 1981), p. 25.

Table 2.3: USSR/US Imports of Strategic Materials

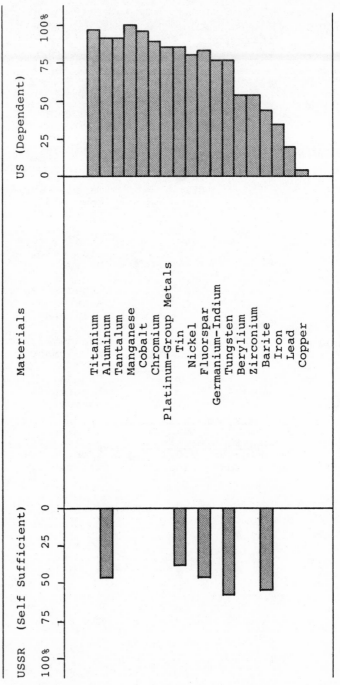

USSR (Self Sufficient)	Materials	US (Dependent)
	Titanium	
	Aluminum	
	Tantalum	
	Manganese	
	Cobalt	
	Chromium	
	Platinum-Group Metals	
	Tin	
	Nickel	
	Fluorspar	
	Germanium-Indium	
	Tungsten	
	Beryllium	
	Zirconium	
	Barite	
	Iron	
	Lead	
	Copper	

SOURCE: Strategic Minerals: A Resource Crisis (Washington, D.C.: Council on Economics and National Security, 1981), p. 26.

Table 2.4: Designated and Potential Wilderness Lands

Total Designated Wilderness

	FS[1]	NPS[1]	FWS[1]	BLM[1]
		(million acres)		
Lower 48 States	19.7	3.1	0.7	--[2]
Alaska	5.5	3.2	18.7	
Agency total	25.2	35.5	19.4	
Total acres	80.1			

Recommended for Wilderness Classification

	FS	NPS	FWS	BLM
		(million acres)		
Lower 48 States	7.2	10.4	3.4	---
Total acres	21.0			

Under Study for Wilderness Inclusion

	FS	NPS	FWS	BLM
		(million acres)		
Lower 48 States	7.4	6.2	0.2	24.3
Alaska	4.3	25.5	57.7	4.5
Agency total	11.7	31.7	57.9	28.8
Total acres	130.1			

SOURCE: U.S. Department of Interior, BLM Wilderness
Office, April 1982.

[1] Agencies of the federal government: FS-Forest
Service, NPS-National Park Service, FWS-Fish and
Wildlife Service, and BLM-Bureau of Land
Management.

[2] Approximately 12,000 acres.

An Economist's Critique
of Privatization

C. Ford Runge

The central premise of the Baden and Lueck paper holds that the private market, rather than government, is the best allocation mechanism for income streams and wealth arising from natural resources -- in this case on wilderness lands. The general argument was made in the sixteenth century for the enclosure of commons in Great Britain, so it is familiar.

In a recent contribution to The Public Interest entitled "Economic Reasoning and the Ethics of Policy," Harvard economist Thomas Schelling commented on the difficulty of disentangling this faith from reason and reality.

> Nothing distinguishes economists from other people as much as a belief in the market system, or what some call the free market system. A perennial difficulty in dealing with economics and policy is the inability of people who are not economists, and some who are, to ascertain how much of an economist's work is faith and how much is analysis and observation. How much is due to...observing the way markets work and judging actual outcomes, and how much is a belief that the process is right and just? (Schelling, 1981, p. 59).

Baden and Lueck's proposal to shift the management of wilderness lands is an example of how non-

---

C. Ford Runge is science and diplomacy fellow, American Association for the Advancement of Science, and assistant professor, Department of Agricultural and Applied Economics, University of Minnesota.

economists' faith in the market process can get confused with the way markets actually work.

I have three main comments on their paper. (1)
The theoretical premise of their argument is based on
a naive faith that private decisions always lead to
the best of all possible worlds. The real world is
not so simple. (2) Even if this theoretical premise
is accepted, their conclusions for policy do not seem
to follow. Granting property rights to conservation
groups does not increase truly private decision-making. (3) Because of these difficulties, the paper's
policy proposals -- if successfully implemented -- may
lead to even greater management problems for wilderness than those of the status quo.

First, consider the Baden and Lueck premise that
the process of private, market-based decision-making
is a more efficient allocation mechanism than government management of public lands. The argument for
market efficiency is technically correct as far as it
goes. However, economists always stress that the
technical argument assumes strict caveats -- perfect
information and foresight, the absence of monopoly
power, and none of the interdependencies or third
party effects called externalities. Unfortunately,
the real world is full of these complexities, all of
which interfere with the technical conditions for
efficient private decision making. In general, the
question of whether private or public choices are the
best allocation mechanism for scarce resources is empirical, requiring consideration of the circumstances
which arise in different cases. These circumstances
include imperfect information, monopoly power, and
externalities. The Baden and Lueck paper appeals to a
purer notion born of faith -- sometimes expressed as
the "tragedy of the commons." This argument holds
that wherever private ownership rights are absent,
resource overexploitation will result. Where private
use rights can be assigned, defined and made transferable, all resource allocation decisions can be made
internally, and no costs can be passed on in the form
of "negative externalities." Where each cultivates
his or her own garden, problems of imperfect information, inordinate influences on the market such as
monopoly, or external effects on others are defined
away. Private use becomes by definition the best of
all possible worlds. Compared with a situation where
resources are managed by government bureaucrats who do
not bear their own costs, this looks like an attractive set of incentives.

While appealing in its simplicity, the premise of
privatization does not confront real problems of
information, imperfectly competitive markets, externalities or the existing structure of property rights.

These are very relevant in the real world. First consider information. To be optimal, private owner-ship or management of resources must yield a rate of consumption consistent with the preferences of society as a whole. Yet evidence suggests that corporate bond rates corrected for inflation, for example, imply a much shorter time frame in the private than in the public sector (Seagraves, 1982). Why? Because avail-able information about the future is limited, and that puts a premium on the present. In the private sector the bottom line is a problem for today, not tomorrow. The considerable risk and uncertainty of doing busi-ness make it difficult for private decision makers to be concerned, for example, with wilderness values for future generations. And, in many ways, this should not be their job.

A second problem with the central Baden and Lueck premise is that it assumes the incentives resulting from new private rights, such as a new homesteading program, will be free from the influence of the existing distribution of property. But privatization can never begin with a clean slate. When railroads were granted large private tracts in the west in the last century, their market power made it unnecessary to put all of these lands to their highest and best use. Once the railroad was built, monopoly power made a competitive use of resources unnecessary. Privati-zation occurs in the context of the existing distribu-tion of property rights, and can promote increased inefficiency if the existing arrangement is one of monopoly or is otherwise inefficient. A similar prob-lem will arise under any new privatization scheme. As Nobel Laureate economist Kenneth Arrow remarked in his study on The Limits of Organization (1974. pp. 21-22):

> (T)here are profound difficulties
> with the price system, even, so to speak,
> within its own logic, and these strengthen
> the view that, valuable though it is in
> certain realms, (the market) cannot be
> made the complete arbiter of social life.

A third problem with the premise is that it is never possible to define and assign away all of the interdependencies or externalities involved in natural resource use. External effects continue because what any given owner or manager of a wilderness area does is likely to affect others as well. The interests of different parties cannot be separated. Because of this interdependence, it is not clear that privatiza-tion is always in the best interest of the affected parties. In technical terms, nonseparabilities make privatization an insufficient basis for the elimina-tion of external effects (Baumol, 1976; Runge, 1981).

All of these factors are of real importance in deciding whether private use is an appropriate institutional response to a given management problem. But they do not imply that government management is always a superior alternataive. "Government failure" is as important a problem as "market failure." The sensible approach is to allow market processes to work where they work best -- and to allow government management where it works best. Universal prescriptions tend to be useless except as statements of faith.

In fact, whether the ratio of costs and benefits of a particular policy is favorable depends on the exact nature of the problem, making generalizations inapplicable. Some government management does not imply a lack of faith in competitive markets. It is simply a recognition of the appreciable gap between the ideal of competitive efficiency and the objective circumstance of economic reality.

A closer look at the intellectual origins of laissez-faire, as developed by the French Physiocrats, emphasizes this common sense point of view. Rather than a sweeping invocation of government non-interference, the true doctrine of laissez-faire followed Thomas Aquinas' view that "when reason argues about particular cases, it needs not only universal but particular principles." (Viner, p. 47) Simply put, government management is justified or unjustified, not as a universal rule, but depending on the circumstances. When, how, and how long government should manage, cannot be answered by faith in general principles. The question then becomes, in the specific case of wilderness, whether the privatization scheme Baden and Lueck propose makes sense.

This brings me to my second main comment. Even if private decisions are superior to government's, it does not follow that environmental groups (even innocuous non-profit conservation organizations under a new Homesteading Act) should be the ones to whom private rights to wilderness are assigned. There are a number of reasons for this. First, it does not appear possible to define these rights in terms of such groups, in lieu of the federal government. Organized in the main for purposes divorced from land management, they are more ill-equipped than government agencies to provide and enforce consistent management practices. Even the one group with the greatest experience in this area -- The Nature Conservancy -- expresses significant reservations about its ability to maintain an adequate level of stewardship on existing preserves, much less an increased level of responsibility (de Buys, 1982).

Second, if allowed to assume such responsibility, there is no guarantee that these groups' management decisions will reflect public preferences for land use. Perhaps, as William Tucker argues, environmentalists are nothing but a bunch of closet aristocrats, seeking to prevent <u>real</u> Americans from enjoying the sights and scenery and riches locked up on public lands. In this case, why should the public hand over its lands to them? Even if they are not the villains of the piece, it is hard to believe that the preferences of the Isaac Walton League will reflect those of consumers as a whole. Why should they have the right to exclude others from these lands? Public ownership retains a right of access for all citizens. And through the democratic process of government, it allows the pluralist expression of individual preferences for the appropriate management of these lands.

Third, it is not clear that environmental interest groups can be considered as private decision makers who bear their own costs. Interest groups do not seem the natural heirs to the promise of privatization. The fact that Baden and Lueck's proposal shifts property rights to interest groups is especially damaging in light of their general indictment of the role of interest groups in encouraging inefficient bureaucratic behavior. Here they differ most fundamentally with their friend Niskanen. In the ideal theory of privatization, one wants entrepreneurs, not interest groups, seeking to protect economic privilege. It is unclear why their concern with interest groups' influence on government suddenly ceases when these groups are denoted as part of the private sector. Because the market for environmental influence is monopolized by a few large organizations, shifting property rights to them would not have the efficiency of a competitive system of private use rights. If Mancur Olson's recent indictment of interest groups and the cartelization of influence is taken seriously, shifting more property rights to such groups is the last thing someone should promote who is sincerely concerned with economic efficiency (Olson, 1982).

In sum, the argument that environmental interest groups should assume responsibility for management of public lands does not follow from the premise that private decisions are superior to government management.

My final comment is designed to open a discussion. Given the realistic problems of managing public lands -- what are the policy implications of Baden and Lueck's proposed shift in property rights?

Their proposal is based on an erroneous historical analogy. The original Homestead Act was designed to overcome a problem of excess supplies of land, not to conserve resources like wilderness lands for which there is excess demand. To propose such a program for wilderness management is really inappropriate. Secondly -- and this is the major issue -- what is the evidence, in the face of imperfect information, noncompetitive markets, and many external effects which cannot be solved by privatization, that such a program will be a net improvement over the admittedly imperfect status quo? The Baden and Lueck paper provides none, because its premise of superior outcomes resulting from privatization is taken on faith. Policy judgments should not rest on arguments without evidence.

A wide range of cases to be examined over the next day-and-a-half will help to provide this evidence. I submit that they will show that institutional alternatives short of privatization may yield better solutions to problems of natural resource allocation. Continued public management of federal lands is not a universal panacea -- but neither is privatization. Public management may be a very poor form of allocation -- but others may be worse. The purpose of this conference is to come to terms with the real issues of improving our management capabilities in whatever way seems appropriate to the specific problems at hand. In some cases, private uses may be indicated. In other cases, they may not. The best way to proceed is to discard universal solutions in favor of more complex, but realistic, policy alternatives.

BIBLIOGRAPHY

Arrow, Kenneth J., The Limits of Organization, New York, W.W. Norton, 1974.

Baumol, William J., "It Takes Two to Tango, or Sind 'Separable Externalities' Uberhaupt Moglich?," Journal of Political Economy 84 (1976): 381-87.

de Buys, William, personal correspondence from the southern regional office of the Conservation Foundation, Chapel Hill, N.C., 1982.

Olson, Mancur, The Rise and Decline of Nations' Economic Growth: Stagflation and Social Rigidities, New Haven: Yale Press, 1982.

Runge, Carlisle Ford, "Common Property Externalities: Isolation, Assurance and Resource Depletion in a Traditional Grazing Context," American Journal of Agricultural Economics (November 1981): 575-606.

Schelling, Thomas, "Economic Reasoning and the Ethics of Policy," The Public Interest, 63 (Spring 1981): 37-61.

Seagraves, J.A., "On the Social Rate of Discount: A Retraction," Faculty Working Papers, North Carolina State University, Department of Economics and Business, September, 1982.

Viner, Jacob, "The Intellectual History of Laissez-Faire," Journal of Law and Economics 3 (October 1960): 45-69.

The Wilderness System Isn't
Broken and Doesn't Need Fixing

M. Rupert Cutler

We have just heard that only through private ownership will land and resources be conserved for future
generations and that legislative protection of public
wilderness areas is relatively worthless.
I could not disagree more.
The National Audubon Society began its seventy-
seven year history of activity by acquiring sanctuaries and encouraging the federal government to do the
same. Audubon sanctuaries are wildlife management
areas administered more like the National Wildlife
Refuge System than the National Wilderness Preservation System. We emphasize non-game species habitat
improvement and are not reluctant to manipulate habitat to that end. Audubon's Rainey Sanctuary on the
Louisiana coast, like federal refuges in that area, is
subject to artificial water level fluctuations, controlled burning and other intensive management techniques to increase its carrying capacity for snow and
blue geese and other wildfowl. The gas-development
activities, closely controlled and monitored by
Audubon, offer opportunities for levee, channel, and
freshwater pond construction to diversify and improve
habitat which Audubon otherwise couldn't afford to
create. Vast areas of salt marsh don't lend themselves to wilderness designation, in public or private
hands, so our development of the Rainey Sanctuary for
wildlife does not prove that Audubon would develop the
wilderness system if it had the chance.
No mineral development occurs on any other part
of Audubon's eighty-unit national sanctuary system.
Most are kept pristine for colonial bird nesting
purposes.

M. Rupert Cutler is senior vice president for programs
and chapter relations, National Audubon Society.

As to the question of the opportunity cost of wilderness designation and the jeopardy in which public wilderness would be placed in the event of a national mineral-shortage emergency, I believe: that the opportunity cost of wilderness generally is low, that the alternative to what some consider a lock-up is a lock-out of the public, and that the chances of our ever having to scrape the bottom of our resources barrel by opening the wilderness system to mineral development are remote.

And I believe that a burgeoning army of wilderness enthusiasts (not just "a small group of rugged outdoorsmen," but local ranchers, scientists and others) will rise to protect the system, just as the farmers and ranchers of Wyoming recently rose to defend the Washakie Wilderness from the oil industry and turned their conservative congressional delegation into supporters of the integrity of the wilderness system.

Excessive population growth is not the only explanation for resource scarcity offered by environmentalists. Perverse government incentives have resulted in the loss of genetic diversity, paving and flooding of prime farmland, and abandonment of urban central business districts. All of the above examples involve government incentives to develop -- to plow up the grasslands, drain the swamps, cut the trees and build the roads, in inefficient (uneconomic) ways. On the other hand, we would support, for example, free market competitive bidding for federal grazing permits.

The wilderness issue is different because it involves government in the role of placing a brake on development -- truly a conservative force. And as Baden and Lueck acknowledge, the opportunity cost of holding these lands in an undeveloped state is near zero. Most contain minimal commodity resources. If their net value is estimated, deducting costs of access, extraction and environmental rehabilitation, most of these lands are not worth entering for resource extraction.

Baden and Lueck characterize conservationists as concerned primarily about resource scarcity and about providing for future generations. But he doesn't mention our concerns regarding ecological diversity (and the resultant diversity of landscapes and recreational opportunities) and equity -- the distributional question involving traditional access to the out-of-doors by all citizens.

Implementing their recommendations could result in the construction of hotels and related tourism facilities at all now-undeveloped key vistas, the lock-out of all but the wealthy few, and probably the deterioration of watersheds resulting from the high-grading of the timber resource, valuable enough to cut once, but on sites not productive enough to re-forest profitably. The result could well be a repeat of what our nation went through fifty years ago -- flooding, the bankrupting of communities, the wasting of people and resources, until the land is repurchased by the government and restored to ecological health at great public expense.

Even so relatively enlightened a private firm as the Weyerhauser Corporation has just been found in violation of good forest practices in the management of its company-owned lands in Arkansas and Oklahoma. A National Wildlife Federation-coordinated review team found evidence of roading and logging near rivers and streams which resulted in loss of key riparian habitat and the degradation of stream water quality.

Baden and Lueck assume that (a) some wilderness areas overlay valuable mineral and fuel deposits and contain valuable timber (high opportunity cost) and (b) when our trading partners refuse to sell us their minerals and the national emergency resource crunch comes, the scramble to dig the last bit of domestic ore and fuel will result in an "unsatisfactory" outcome when politicians rush to breach the wilderness barricades.

Wilderness areas have been open to exploration, claim and patent. Where high mineralization was known, as in the primitive areas of southwestern Colorado and more recently in the new Misty Fjords and Admiralty Island wildernesses in Alaska, boundaries were adjusted to exclude the highly mineralized zones.

This precaution, to avoid conflict and excessive opportunity cost, was taken when Bob Marshall set aside the primitive areas, when the Forest Service reclassified them as wilderness and wild areas, when the Congress held hearings on the initial wilderness system and on every addition thereto (referring to U.S. Geological Survey studies of every primitive area), and during the RARE II Development Opportunity Rating System process.

Little of high commodity value is thought to be held within these reserves, so decisions have been made -- with great deliberation -- to place this small proportion of the nation's land with extraordinary surface features off-limits to development.

Yes, wilderness management is an embryonic art, but I believe we'll soon succeed in establishing human carrying capacities, regulating use, rotating trails and campsites, and providing a sustainable wilderness-use program without irreversible resource loss.

Public-agency bureaucrats come in for a lot of condemnation by Baden and Lueck, who characterize them

as empire builders. I've seen otherwise. Bureaucrats
of large private corporations, on the other hand, may
be less idealistic. They have to produce profits...
and in an inflationary economy, over a period of a
very few years...and thus might tend to exhaust a resource more quickly and not conserve it for future
generations.

Users of wilderness areas are willing to pay
their way. User fees are attractive means of
recovering public administrative costs. Hunters and
fishermen have anted up for decades. Hikers, photo-
graphers and birders would be happy to do so. Let's
be more creative as to how to tax wilderness users.
They'd like to be counted in and thereby credited with
a vested interest in the well-being of the resource.
A stamp could be used, like the federal "duck stamp"
or Virginia's national forest hunting and fishing
stamp.

To suggest that conservation groups, with their
tens of millions of dollars of assets, could
"reasonably compete" for ownership of wilderness areas
with wealthy corporations, with their billions, is
unrealistic, to say the least. Only the Nature
Conservancy and the Trust for the Public Lands work
full-time at land acquisition (and then, oftentimes,
as advance agents for federal agencies). We don't
have the money. It's not the reason we were
organized. And basically, the wilderness system isn't
broken, and doesn't need fixing.

To suggest that National Audubon and The Wilderness Society supplant the Bureau of Land Management
and the Forest Service as managers of U.S. wildlands
after competing for those lands on the open market
with Exxon, AMAX and TENNECO reminds me of one of
Stewart Brandborg's favorite sayings, "It's every man
for himself, said the elephant as he danced among the
chickens." We environmental organization chickens
will, on balance, trust the people and their representatives in the Congress to determine the highest
and best use of the scenic and ecological best our
nation has to offer.

We have relatively little fear of "political
whims." We are more comfortable with the political
debate and the democratic process than with the
results of benefit/cost analysis and the rule of the
invisible hand when it comes to the care over time of
the public trust in our wilderness heritage.

I'll go with conservative columnist George F.
Will's recent characterization of wilderness as "an
aristocratic pleasure democratically open to all" and
with his conclusion: "Some {community} assets, such
as wilderness areas, cannot survive if unprotected
from the morals of the marketplace."

3
Public Land Politics in the 1980s

D. Michael Harvey

Abstract: Increasing scarcity of basic commodities; a rapid shift of the urbanized demographic
center of the nation to the west and south; and a
growing appreciation of environmental values have
increased pressures for the use of the federal lands
for such competing purposes as energy production,
urban growth, recreation, wildlife management, and
wilderness preservation -- as well as for the traditional uses. Philosophical and political debates
between "environmental protection" and "resource
development" usually ignore the central issue: that
man's survival does not depend on one or another -- it
depends on both. Issues in federal land politics will
be: 1) the size and shape of the federal budget; 2)
relationships among federal, state, and local governments; 3) protection and preservation of the natural
environment; 4) improvement of the decision-making and
conflict resolution processes and; 5) implementation
of the Alaska land tenure adjustment program. Successful balancing of different uses of the federal
lands involves implementation of the land-use planning
and decision-making processes of the National Forest
Management Act of 1976 and the Federal Land Policy and
Management Act of 1976, as well as reducing recent
polarization of the debate. Federal land issues are a
complex web, but using the policies and processes of
existing laws can help achieve a broadly balanced
program.
Key words: politics, Congress, public land laws,
Alaska, decision-making process.

D. Michael Harvey is chief counsel for the minority,
Committee on Energy and Natural Resources, U.S.
Senate.

INTRODUCTION

Natural resources must be developed
and preserved for the benefit of the many,
and not merely for the profit of the few.
Gifford Pinchot

We abuse land because we regard it as
a commodity belonging to us. When we see
land as a community to which we belong, we
may begin to use it with love and respect.
There is no other way for land to survive
the impact of mechanized man.
Aldo Leopold

The purpose of this conference is "to encourage a
wide-ranging discussion of ways in which the public
lands and resources administered by the Forest Service
and the Bureau of Land Management can be better used
to serve the present and future needs of all
Americans."

My assignment is to focus on "the political
constraints and uncertainties that help to shape
public land policy." I approach this task with
considerable trepidation, for it is almost certain
that the next ten to fifteen years will involve
considerable debate over federal land questions that
none of us would dream of here today. On the other
hand, there are many policy issues that seem to be
always with us.

What Are the Federal Lands?

For my purpose the federal lands are the lands
managed by the Forest Service (FS) and the Bureau of
Land Management (BLM) in the contiguous forty-eight
states. Thus, the Outer Continental Shelf (OCS) and
lands in Alaska and Hawaii are not included, nor are
national parks and wildlife refuges. Alaska is a very
special situation that I will discuss later.

The lands managed by the Forest Service are the
national forests and grasslands (166 million acres),
some of which (130 million acres) were reserved from
the public domain while others (twenty-seven million
acres) were acquired by purchase or otherwise. The
BLM lands (175 million acres) are almost entirely the
unappropriated and unreserved remnants of the original
public domain. These were called "public lands" in
the Federal Land Policy and Management Act of 1976.

Most of the national forests (139 million acres)
and essentially all the public lands are in the eleven
western states.

What is Politics?

As defined in my dictionary, politics has several meanings. One is the "art or science of political government." A second is "the methods or tactics involved in managing a state or government." A third is "the policies, goals or affairs of a government or of the groups or parties within it."

What Parties are Involved?

Who or what are the "groups of parties" involved in federal land policy and thus federal land politics? The Public Land Law Review Commission has identified six "publics" that together make up the general public:

(1) the national public;
(2) the regional public;
(3) the federal government as sovereign;
(4) the federal government as proprietor;
(5) state and local governments; and
(6) the users of the public lands.

The National Public. Although the federal lands are not distributed proportionally throughout the nation, they and their resources belong to all the people of the United States.

The national public has an interest in reducing the burden on taxpayers either by maximizing the net revenue from the federal lands, or by assuring more efficient management, or both. The national public also has an interest in having consumer goods and services derived from the federal lands made available at the lowest possible price consistent with good conservation practices.

The national public is concerned that the federal lands should contribute to the maintenance of a quality environment and that people who use these lands be treated equally.

The Regional Public. Those who live and work on and near the federal lands have separate, identifiable and special concerns. They want these lands to contribute meaningfully to the quality of the environment in which they live, and contribute to regional growth, development, and employment.

Taxes on private property ownership are a major source of revenue in federal land states, particularly at the local level. It is in the regional public interest to have the federal government, as a landowner, pay its fair share of the costs of adequate local and state governmental services.

The Federal Government as Sovereign. While there
is no legal significance in the different roles of the
federal government as sovereign and as proprietor, it
is useful to separate those interests which relate to
governmental functions from those which are similar to
the interests of any other landowner.

Federal lands must be viewed as one of the tools
that the federal government has available in pursuing
its sovereign objectives.

The federal sovereign interest lies in the efficient economic and noneconomic utilization of all the
resources of our nation and the avoidance of diversion
of labor and capital to less productive enterprises.
Consequently, from the sovereign point of view, laws
and policies should not permit federal lands and resources to be used in unfair competition with resources from other sources. Withholding of federal land
resources from development may, in different circumstances, either further or thwart the sovereign interest.

The national interest requires users of federal
lands and resources to contribute their fair share of
federal revenues. This precludes tax or pricing
policies which unduly favor the users of federal
lands. There is a sovereign interest in assuring
access on equal terms to all potential users of the
goods and services from those lands. There is also a
sovereign interest in the maintenance of environmental
conditions on federal lands at least equal to those
generally required by law.

The Federal Government as Proprietor. In its
role as proprietor, the federal government has much
the same interest as other landowners. It wants at
least the same freedom other landowners have in
managing and using its resources.

As a proprietor, the federal government wants to
maximize the net economic return from sales or use of
its land and resources.

The federal proprietor also has an interest in
controlling land users in order to maintain the
resource base and minimize damage or adverse environmental impacts.

State and Local Governments. In the absence of
conflicting federal legislation, state and local
governments have legislative jurisdiction over federal
lands for many purposes. Exceptions are those
instances where exclusive federal jurisdiction over
specific areas has been ceded. State and local governments therefore have an interest in obtaining from
the federal government an equitable share of their
governmental costs as a proprietor of federal lands.

State and local governments affected by land use decisions expect to be consulted and have a voice in the federal decision-making process. They expect the United States to give consideration to relevant state and local programs and to consider the impact of federal land actions on state and local governments.

Because they use federal lands for public purposes, these units of government expect a preference over competing potential users. They also expect to purchase or lease federal land at less than market value.

Users of Federal Lands and Resources. Those who use the federal lands as a basis for economic enterprise and those who use the federal lands for such non-commercial purposes as personal recreation have an interest in federal land policies that will provide an opportunity for the satisfaction of future requirements as well as present needs.

As a group, users have a common interest in the federal lands. But different classes of users, and, indeed, individual users within classes, often must compete for the opportunity to use the federal lands. Many of the controversies over federal land policy involve such conflicts.

Users want equal opportunity for access and equal treatment in their relations with the federal government and with other users. They want a voice in decision-making from the time that plans are made for general use through the chain of events that may involve decisions affecting their particular uses. And all users desire prompt and fair consideration of disputes with federal land administrators.

Users want the terms and conditions of usage specifically stated in advance. They also seek pricing and other conditions competitive with the use of other lands, and they want their investment secured, usually through assured tenure of use. Users expect to be compensated if use is disrupted before the expiration of the term of the lease or permit.

SPECIAL ROLE OF THE CONGRESS

The Congress has a special role in federal lands policy and politics. The famous Maryland-Virginia compromise at the Constitutional Convention in 1788 is spelled out in Article IV, Section 3, Clause 2 of the Constitution, which provides that,

The Congress shall have Power to dispose of and make all needful Rules and Regulations respecting the Territory or other Property belonging to the United States.

This is a sweeping grant of authority. As the Supreme Court indicated in 1976 in Kleppe v. New Mexico, "while the furthermost reaches of the power granted by the Property Clause have not yet been definitively resolved, we have repeatedly observed that 'the power over the public land thus entrusted to Congress is without limitation.'"

Thus, like it or not, Congress will undoubtedly be involved in most of the federal land issues in the years ahead, just as Congress has been involved in the past. To evaluate realistically the impact of congressional participation in federal land issues, two fundamental principles must be kept in mind.

The first is that the legislative process, set forth by the Founding Fathers and amplified by precedent over the years, is designed to prevent the enactment of legislation.

Paradoxically, the second is that, as a New York judge once noted, "No man's life or property are safe while the legislature is in session."

Where Are We Now?

As we look for ways to meet our growing energy, food and fiber, timber, water, recreational and other demands, long overdue national attention has turned to the resources of the federal lands.

But, because of their richness and diversity, use of these lands provides a classic formula for conflict. Historically, they were used predominantly by western livestock and timber operators and mining interests, and there were few rules or competing demands. Recently, however, awareness of the importance of these lands for a much wider variety of uses has increased substantially. A growing scarcity of basic commodities; a rapid shift of the demographic center of the nation to the west and south; and a burgeoning appreciation of environmental values have increased pressures to use these lands for such competing purposes as energy production, urban growth, recreation, wildlife management, and wilderness preservation -- as well as for their traditional uses. In turn, these demands have broadened the range of people who feel they have a stake in, and something to say about, how the federal lands are managed. As a result, there are new definitions of the public interest, new constituencies to be served, and new claims on the resources of the federal lands.

The Congressional Response. Congress has been the leader in recognizing this evolution of demands, values, and attitudes. During the 1970s it enacted a number of laws affecting federal land management including requirements for environmental impact analyses; changes in federal oil, gas, and coal leasing; regulation of surface coal mining; protection of endangered species; and improvement of public rangelands.

The three most important are the Forest and Rangeland Renewable Resources Planning Act of 1974 (RPA), National Forest Management Act of 1976 (NFMA), much of which consists of major amendments of RPA, and the Federal Land Policy and Management Act of 1976 (FLPMA).

These laws established that the national forests and the public lands are to be managed under principles of multiple use and sustained yield. They expressly recognize that the many and varied resources of these lands are important but not limitless. They require balanced use to realize their many potential benefits. The laws do not specify which uses would be allowed on which areas. Instead, they establish goals and principles and set out a planning process to be used for making land use decisions.

Multiple use and sustained yield are the basic goals of federal land management, and the laws require federal land managers to follow four basic principles in striving to achieve them:

(1) Decisions must be based on comprehensive land use planning accomplished with ample public participation.

(2) Activities on the land must be designed to prevent or minimize environmental damage, and resource users, rather than the general public, should pay the costs of doing so.

(3) The public should receive fair market value for private use of public resources.

(4) Management decisions and programs must be coordinated with state and local land use plans and carried out in close cooperation with state and local government officials, and local citizens.

Implementation of New Laws. During the years that Congress was considering NFMA and FLPMA prior to their passage and approval by President Ford in October 1976, these general principles and the land use planning process were accepted by both preservationists and developers. However, implementation of the new laws by the Carter administration started a fierce debate that is frequently character- ized as being over the "choice" between preservation and development.

These philosophical and political debates between "environmental protection" and "resource development" usually ignored a central reality: man's survival does not depend on one or the other -- it depends on both. NFMA and FLPMA recognize that fact. The laws do not mandate one or the other on any or all federal lands. They recognize that both are necessary, and achievable.

More and more frequently these issues also were characterized as east versus west. The ultimate expression of this view is found in the so-called "Sagebrush Rebellion." The goal of the rebellion is federal legislation directing the transfer of the national forests and public lands to the states. The rebellion had a rapid rise to national prominence, perhaps reaching its high point in late 1980, when then-candidate Ronald Reagan said "Count me in as a rebel," and secretary of the interior-designate James Watt said "I am a Sagebrush Rebel."

But the rebellion has waned considerably. There have been no hearings on the legislation. Secretary Watt believes his "good neighbor" policy with state and local governments makes the transfer unnecessary. Moreover, any administration, particularly one interested in budget balancing, would be loath to give up the large revenues from these lands -- revenues which far exceed management costs.

As an alternative, some in the administration and elsewhere favor "privatization," a concept which is opposed by the original "rebels." The president's budget, for example, assumes substantial revenue from sales of public lands, and new legislation to fa- cilitate such sales has been proposed and is being drafted.

In addition to starting an ambitious program of selling federal lands, particularly public lands, the administration has launched accelerated energy re- source leasing programs for oil, gas, coal, and geo- thermal. There are plans for oil shale and tar sands, despite the fact that the marketplace indicates that there is no strong industry interest.

One ironic result of all this activity is that state and local governments are up in arms. They cite total lack of consultation in land sales, reduction of the state role in coal leasing, and lack of coordination on nuclear waste disposal sites, and rights-of-way.

WHAT ARE THE ISSUES FOR THE '80s?

I have been asked to speculate about what the people will want and expect from the federal lands in order to identify the issues of the '80s.

My not-entirely-facetious reaction is that the people will want <u>everything</u> the national forests and public lands can provide! Certainly they will want, among other things: oil, gas, and coal; good hunting and fishing; wilderness preservation; new homes and other good things made from wood; varied outdoor recreation opportunities; wild free-roaming horses; beef and mutton; healthy wildlife populations, including coyotes and eagles; clean air and clean water, and a balanced budget!

How will this wish list manifest itself in federal land policy and politics?

On our conference program we see timber, nonfuel minerals, and energy resources. We also see wilderness and rangeland which involve different concepts, but obviously overlap the first three.

Federal land politics also will involve matters of a more generic nature. Some that come to mind are:

(1) commodity pricing - fair market value or subsidy, competition or negotiation?

(2) the role of state and local governments - land use plans and regulation, law enforcement.

(3) disposition of federal land revenues - revenue sharing, Payment In-Lieu of Taxes (PILT), Land and Water Conservation Fund (L&WCF), retiring the national debt?

(4) the Forest Service and BLM decision-making processes

-- land use planning, public participation, and EIS - aids to decision or paralysis by analysis?

-- action forcing devices - Energy Mobilization Board or what?

-- judicial review - standing to sue, and payment of costs?

-- congressional review, perhaps in lieu of judicial review?

Each of you undoubtedly can think of other subjects that could be the subject of political debate in the '80s.

There are five categories of issues that I believe will be part of federal land politics during the next ten years and might well have a dramatic impact on federal land management.

They are:

(1) the size and shape of the federal budget;

(2) relationships among federal, state and local governments;

(3) protection and preservation of the natural
    environment;
(4) improvement of the decision-making and
    conflict resolution processes;
(5) implementation of the Alaska land tenure
    adjustment program.

Each of these categories includes a variety of specific issues. Let's look at each category briefly.

Size and Shape of the Federal Budget

It seems inevitable that Congress will continue to try to reduce the size of the federal deficit. For federal lands programs this means looking at ways to cut costs and increase revenues.

Revenue Raising. Mineral leasing and timber sales are the biggest present and potential sources of revenue. Emphasis on each will tend to reduce support for wilderness or other designations which would eliminate or limit revenue. Perhaps more significant will be a continuing shift in FS and BLM budgets toward funding mineral leasing and timber sales at the expense of planning, recreation, wildlife, and range management functions. If pushed too far this trend can lead to poor decisions -- which will lead to unnecessary conflict and may not withstand judicial review.

Funds for land acquisition by federal agencies will be very hard to come by. Witness what has already happened to L&WCF. Exchange programs also will be hamstrung.

Sales of federal lands are another way to raise revenue. Indeed the Reagan FY '83 budget predicted $17 billion in sales revenue over five years. This program will be highly controversial if it is viewed as implementation of the "privatization" philosophy, i.e., that private ownership of lands is the way to achieve the highest national benefit. However, if it is viewed as a logical outcome of rational land use planning and sales under FLPMA and other laws, it could be relatively noncontroversial. The Senate has already passed -- by unanimous consent -- legislation (S. 705) authorizing the sale of as much as 700,000 acres of national forest lands.

Calling the sale program "asset management" sounds "business-like." But saying the proceeds will be used to retire the national debt is pure baloney.

Incidentally, if we really want to be business-like in dealing with our national real estate, we should be treating much of our FS and BLM budgets as capital improvements - not annual expenditures. Shouldn't we be depreciating capital assets as well as selling them?

Review of Subsidies. Closer attention to the federal lands budget will result in a harder look at federal resource pricing, investment and revenue sharing policies. The non-federal land states already are beginning to question why fifty percent of mineral revenues and twenty-five percent of timber revenues go to the federal land states -- an allocation that may amount to $1 billion in 1983.

Another obvious target will be what are perceived to be federal subsidies in the establishment of federal prices for recreation, livestock, grazing, timber, water, and other uses. The recently enacted reform of the Reclamation Act of 1902 is a good example of this trend. Another is the administration proposal for an increase in park and recreation user fees, which originally included even a federal fee for hunting and fishing in national forests and public lands.

The current statutory fee formula for livestock grazing on public lands expires in 1985. This may trigger a renewal of the grazing fee controversy of the 30s, 40s, 50s, 60s and 70s, although the amount of money involved is relatively small.

Questions also may be raised about non-competitive oil and gas leasing, free disposal of hardrock minerals, and relatively low royalty rates on energy mineral leases. Accelerated leasing raises the question of whether we are reducing long-term revenues in an attempt to get larger near-term income.

Lest one think that western state representatives can easily block increases in resource prices or reduction in payments, consider where the votes are. Even if Alaska is included, federal land states have only twenty-four votes in the Senate where their power is greatest. In the House of Representatives, the total is eighty-three of 435 votes, with forty-five of the eighty-three from California, where most congressional districts contain no federal lands.

On the other side, the northeast-midwest coalition will be challenging the existing federal land system on many issues. They take the position -- often resented by western beneficiaries of the system -- that citizens from their states have a legitimate and genuine interest in federal lands.

Review of Investment Policy. A third outgrowth of the emphasis on the budget probably will be a review of federal land investment policies and priorities. Are we putting scarce dollars into the most productive lands? Should timber stand

improvement, harvest and reforestation be limited to
such lands? This kind of review will, inevitably,
precipitate debate over sustained yield harvest rates,
and cutting methods, with particular emphasis on the
old-growth soft wood in the Pacific northwest.

Is it time to review the Public Land Law Review
Commission's recommendation for dominant use designations to focus investments in timber, range, and
recreation on the areas where the return will be
greatest? Part of a business-like approach would
include multi-year budgets and appropriations that
distinguish between capital improvements and operating
expenses. Surely, this would also involve tenure
adjustments, including sales, purchases, and exchanges. If exchanges are to be a major management
tool, there is a need for broader, more flexible legal
authority, including less costly ways of determining
"equal value" or perhaps just a simple "public interest" finding. How to balance the desirability of
flexibility with the potential for administrative
abuse and hanky-panky is a problem.

In any event, there is a strong case to be made
for a more analytical cost-benefit approach to federal
land programs, despite much popular concern that they
will tend to favor commodity uses over non-commodity
uses.

Federal-State Relationships

Federal-state relationships in federal land and
resource management has been a major policy issue in
the last ten years. NFMA,FLPMA, the Surface Mining
Control and Reclamation Act, Coastal Zone Management
Act, OCS Amendments of 1978, Federal Coal Leasing
Amendments Act, and PILT all dealt with this issue.
Particular emphasis was placed on coordination of
federal activity with state and local land use plans.
Despite the concern for coordination, problems
persist.

Current Problems. Problems with the highest
current visibility involve the role of state government in federal programs and proposals to increase
domestic energy self- sufficiency through the
development of federally-owned energy resources. For
the longer term, all these issues assume constitutional dimensions and involve fundamental questions
concerning institutional arrangements for regional and
national planning, balancing environmental concerns
with developmental requirements, national, regional,
and state allocation of costs and benefits, and the
manner in which state concerns and interests are to be

reflected and accommodated in national policies and
decisions. They often involve multi-state and national interests which go beyond the jurisdiction or the
financial and technical capabilities of single state
governments.

At present, no comprehensive set of institutional
arrangements has been developed to facilitate a
coordinated federal and state response to these
issues. Traditionally, when the national consequences
of particular developmental programs are discovered, a
national program or policy is prepared in response.
To the extent that the affected states and regions are
able to make their views known at the federal level --
whether through public opinion, congressional influence, or legal obstruction of particular federal proposals -- accommodation of state interests is made on
a case-by-case or issue-by-issue basis.

When the traditional approach to accommodation of
state interests fails, proposals for federal preemption often are advanced without a genuine effort to
resolve or accommodate potentially divergent federal
and state interests.

Neither of these approaches -- federal preemption
or case-by-case resolution -- is satisfactory. Both
create uncertainty, invite conflict, and impede
orderly and logical planning at the federal and state
levels. Neither directly addresses the difficult
question of how best to resolve those energy, natural
resource, and environmental controversies which bring
national requirements into conflict with the economic,
social, and environmental objectives of individual
states.

Future Concerns. These problems must be addressed. Congress undoubtedly be asked by the western
governors to strengthen the consistency requirements
of FLPMA. There may also be legislative attempts to
overturn the Ventura County decision, which held that
the Mineral Leasing Act pre-empts local zoning if such
zoning thwarted oil and gas development in national
forests.

Obviously, there are serious obstacles to the
fullest participation of states in federal
decision-making. The legal and political structures
of federal government tend to compartmentalize
governmental responsibility and sovereignty regarding
critical decisions, making both state and federal
parties reluctant to accept compromises for which they
must be accountable within their respective political
systems. Furthermore, although full state participation in planning may be invited, the relative lack of
manpower, technical expertise, and funding at the
state level often serves to reduce actual state

participation. The states are, in effect, implicated in decisions when in reality they have been only observers in the decision-making process.

I believe the Congress will consider the need to devise a better institutional mechanism for integrating federal, state and local interests and plans in land use. Perhaps the Alaska Land Use Council established by Alaska National Interest Lands Conservation Act (ANILCA) will prove to be a prototype that other states or groups of states can adopt.

The council is made up of the federal officials responsible for all federal programs in Alaska and their state counterparts. A presidential appointee and the governor are co-chairmen. The council can make recommendations about all aspects of federal and state land and resource management programs. Any official who does not accept the council's recommendations must explain his reasons for not doing so within thirty days. To make certain that Washington is kept apprised, a cabinet-level federal coordination committee, chaired by the federal co-chairman, has been established. The co-chairman sets the agenda for committee meetings, which must be held at least three times a year.

Even if this, or an alternative approach is adopted by other states, federal-state relationship issues will continue because they involve the fundamentals of our governmental system.

Protection and Preservation of the Natural Environment

The popular support for environmental protection that led some to call the '70s the "Environmental Decade" will not disappear in the '80s. But that support may well be more tempered by concerns about the economy than it was at times in the past. In any event, the "Green Vote" will continue to be a significant force in federal land politics.

I do not believe that Congress will weaken significantly any of the environmental protection laws, almost all of which affect federal land management in some way. These effects take two forms. One is the imposition of terms and conditions on use of federal lands. The other is by generic regulation, e.g., air, water, and toxic waste. I do not believe that there will be many serious efforts to change these laws. Instead, I see the regulatory process and the budget as the critical battleground.

Jim Watt wasn't kidding when he said, "We will use the budget as the means to make policy changes." Underfunded or zero-funded programs result in inadequate enforcement of environmental protection

laws and regulations. Inadequate planning can result
in failure to prevent or minimize damage that could be
avoided.
    The result can be the same as an amendment to the
applicable law.   Some find it ironic that those who
stress "law and order" seem quite willing, in effect,
to change or repeal a law by lack of enforcement.
Whenever this happens, the Congress and the public
eventually will become aware of it and will, I
believe, insist upon enforcement, unless and until
Congress changes the law.
    I should note two factors that could easily lead
to different outcomes of environmental protection
issues involving national forests and public lands.
    The first is the historical difference in public
understanding of and support for the programs of the
Forest Service and the BLM.   Historically, the Forest
Service has been much more respected and supported by
the general public, commodity users and environmental
and conservation groups than BLM. While this difference in attitude is lessening, it still exists.
    The second is based on the different regional
publics that are involved. Public lands and national
forests are both important to the people in the eleven
western states.   Their importance lies in commodity
uses -- timber, minerals, and livestock grazing -- and
in environmental values -- wilderness, recreation, and
open space. However, the national forests are also
important to the public in a number of other states,
including those in the southern, mid-Atlantic, and New
England states.   In these areas, the public looks to
the national forests primarily for their environmental
values.   The commodity values are much less significant than they are in the west. These factors should
be kept in mind when one considers what Congress may
do on a federal lands issue.
    There are a few specific environmental protection
issues that undoubtedly will be actively considered in
the '80s. Congress will, of course, continue to deal
with wilderness designation and rules for management
of wilderness areas.   This includes the RARE II
recommendations, including release and sufficiency.
The debate continues over the national or
state-by-state approach, although state-by-state seems
to be winning in the sense that what little is getting
done is getting done through this approach.
    While Congress is beginning to get recommenda-
tions for BLM wilderness, so far the whole process set
in motion by Section 603 of FLPMA hasn't attracted a
lot of congressional attention. However, we did fin-
ish BLM wilderness in Alaska in ANILCA!
    If the courts rule invalid the contingent right
or no surface occupancy stipulations in oil and gas

leases, then I believe Congress will step in. I would hate to see another all-or-nothing situation like the 1872 Mining Law, i.e., either development without adequate mitigation measures or no development at all.

Speaking of the Mining Law, if there is renewed interest in what is euphemistically called a "mineral inventory" of federal lands for strategic minerals, the long-dormant subject of reform of that law will be raised again. It is not clear whether the administration still places a high priority on the so-called "strategic minerals" issue. The president's April 1982 message is ambivalent. There may also be questions about the fact that valuable minerals are given away under the Mining Law.

Finally, the Congress is going to deal with the question of oil and gas leasing in wilderness areas. I think the administration made a very serious mistake in its approach to this issue. Secretary Watt's statement that the law forced him to lease flies in the face of the law. It also conveniently overlooks his own management objective to "open wilderness areas to leasing." Legislation to stop oil and gas leasing in wilderness has already achieved widespread support in Congress.

Improvement of the Decision-Making and Conflict Resolution Processes

This issue is easy to identify but very difficult to deal with. The problem is a growing sense of frustration. More and more people are concerned that the many new laws Congress enacted in the brief period since 1970 have created a tangled web preventing any action. Some look at land use planning and environmental impact studies as "paralysis by analysis." Others believe litigation brought by various interest groups on the grounds that the FS or BLM failed to comply with the law has resulted in complex court orders; they decry what they perceive as judges running the government.

The scores of permit requirements in existing laws may delay construction for months or even years, ultimately requiring consumers to pay higher costs. As one commentator noted, "the movement for regulatory reform has immediate, visceral appeal to anyone who has tangled with the mind-numbing complexities of the bureaucracy." Sponsors of important projects often must go through seemingly limitless numbers of hoops before they even know whether the government will allow their projects to be built. The burden of these requirements falls not only on project sponsors, but on the general public as well. Delay costs money.

Many of the regulatory requirements are designed
to promote laudable public objectives. But, in
implementing these requirements, courts and agencies
have set up procedural hurdles that cause needless
delay and undermine public confidence in the very
ability of government to accomplish its stated goals.
Kierkegaard once observed that not to choose is itself
a choice, and it often seems that both agencies and
courts hope that by refraining from considering an
issue the problem will go away.

According to the Study on Federal Regulation
prepared by the Senate Committee on Governmental
Affairs in 1977, administrative agency proceedings
average more than nineteen months for licensing,
twenty-one months for ratemaking, and three years for
enforcement actions. In licensing and ratemaking
proceedings, it took an average of 160 days for
matters to reach even the hearings stage; enforcement
actions average well over a year before a hearing is
even convened. The committee study concluded, "We
find no justification for delay of this magnitude."

Despite recent actions to reduce regulatory
requirements, the problem remains. This kind of frustration already has caused some reaction in Congress
and could lead to more.

What kind of reaction? Well, the most prominent
example is the attempt to establish the Energy
Mobilization Board (EMB). The required legislation
passed both Houses in the 96th Congress before the
conference report was defeated by the House of
Representatives. This proposal would have set up a
federal agency that could force federal, state, and
local agencies to decide issues relating to "priority
energy projects." There were provisions for expedited
administrative procedures and judicial review. There
were also special procedures for congressional approval of waivers of federal law for a specific project.

I don't think that EMB will be resurrected, but I
do believe that there will continue to be concern
about what many reasonable people believe to be a
breakdown of the government process. The '80s will
see a continuation of proposals for reducing or
limiting judicial review, regulatory reform, changes
of standards of judicial review as in the Bumpers
amendment, and use of arbitration or congressional
review as a substitute for judicial review.

Ways will be sought to resolve conflicts without
confrontation. Some of you are familiar with the Coal
Policy Project sponsored by Georgetown University.
That project brought industry and environmental
representatives together in an attempt to resolve
differences. The American Bar Association has started
a major project on dispute settlement without litiga-

tion, a subject with special pertinence to the ABA
Section of Natural Resources Law.
   While it is difficult to predict what these
activities will lead to in the '80s, I'm sure that
there will be efforts to improve the decision-making
and conflict resolution process.

IMPLEMENTATION OF THE ALASKA
LAND TENURE ADJUSTMENT PROGRAM

The Alaska Setting

   Alaska's lands and its inland and coastal waters
are a treasure trove of wildlife, timber, fish, marine
mammals, migratory birds, and many hardrock minerals.
   Alaska is also a place of special beauty. After
extolling the many possibilities he foresaw for
development of Alaska's rich and varied resources,
Henry Gannett, chronicler of the 1898 Harriman expedi-
tion to Alaska, had this warning:

>   There is one word of advice and
> caution to be given those intending to
> visit Alaska for pleasure, for sight-
> seeing. If you are old, go by all means;
> but if you are young, wait. The scenery
> of Alaska is much grander than anything
> else of the kind in the world, and it is
> not well to dull one's capacity for enjoy-
> ment by seeing the finest first.

Alaska's Oil and Gas Resources

   Most significant to this conference, Alaska is
the most likely place in the U.S. for major new
discoveries of oil and gas. There are twenty-three
possible sedimentary basins in Alaska and its
continental shelf. Nearly 1,000 wells have been
drilled in Alaska and nineteen proven oil and gas
fields have been discovered. Oil and gas are being
produced from the Swanson River field in the Kenai
National Moose Range and in upper Cook Inlet. Oil is
being produced at Prudhoe Bay.
   The Arctic region of Alaska, north of the Brooks
Range and extending from the Canadian border westward
to the Chukchi Sea, is strong in environmental and
wildlife values. It is also an area containing some
of the best possibilities for major new petroleum
discoveries under United States jurisdiction.
According to studies by the federal government and the
State of Alaska, the areas of highest energy potential
lie accross the entire midsection of the National

Petroleum Reserve-Alaska, extend into the current producing area surrounding Prudhoe Bay and continue along the coastal plain into the Arctic National Wildlife Range.

History of Resource Conflict

For decades, Alaska and its resources have been a focal point for fiercely competing resource protection and development demands. The national importance of these contests has grown as citizens of all states become increasingly dependent on the development of Alaska's energy resources -- now oil, perhaps by the '90s gas, and possibly in the more distant future, coal. Simultaneously, Americans have become increasingly aware of Alaska's superb scenic, wildlife and recreational sources.

In the Alaska Statehood Act of 1958, the federal government agreed to deed over 103 million acres of federal land -- almost one-third of the land area of Alaska -- to the state. This is the most generous land grant in U.S. history. In 1971, under the Alaska Native Claims Settlement Act, the federal government agreed to grant forty-four million acres to Alaskan native groups.

Section 17(d)(2) of the Settlement Act, which called for identification and study of national interest lands reflected congressional concern that the implementation of the massive land grants under the Statehood and Native Claims Acts must be accompanied by careful planning and management of the remaining public lands in Alaska. That concern was based on the historical record of haphazard and ill-advised development in the land rushes associated with earlier disposals of public lands.

In December 1980, after one of the most intense lobbying campaigns in history, the Alaska National Interest Lands Conservation Act (ANILCA) became law. It designated approximately 105 million acres of federal lands for protection of their resource values under permanent federal ownership and management. The act more than doubled the size of the National Park and Wildlife Refuge Systems. It tripled the size of the National Wilderness Preservation System.

ANILCA also is important for national forest and public lands. Once the entire tenure adjustment process is over, BLM will still manage seventy-four million acres and the Forest Service about twenty-four million acres.

During the painstaking crafting of this legislation, Congress recognized the importance of striking a viable balance between resource protection

and resource development. Congress was ever mindful
of other national goals. Not the least of these was
energy independence that could be met, at least in
part, through properly managed development of Alaska's
vast lands and abundant natural resources. Therefore,
in the designation of specific areas to be preserved
as national parks, refuges, wild and scenic rivers,
wilderness, and national monuments, great care was
taken -- in fact Congress went out of its way -- to
avoid resource conflicts by leaving most high-value
mineral, oil, gas, and timber lands outside of
conservation system units.

Thus, a proper balance was achieved between the
protection of Alaska's "crown jewels" and the economic
development potential in Alaska's wealth of resources.
Section 101(d) of the act reads in part:

> The designation and disposition of public
> lands in Alaska pursuant to this Act are
> found to represent a proper balance be-
> tween the preservation of national con-
> servation system units and those public
> lands necessary and appropriate for more
> intensive use.

There will, however, be considerable concern
about these lands during the coming years, and in my
judgment there should be.

Many provisions of ANILCA directly affect both
national forests and public lands. These include:

(1) subsistence management and use (Title VII);
(2) the oil and gas leasing and mineral
     assessment programs (Title X);
(3) transportation access (Title XI);
(4) the Alaska Land Use Council (Title XII);
(5) many of the administrative provisions (Title
     XIII);
(6) the national need mineral activity recom-
     mendation process (Title XV).

Management by BLM of the Steese National Conservation and White Mountain National Recreation areas
established by Title IV will be reviewed. So will the
Forest Service's implementation of the special timber
utilization program in the Tongass National Forest
under Section 705.

During the last two years Congress has not
devoted much attention to the administration's
implementation of ANILCA, or to management of the
National Petroleum Reserve-Alaska and the new
congressionally-mandated oil and gas leasing program
there.

This will change. If nothing else the Alaska
Coalition will call attention to what they may regard

as "violations" of the act. Industry undoubtedly will have problems, too. Obviously if oil and gas leasing is proposed for the "coastal plain" in the Arctic Wildlife Refuge, Congress will be deeply involved because no leasing can take place unless Congress passes a new law.

If the Alaska delegation pursues the legislation it has introduced to allow sport hunting in twenty-five million acres of Alaska National Parks that, too, will trigger congressional review. I might add that there would be no way to prevent that review from reconsidering the entire panoply of compromises and trade offs that went into the ultimate legislative package.

Anyone seeking changes should think twice before starting the legislative process, because once started it may be impossible to stop. This would be particularly true if the changes proposed were perceived to be primarily of benefit to the state of Alaska. While there has been considerable deference to the feelings of Alaskans that they are besieged by "outside" interests -- federal and private -- that feeling is declining. With the state government distributing the fruits of the federal land grant -- $1,000 checks to every man, woman and child -- the national public's interest is more likely to be asserted from both a development and preservation standpoint.

THE POLITICAL BALANCE

In closing, I would like to present some ideas on the best means of balancing our conservation and preservation goals with our resource development needs.

First, implement the land-use planning and decision-making processes established by NFMA and FLPMA. We don't need new laws. We may very well need to continue to streamline existing regulations and procedures based on experience. We do need to get on with making the hundreds of thousands of individual decisions that are required every year. Some of these decisions will be to sell or exchange lands.

Decisions must be based on full information about resource capability and the costs and benefits of alternative uses. There must be full representation of conflicting interests and viewpoints. This means not only interests like timber, mining, recreation and wildlife, but also urban consumers, state and local government, local industries, and neighboring land-owners. Once made, decisions should be carried out so that land users can safely make investment decisions.

Most users are ready and willing to take steps, sometimes costly ones, to prevent or minimize damage to the land and the environment from their activities. They need to know what is required. They also need to believe that the requirements will be enforced reasonably, and promptly.

This means that the executive branch and the Congress must provide adequate manpower and funding so that professional land managers can do their job properly. It also requires delegation of decision-making authority out of Washington, D.C., to the lowest possible level in the field. Congress and political appointees in the executive branch must provide adequate guidance for exercise of that authority. They must also refrain from second-guessing decisions of on-the-ground managers unless they are clearly inconsistent with established law, regulation, or policy. They must be willing to praise dedicated public servants as well as badger bumbling bureaucrats.

Second, and most important, reduce the polarization that has characterized much of the recent federal land policy debate. Cecil Andrus called traditional federal land users the "rape, ruin and run boys." I suspect he heard from third-generation Idaho ranchers about that! James Watt has referred to "toadstool worshippers" and "environmental extremists" who are always selfish, usually easterners, and possibly communists. I know he heard from a lot of life-long Republican capitalists about that. He even may have heard from Teddy Roosevelt! These and other colorful statements may make good copy, but they don't help make good federal land decisions.

Congress did not side with any user group. It took the middle ground, not just out of political expediency but out of recognition of reality. Federal land issues are never black and white. Neither are they simply development versus preservation, east versus west, urban versus rural, public versus private, or federal versus state. They are all these and more, wrapped together in a complex web.

All interested parties must be willing to enter into dialogue, not indulge in diatribe. We need reasoned responses, not knee-jerk reactions; cooperation, not confrontation or litigation. All must be willing to work within the NFMA and FLPMA processes to identify areas of agreement and disagreement, make their arguments, and work to develop acceptable solutions.

To ignore acceptable solutions or to attempt radical changes is to invite suspicion, stridency, and, eventually, stalemate. Instead of the cooperation and accommodation that is necessary to make any

society work, we shall see more polarization as "preservationists" and "developers" try in Congress and in
the courts to stop each other. Any hope for the certainty needed to preserve land or to develop it wisely
will disappear.

Let's commit ourselves to use those policies and
processes of existing law that are designed to achieve
broadly balanced federal land programs. It will be
hard work, often frustrating, sometimes infuriating,
but ultimately immensely rewarding. No one of us can
change the outcome, but together we can insure that
these lands and their rich and varied resources are
used as Congress intends them to be used -- "in the
combination that will best meet the present and future
needs of the American people."

Federal-State Cooperation and Public Land Policy

Timothy E. Gallagher

We in the west largely concur with the prescription for implementing the planning and decision-making processes established by the National Forest Management Act (NFMA) and the Federal Land Policy and Management Act (FLPMA); of the federal government committing itself to funding these processes and delegating decision-making to the lowest level possible; of stopping the polarization of public land policy created by radical swings in federal administrative policy; and of choosing cooperation in resolving public land issues rather than litigation and confrontation. A lean compromise is far better than a fat lawsuit. We believe that with some fine tuning of the law and with a substantial commitment by the federal government to cooperative, shared decision-making between the states and the federal government, the promises of FLPMA can be achieved.

THE MONTANA BALANCE

We in Montana have a prescription for public land maladies. It is called meaningful state involvement in federal land management decisions, and stability and responsiveness to local conditions. To date, these ingredients have been quite rare, in spite of the objectives of FLPMA and the administration's often stated but rarely implemented "good neighbor" policy.

Despite common misperception, western states are not biased in favor of development over the preservation of the public lands. If anything,

Timothy E. Gallagher is senior administrative assistant for natural resources, Governor's Office, State of Montana.

western states are committed to balance. To those who
fear the development bias, for instance, let me point
out the following.
    We in Montana recognized the poisoning of our
waterfowl by a variety of pesticides -- well before
the Environmental Protection Agency (EPA) acknowledged
the problem.   We had in place one of the most stringent surface mining reclamation programs in the nation
well before the federal government enacted the Surface
Mining Control and Reclamation Act (SMCRA).   Indeed,
Montana was the only authority protecting federal
lands from uncontrolled surface mining prior to SMCRA;
the federal government was the Johnny-come-lately to
protection of "its own" land. In water issues, Montana is unique in systematically planning the allocation of water from the Yellowstone River, an area of
rich energy resources. Quite plainly, decisions governing the use of natural resources in Montana are not
seen as either-or propositions.   Instead, we have
looked for solutions benefiting all concerned.   The
real successes of resource management in Montana are
balancing acts we are dedicated to continuing and
enhancing.
    In like manner, Alaska and California have pushed
hard to ensure a balanced federal program for Outer
Continental Shelf oil and gas leasing.   Wyoming has
sued to prevent oil and gas drilling at Little Granite
Creek, a federal wilderness area near Jackson Hole.
Washington State has prodded the Forest Service to
prevent damage to a critical watershed above   Seattle.
Utah has demanded an Environmental Impact Statement
(EIS) on a potential high-level radioactive waste
disposal site near Canyon Lands National Park.
    My point is that in a cooperative scheme of
shared decision-making, states can be trusted to press
for a balanced program.   Please remember western
states' stake in federal land management decisions.
Federal land commonly takes up from one-third to
nine-tenths of western states' land area. Everything
from western states economies to their very authority
as sovereigns in their own right is heavily affected
by the presence of such huge quantities of federal
land. If the federal government wants to do something
on federal land, it can. But, if it really wants to
achieve the kind of balance which FLPMA and NFMA
"allow" (but may not necessarily require), then it's
not only SMART, but imperative to include states as
meaningfully as possible in the decision-making
process.
    The federal government is not the only entity
with a responsibility for a balancing of interests.
The states also have that responsibility and have

exercised that role responsibly when given an opportunity to participate in federal decisions.

I am not saying that states should be allowed to
manage federal land. But I am saying that states
should participate meaningfully in federal land management. In 1775 Edmund Burke said, "All government
-- indeed every human benefit and enjoyment, every
virtue and every prudent act -- is founded on compromise and barter." Those words hold true today. Let
me elaborate.

I think we can all agree that balanced management
of federal land is a worthy objective. But there are
really two levels on which balance must be struck.
The first is the national level. Some land management
issues have national significance and require a
national-level decision-maker. Such issues are:
Should we, as a nation, lease federal coal? Should
we, as a nation, protect and preserve wilderness
areas? Should we, as a nation, lease oil and gas on
the Outer Continental Shelf? How do we, as a nation,
receive fair market value for the use and development
of our federal resources? These questions, and many
others, rightfully and logically involve decisions for
Congress and the federal administration.

But there is a second level where balance also
must be struck -- the level of the states and such
state-level federal land management officials as
Bureau of Land Management (BLM) state, district and
area managers. For instance, pursuant to a balancing
process at the national level, the Congress, or the
secretary of the interior under authority delegated by
Congress, decides that it is in the national interest
to lease federal coal. Fine. But when it comes down
to the selection, for instance, of which tracts to
lease in which places and under what environmental
stipulations, are we still performing a national level
balancing act? No! These on-the-ground decisions are
important land management decisions that are best made
by states and federal field officials. Why should
states be involved at this level? Because states are
uniquely suited and, in fact, obligated to make these
kinds of decisions. Remember, states are not interest
groups. They are, instead, sovereign representatives
of all the people in the state. We don't expect
issues in New Mexico to be the same issues in Montana,
so why should federal land management in New Mexico be
the same as federal land management in Montana? The
best way to ensure balanced adjustment to the uniqueness of each state is to include states in the state-
level decision-making process.

Thus, I argue for a role for states in state
level federal land management decision-making and
incorporation of that role in the text of federal land

management statutes. I believe this would provide for stablility of federal land management policy across administrations, something we desperately need. It would also provide for responding to local conditions, while remaining within the bounds of national land management objectives. The Alaska Land Use Council is a very good example. In fact, a similar council exists in Montana. The Montana Natural Resources Council consists of the governor, the state BLM director, and the regional forester in Montana. The difference between the Montana and the Alaska councils, however, is that the Alaska council is provided for by statute, whereas the Montana council is a product of an administrative Memorandum of Understanding (MOU). This difference does not mean that the Montana council need be less effective. Already, for instance, significant state-federal cooperative transportation and utility corridor planning in Montana has taken place under the auspices of the council and general guidelines of Title V of FLPMA. Still, I wish the state's role in federal land management decision-making in Montana had greater protection in federal statute. Let me illustrate my concern with an example of a federal land management mechanism that worked well with state participation, but -- because it lacked congressional statutory protection -- is now seriously threatened by administrative fiat from an insensitive Department of Interior.

REGIONAL COAL TEAMS (RCT)

The federal coal leasing program, established in 1979, under the previous administraiton, was a remarkable and productive departure from the way the federal government had made coal leasing decisions in the past. Prior to 1979, the federal government's record in providing for the orderly leasing of federal coal resources was abysmal by any standard -- uncontrolled leasing with little production and small returns to the federal treasury, culminating in a leasing moratorium that began in 1971 and lasted almost a decade; two flawed leasing program proposals that ended in litigation precluding a lifting of the moratorium; and a wholesale rewrite of the law under which coal is leased. It is important that throughout this period the states did not have a role in the decision-making process. All the key decisions were made in Washington, D.C. and usually in private.

After fourteen months of negotiations between the Interior Department and the states, a new coal leasing program was finalized in July 1979. The program in-

cluded new regulations complying with the legal requirements laid down by Congress in FLPMA, the Federal
Coal Leasing Amendments Act and the Surface Mining
Control and Reclamation Act. The program was accompanied by a programmatic EIS that has not been challenged in court. The major difference between the
1979 program and previous, unsuccessful programs is
the significant role for states in the leasing decisions.

The 1979 leasing program provided two direct
methods for gubernatorial participation in coal
leasing decisions:

(1) mandatory consultation of the governor
by the secretary of interior prior to the final lease
sale decision, on the initial estimate of the amount
of coal to be leased, on the unsuitability criteria,
on intiation or stopping of the leasing process and on
lease exchanges; and

(2) the creation of regional coal teams
consisting of the governor and the BLM state director
from each state in a coal basin and a team chairman
appointed by the director of the BLM.

The mandatory consultation provisions parallelled
many other such consultation provisions, historically
little more than polite gestures by the federal agency
after the decision has already been made. But the
creation of the regional coal team was a unique
departure from the way the states had participated in
federal decisions, and it was a success. Under the
1979 rules, the RCTs would guide the coal leasing
program from the earliest initial discussion through
the coal lease sale and beyond. Since 1979 more than
two dozen coal leases have been issued with little
controversy.

The following principles behind the regional coal
teams illustrate why the 1979 program had been free of
litigation and had resulted in coal being leased in an
orderly manner:

1. The key on-the-ground decisions on how much
   coal to lease, where and when to lease and
   under what conditions to lease must be debated
   and essentially made in the region impacted by
   the development, not on the shores of the
   Potomac where they are subject to pressures
   irrelevant to the well-being of the states
   affected. The decisions must be made by the
   governors and the BLM people in the field --
   people more knowledgeable of and responsive to
   local needs and concerns but still cognizant
   of the national picture.

2. Decisions must be made in public through a
   consensus-building process. When all interested parties are given the full opportunity

to express their views, chances of litigation are reduced.

3. The <u>federal government must realize that the states' interests</u> in many leasing issues are paramount to the federal interests. Specifically the federal government has the responsibility for insuring that there will be adequate coal to meet the nation's energy needs; the states have the primary responsibility of dealing with the social and economic impacts from leasing and development; and each level of government must respect the importance of the other's sphere of responsibilities.

4. The program must be designed to <u>eliminate potential obstacles early in the development process</u>, at the leasing stage, before huge financial investments and commitments are made and parties become intransigent to compromise.

Unfortunately, this unique and successful experiment in state-federal relations in public land management was not well received by some at Interior who believe that key decisions, such as coal leasing, should be Washington's prerogative. They do not trust their own people in the field and they do not trust the states. They want a free hand to implement their perception of how coal leasing should be done without the annoyance and political embarrassment of having to override a consensus view of the states, local governments, BLM field people and frequently the industry and environmentalists. Thus, in the name of regulatory reform and streamlining, the Interior Department issued new coal leasing regulations last summer. The new regulations diminished the role of the regional coal teams and the governors while increasing secretarial discretion. Thus both stability of policy and federal responsiveness to local concerns are neutralized. No sooner had the regulations been issued, than the department was sued for, among other things, failure to prepare an EIS on what is alleged to be a completely new coal leasing program. Thus, a workable, cooperative federal land management program was unilaterally gutted at the Washington, D.C. level and immediately the program was embroiled in controversy.

According to Mike Harvey, "While there is no legal significance in the different roles of the federal government as sovereign and as proprietor, it is useful to separate these two institutional interests in federal land." There is no legal difference because whether they be sovereign or proprietary, congressional acts respecting federal land can preempt state law that might otherwise reach those lands. That is the result of the Supreme Court decision in the famous Kleppe v. New Mexico case. That should remind those who fear that states would abuse any authority that Congress can stop and take complete control whenever it wants. However, it is not only useful, but necessary to separate the proprietary and sovereign roles of the federal government if we are to solve the important problem of federal-state relations in the western public land states and achieve the desired balance in federal land management. One way to do this is for Congress, whose property clause power over federal land is supreme, to distinguish clearly between the federal government's proprietary and sovereign interests in the text of its federal land enactments. If Congress wants to preempt state decision-making power over federal land in its sovereign capacity and simply set national objectives under national guidelines, it should say so in the statute; when it does not intend to preempt, it should say that too. Instead, we have a situation where lengthy court battles raise and occasionally settle issues in gaps which Congress could have filled in the legislative drafting stage. Of course, no one could write a law anticipating and settling all the issues which may arise under it. Yet, it is reasonable to expect Congress, where it can distinguish between its proprietary and sovereign interests, to be clear about its intent to preempt a state role. Congress should not leave it to courts and interior secretaries to decide the extent of impermissible conflict between state and federal authority.

FLPMA/MINERAL LEASING ACT

We recognize FLPMA is a substantial improvement over previous law involving state participation in federal government decisions regarding the public lands. At the time it was passed, it was a novel leap into the unknown area of state participation. However, western states' capabilities to participate in public land decisions have grown substantially since 1976 and at the same time some new, previously unrecognized, mechanisms have been developed for the type of shared decision-making needed.

In 1976 Congress favored granting states a major role in federal land management decisions and made clear it believed that the primary way to do that was through requiring a consistency of federal land use plans with state and local land use plans. Recognizing that there were very few state or local land use plans of the same quality as state coastal zone management plans, the Congress required consistency only to an extent determined by the secretary of interior. FLPMA also contemplated that all federal actions on the public lands would be pursuant to land use plans.

The federal land use planning effort has not yet lived up to those expectations. Indeed, nearly all significant BLM decisions are made on a separate decision track, independent of what the BLM land use plans state. Clearly, planning does not currently drive decision-making at Interior.

However, new cooperative decision-making mechanisms have emerged, among them the regional coal team and the Montana Natural Resource Council. These schemes have achieved many of the objectives of coordinating state and federal actions that were contemplated under the land use planning section of FLPMA (Section 202).

While continuing to support the planning approaches outlined in FLPMA, I believe that the largely unfulfilled consistency objectives of FLPMA can be enhanced substantially and immediately with the following amendments to the law.

1. An amendment to FLPMA and the Mineral Leasing Act (MLA) stating that users of the public lands are required to comply with state and local laws, unless Congress clearly and explicitly excludes the application of state law.

2. An amendment to FLPMA requiring that activities on public lands be consistent with state land use plans and management programs, unless such consistency would violate federal law.

3. An amendment to the MLA establishing in statute the regional coal team and regional oil shale team concept and requiring that any secretarial override of such team recommendations be fully explained and documented to assure accountability.

4. An amendment to Title V of FLPMA clearly stating that federal agencies, such as the Bonneville Power Administration, must comply with state facility siting laws as a condition of receiving a BLM right-of-way permit. Private firms are currently required to comply by FLPMA, but federal agencies are exempted from procedural certification requirements.

5. An amendment to the MLA and possibly the Surface Mining Control and Reclamation Act (SMCRA) making clear that states with approved reclamation programs and cooperative agreements with the Interior Department are solely responsible for applying the SMCRA standards to mines involving federal coal. Such amendments are needed to eliminate the duplication

of mine plan reviews by the state and the
Office of Surface Mining for mines containing
federal coal. This would not reduce the federal government's control over mining on federal land, because the Secretary would still
control the actions of the federal leasee
through the terms and conditions of the lease
itself.

I believe that such amendments would add significantly to the stability and responsiveness of federal
land management decisions, but it will also take a
significant measure of goodwill on the part of the
Interior Department and the states to achieve the
degree of cooperation needed to manage the public
lands prudently in the '80s and '90s. The states have
demonstrated their willingness and ability to be constructive partners. We urge the administration (if
needed, by congressional directives) to make a good
faith effort to achieve shared decision-making on the
management of public lands.

A final comment on one issue that is vital to
western states and the federal resources in the west:
water. The recent Sporhase v. Nebraska decision of
the Supreme Court has cast doubt upon the heretofore
preeminent position of state water law. The court
held that water is an article of interstate commerce
and, therefore, state laws regulating water are subject to review under the Commerce Clause. This review
requires that state law not unduly burden interstate
commerce. The court in Sporhase found Nebraska's
water law to be facially discriminatory. Congress, to
its credit, reacted quickly to Sporhase with amendments to the coal slurry legislation. Committees in
both houses of Congress clearly and specifically said
in the legislation that Congress delegates its power
under the Commerce Clause to states so that states may
use their own water law to grant or deny water rights.
This degree of congressional clarity is commendable.
Though this particular example cuts in states' favor,
even if it did not, clarity of congressional intent is
preferable to the uncertainty and litigation over
other public land issues where Congress was not so
clear.

There are no miracle cures to federal land
management. Albert Einstein rightly observed that
"the quality of thought in solving problems must be
better than that which got us into difficulty."
Solutions for the difficulties facing federal land
management demand innovation, creativity, hard work
and vision.

Part 2

Timber Issues

4
The Federal Preserve in the West: Environmental Champion or Economic Despoiler?

William F. Hyde

Abstract: This paper explores the consequences of selling federal lands in the west. The effects on the federal treasury, the local tax base, and environmental preservation are specifically treated. Land ownership and productivity, intraregional land use differences, and the impact of federal agency budgets are discussed. The author concludes that nearly 200 million acres would fail to attract private purchasers, resulting in a large amount of de facto wilderness. Also the federal treasury would be insignificantly affected by such sales.
Key words: productivity, land ownership, environmental protection, federal agency budgets.

INTRODUCTION

Environmental protection versus economic growth and development has proven to be a divisive political issue. Too often, however, the implied polarity is artificial and based more on emotion than on a rational examination of the economic facts. Witness the Sagebrush Rebellion. Sagebrush rebels have the opinion that federal land management deprives the

William F. Hyde is associate professor, Center for Resource and Environmental Policy Research, Duke University. Thanks to David Newman and Peter Gilruth for their assistance collecting and organizing data and to James Vaupel, Peter Emerson and an unidentified reviewer for their helpful comments. This study was partially funded by the U.S. Forest Service. This paper appeared in a different version in The Journal of Policy Analysis and Management, Volume 2, Number 4 (Summer 1983) pp. 605-613.

western United States of access to local resources and
opportunities for economic development. They argue
that federal management is too restrictive, too slow
and too insensitive to local issues. The rebels posit
state management as a preferable alternative. More
recently, Congressmen Kramer and Winn and Senator
Percy have gone a step further. They argue for
divestiture and private ownership of the federal
lands, forecasting improved resource stewardship and
production efficiency as well as both local financial
gains and substantial gains to the federal treasury.
The Heritage Foundation/Reagan administration transition team drew on a belief in the innate superiority
of private property as justification for divestiture
-- excluding unidentified "national treasures."

Environmentalists, on the other hand, see federal
ownership as the best means of securing protection for
the west's varied and fragile ecosystems. The states
are perceived as both poorly endowed (relative to the
federal government) and easily captured by local,
often pro-development groups. The potential private
owners of these lands are depicted by environmentalists as modern-day cowboys who show little respect for
the fragile nature or sustainable productivity of the
land.

Those who argue for economic growth and development often see federal disposition to the states or
the private sector as a necessary measure; those who
favor environmental preservation/conservation perceive
the status quo as the best means of securing their
objectives.

There is enough evidence, however, to hypothesize
that the environmental protection vs. economic growth
argument, as it pertains to the federal presence in
the west, is both naive and over-simplistic. Federal
divestiture may prove to be neither the economic
elixir predicted initially by the Sagebrush rebels and
later by privatization advocates, nor the anathema
feared by the environmentalists. Property taxes and
other liabilities of land ownership would exceed
commercial values and prevent some federal land from
selling at any positive price. The federal government
currently assumes these liabilities. Federal agencies
also subsidize commercial uses of some public lands
while restricting commercial uses to less than their
profit maximizing level on other public lands.

Were the federal government to cease managing its
western lands for their commercial bounty, selling its
holdings (exclusive of national treasures) either to
the states or to private individuals, and managing for
their noncommercial (i.e. recreational, environmental
and aesthetic) values only those lands on which the
liabilities are such that the lands would receive no

purchase bids, then I predict the following outcomes:
(1) immediate gains to the federal treasury of less
than nine billion dollars and small gains to state and
private managers in those localized cases where profit
maximizing operations would expand upon current
commercial production, (2) generally increased burdens
for the local tax base as the federal presence (i.e.
federal employment and subsidy) is removed, and (3)
de facto environmental preservation of those federal
lands which would receive no purchase bids from either
the state or private sectors owing to their low (or
negative) commercial value. Removing current subsidies for mineral, timber, and livestock operations
would result, I predict, in a twentyfold expansion of
lands in a currently preserved status. This third
point may surprise many observers of the situation who
have yet to consider the scattered empirical evidence.
Let us consider the lands and budgets in question and
make some casual observations on desert and mountain
land in general.

LAND OWNERSHIP AND PRODUCTIVITY

The present argument for reduction or elimination
of federal land holdings in the west is but another
round in a century-old debate.[1] The argument has
focused on lands located in the Rocky Mountains and
intermountain west which are managed by the U.S.
Forest Service (USFS) and the Bureau of Land
Management (BLM). The argument occurs less frequently
and is made less emphatically in populous California
and coastal Oregon and Washington.
Appendix Table 4.1 shows USFS, BLM and total
federal land holdings (including National Park Service, Department of Defense, etc.) within eleven
western states. Clearly USFS and BLM are the dominant
land management agencies. The mere size of the federal land holdings (48.1 percent of the total land area)
invites political movements, like the Sagebrush
Rebellion, which assert that the federal presence
dominates local life. Furthermore, it is not surprising that the Sagebrush Rebellion appears strongest
in the intermountain states of Utah, Idaho and Nevada
where the federal share is largest -- in excess of
sixty percent.
This comparison of public and private lands
emphasizes the large federal share but overlooks
productivity differences. Only forty-six percent of
federal timberland, or 64.9 million acres, is
classified by USFS as potentially "commercial;" the
remaining 76.1 million acres are classified unproductive.[2] Furthermore, the potential productivity of

these federally-owned commercial acres (71 ft^3/acre/ year) is less than the potential productivity of private timberlands (83 ft^3/ acre/year).[3] Range quality, measured in animal-unit-months per acre of rangeland, similarly favors private (0.4) over federal (0.1) lands.[4] Measures of recoverable minerals, no doubt, also favor privately owned deposits.[5] Thus, it is a reasonable hypothesis that commodity values on private lands exceed those on federal lands. This comes as no surprise; the private lands were originally selected from the public domain because of their greater commodity values. In general, the federal government manages today what remained after that earlier selection.

The relative productivity of non-market services on private and federal lands may be altogether different, however. Certainly recreational use of the federal lands exceeds recreational use of the private lands. Perhaps this is because exclusion of recreational users often is difficult, therefore many recreational activities fail to attract user fees and there is no incentive for their private production. Perhaps it is because federal lands are topographically and biologically more diverse, and therefore more scenic. Perhaps both explanations are valid.

In sum, the federal lands, taken altogether, are comparatively poorer providers of commodity values but perhaps comparatively better providers of non-market services. This suggests, first, that their transfer to (financially more constrained) state management would either cause a reduction in the flow of non-market services which they provide citizens of the entire country or create a heavy burden on the state treasuries if the flow were to be maintained. Second, transfer to private ownership would depend on the transfer price. It would fail to occur for the bulk of federal lands which have either no commodity value or which would be taxed in excess of their commodity values.[6] (Furthermore, non-market recreational values and the values of options on future land uses justify continued federal management of some lands with positive net commodity values.)

BUDGETS AND THEIR IMPACTS

Federal agency budgets provide some support for these observations. Appendix Table 4.2 summarizes USFS and BLM budgets for fiscal year 1978, the latest year for which complete budgets were available. The first column shows federal receipts from the sale of goods and services in each state. Its entries are large enough to suggest that some federal lands

support profitable private management. The second
column shows the obligated expenditures within each
state, including expenditures for both salaries and
equipment. A portion of gross receipts are returned
to the state in lieu of state and local taxation of
the federal lands. Column three records this
transfer. There are many individual cases where
payments in lieu of taxes exceed net receipts for
resource services. This is particularly true for BLM
timber sales in Oregon. The fourth column shows the
net flow, in every case an outflow from the federal
treasury to either the state or its citizens. These
outflows suggest some combination of (1) the high cost
of managing for non-market-valued services and (2)
inefficient management.

There is no a priori reason to believe that state
management would be more efficient than federal
management, therefore the net dollar flows support a
contention that transfer of federal lands to the
states would either create a heavy burden on state
budgets or require a reduction in services provided.
A sense of the magnitude of this burden can be found
in column five which shows the net flows as portions
of the state budgets (expenditures). They average
five percent and exceed two percent in every state
except California and Washington, states where neither
the Sagebrush Rebellion nor divestiture are important
political issues. Federal withdrawal, suggesting five
percent budget reductions, would cause attention in
any state; the eleven percent budget reduction in
Montana and fifteen percent reduction in Idaho would
be severe.

In the event of private ownership, the level of
receipts minus expenditures is indeterminant. Receipts would be larger where federal agencies currently constrain commodity production but smaller where
they currently subsidize production. Expenditures
would be smaller to the extent that private operations
would be more efficient than public management. Taxes
are also indeterminant, as would be the net effect on
regional welfare.

INTRAREGIONAL LAND USE DIFFERENCES

The evidence on which to base judgments regarding
location and number of commercially profitable acres
is sparse. Nevertheless, an attempt might be instruc-
tive.

Commercially profitable timberland can be divided
into two categories: that on which it is profitable
to grow successive crops of timber, and that which has
standing timber which might be harvested profitably

but which cannot grow successive crops big enough,
fast enough or dense enough to support even minimal
continuous management costs. Operations on the first
are known by the term "sustained yield" and on the
second by the term "timber mining." Most knowledgeable observers agree that coastal Oregon and
Washington, northern California, and much of northern
Idaho and western Montana qualify for sustained-yield
operations. Indeed, these are the only locations
where significant amounts of privately owned
timberland can also be found.

Timberland is classified by biological productivity from best to poorest or from Site Class I through
Site Class V. Even in the aforementioned locations,
land below Site Class IV can, at best, justify timber
mining.[8] Elsewhere (southern and central Rocky
Mountains and the intermountain region) the market is
less accessible, the land more arid, the timber
sparser, and the species of lower commercial value.
Two studies have shown that growing timber on the
Beaverhead National Forest in southwestern Montana has
a benefit-cost ratio less than one (even using the
questionable calculations and discount rates of the
USFS) and that harvesting timber on the San Juan
National Forest in southwestern Colorado costs $38.70
per thousand board feet yet returns only $2.65 per
thousand.[9] It might be generous to suggest that
timber may be mineable on one-third of the land of
Site Class IV or better in these locations. On the
remaining land, timber is so inaccessible, so sparse,
or of such poor quality that, in absence of some form
of subsidy, it would attract no timber sale bidders at
any positive price.

The commercially profitable share of public range
within each state probably does not exceed the
commercially sustainable plus mineable share of
timberland within each state. Some rangeland also is
too arid or inaccessible for grazing livestock.
Moreover, the steady regionwide decline in
animal-unit-months from 12.45 million to 8.88 million
since 1960 suggests that the share of profitable
rangeland is declining rapidly.[10] Public range is
currently transferred to private usage under a system
of noncompetitive leases. The price for these leases
is less than the discounted flow of the market value
of their resource services.[11] Furthermore, the BLM
matches range improvement costs on private investments, and federal water projects and agricultural
price supports provide additional subsidy. Without
these inducements, the commercial share of public
range would decline further still.

Finally, there are surely many scattered and
isolated sites of high commercial value for minerals,

for resort homes, and for ski areas. While the dollar
value of these sites undoubtedly is high, greater than
the per acre values for either timber or range, the
total number of acres involved must be insignificant
relative to the number of commercially profitable
acres of timber and rangeland.

We might also argue that someone would be willing
to hold almost any acre of remaining, low-valued
land -- if only for its potential future value or to
satisfy a personal bequest motive. The remaining
lands are so low-valued, however, that their transfer
would have little effect either on federal or state
treasuries or on the local economy. Meanwhile, demand
for public expenditures on such lands would continue
because private owners could not justify the fire or
watershed expenditure necessary to protect neighboring
offsite values. If transfers were restricted to those
lands which attracted prices sufficient to pay these
offsite liabilities, then very few remaining acres
would be attractive for private ownership.

Appendix Table 4.3 puts these land use observations into a quantitative form. It also provides some
very uncertain, but (in my judgment) generous, estimates of the commercial market value of these lands.
Of special interest is the number of residual acres
and the aggregate value of those acres which might
have commercial value.

CONCLUSIONS

Were federal lands in these states offered for
sale, nearly two hundred million acres would fail to
attract private purchasers at a price sufficient to
compensate for public protection against the offsite
liabilities of land ownership. Therefore, these lands
would probably continue under public management. In
the absence of either successful sale to private
owners or continued public agency subsidy of commercial values, then decisions either to manage these two
hundred million acres for their noncommercial values
or to hold them as de facto wilderness would result in
a twentyfold expansion of current USFS wilderness and
total National Park Service and Fish and Wildlife
Service acres.[12] The eventual increase would be even
greater as some land mined of its timber would be
abandoned and revert to public protection. No doubt
considerable rangeland acreage eventually would revert
to public protection for the same reason.

Sale of federal lands would affect the federal
treasury insignificantly. The treasury might receive
an inflow of funds approximately less than one percent
of the one trillion dollar national debt (or between

six and nine percent of the annual federal deficit
-- a frequent but less meaningful comparison because
the budget deficit is a flow while land value is a
stock). We must be very careful, however, even of
this datum. It would take the regional economy a
large number of years to absorb this transfer, and one
result of paying for these lands could be a new
"landed-poor" western population. Furthermore, while
there may be good economic arguments for it, we must
recognize that after the sale of the commercially
valuable public lands, this revenue source would be
gone forever and the remaining public lands, managed
for public goods, would be a permanent, if socially
justifiable, drain on the treasury.

Neither state nor private management would have
the generally favorable impacts expected by groups
like the Sagebrush Rebellion. Either state of private
management could realize a few localized gains and
many localized burdens. States like Idaho and
Montana, with large budget deficits to overcome, and
the arid southwestern states, whose federal lands have
low commercial value, would lose. State management,
depending on the level of state provision of public
goods, likely would require increased state tax
burdens. Timber and range interests on the Pacific
coast and in the northern Rockies might gain;
elsewhere they would lose their current federal
subsidies. Indeed, in the absence of federal agency
support for these commercial uses of the public lands,
the greatest beneficiaries might be private timber and
livestock producers external to the west who would now
face reduced western competition. The greatest losers
might be the intermountain region stockmen who seem to
be the strongest supporters of the Sagebrush Rebellion
and most vocal opponents of federal ownership.
Finally, environmentalists, with their interests in
non-market values, would be heavy losers with regards
to the newly private lands; their status with state
management would be less certain, but they would be
absolute and immediate gainers on the vast numbers of
commercially unprofitable acres which are currently
managed for timber, livestock and minerals. In
addition, environmentalists would be the eventual
gainers on mineable land which would someday revert to
public protection. The acreage gains for non-market
environmental interests could be astounding.

While this assessment is casual at best, it
cautions against automatically assuming anything about
gains from transferring the western federal lands to
either state management or private ownership. Small
transfers of land from public or private ownership may
be reasonable. But localized transfers in the
opposite direction may also be justifiable -- if not

politically fashionable. Transfers of federal lands
to either state management or private ownership will
have neither the generalized favorable economic
development impact which the Sagebrush rebels
anticipate nor the budget impact which the Reagan
administration desires. Indeed, the impacts may be
the opposite. Imagine environmentalists and the
Sagebrush Rebellion joining efforts to remove federal
presence from the west! Imagine them successful!

NOTES

1. Consider, for example, the Homestead Act of
1862, the debate over the 1934 Taylor Grazing Act, or
Milton Friedman's call to sell the U.S. Forest Service
{Capitalism and Freedom (Chicago: University of
Chicago Press, 1962} p. 31).
2. The USFS "commercial" classification is based
on a biological criterion. It overstates the area of
financially profitable timberland.
3. Lands owned by the forest industry have an
even greater potential of 103 ft^3/acre/year. Calculated from USDA Forest Service, An Analysis of the
Timber Situation in the United States: 1952-2030
(Washington, 1980) Appendix 3, Table 6.
4. These are approximate measures more accurately
reflecting federal/non-federal than federal/private
proportions. I assume the non-federal non-private
shares of both AUMs and land is small. Gathered from
USDA Forest Service, An Assessment of the Forest and
Rangeland Situation in the United States (Washington:
FRR-22, 1981) Tables 2-3 and 5-8; USDI Bureau of Land
Management, Public Land Statistics 1980 (Washington:
USGPO, 1981) Table 52; and USDA Forest Service,
"Forest Service Annual Grazing Statistical Report Use
Summary 1980" (internal document, Range Management
Staff, 1981).
5. Consider two recent empirical papers refuting
claims that the wilderness lands are significant oil
and gas depositories. C.F. Runge, "Wilderness Land
and Energy Exploration: A Policy Analysis" (unpublished research paper, Political Science Department,
University of North Carolina, 1982) and L. Fischman,
"Potentially Producible Petroleum and Natural Gas in
the United States and the Western Overthrust Belt"
Economic Policy Report No. 1, The Wilderness Society,
1982.
6. It is not unusual for property taxes to exceed
commodity values originating from the land. Indeed,

this explains why timber and mining interests have often "high-graded" their resource and departed from the land, leaving it unclaimed, often to revert to public ownership in absence of tax payments.

7. For a collection of examples of the latter, see J. Baden and R.L. Stroup, eds. Bureaucracy vs. Environment (Ann Arbor: University of Michigan Press, 1981).

8. General empirical support can be found in: H.J. Vaux, "How Much Land Do We Need for Timber Growing," J. Forestry 71 (1973): 399-403; W. Hyde, Timber Supply, Land Allocation and Economic Efficiency (Baltimore: Johns Hopkins Press, 1980); M. Clawson, "Economic Classification of U.S. 'Commercial' Forests" J. Forestry 79 (1981): 727 ff.; and J. Walker "Timber Management Planning" (Western Timber Assn. mimeo, August 1974).

9. USDA Forest Service, "Timber Management Plan" (Dillon, Montana: Beaverhead N.F. mimeo, 1977); and W. Hyde "Timber Economics in the Rockies" Land Economics 57 (1981) 630-38.

10. USDI Bureau of Land Management (1981) Table 52 and USDI Bureau of Land Management, Statistical Appendix to the Annual Report of the Director, 1961 (Washington: USGPO, 1962) Table 83.

11. For a bibliography, see E. Castle "Natural Resource Economics" in L. Martin, ed., Economics of Welfare, Rural Development and Natural Resources In Agriculture. Minneapolis: Univ. Minnesota, 1981, p. 451.

12. USDA Forest Service, (1981) Table 3-13. Calculated by subtracting an estimated 5,646,984 acres for Alaska lands.

APPENDIX

Table 4.1: Federal Land Area in Eleven Western States

State	USFS and BLM[1] (000s of acres)	Total Federal[2] (000s of acres)	Federal Share[3] (000s of acres)
Arizona	23,866	32,034	44.1
California	36,954	47,610	47.5
Colorado	23,510	24,783	37.3
Idaho	32,360	33,748	63.8
Montana	24,909	27,662	29.7
Nevada	54,261	61,617	87.7
New Mexico	22,093	25,825	33.2
Oregon	31,334	32,413	52.6
Utah	30,121	33,491	63.6
Washington	9,379	12,863	30.1
Wyoming	27,045	30,311	48.6
Total	315,832	362,357	48.1

[1] USDI Bureau of Land Management Public Land Statistics, 1978, (Washington: USGPO, 1980). Calculated from Table 9, pp. 14-5, 21-2.

[2] Ibid. Table 7, p. 10.

[3] Ibid. Calculated from Table 7, p. 10.

Table 4.2: Bureau of Land Management and Forest Service Receipts and Outlays in Eleven Western States, 1978

| State | BLM plus USFS ($000) | | | | |
	Receipts[1]	Obligated Expenditures[2]	Payments in Lieu of Taxes[3]	Net Flow[4]	Net Flow as % of State Budget[5]
Arizona	24,617	72,716	6,203	- 54,302	2.63
California	187,154	352,244	60,242	-225,332	0.92
Colorado	37,180	136,273	16,714	-115,807	5.08
Idaho	51,767	164,391	14,139	-126,763	15.14
Montana	53,603	135,329	16,217	- 97,943	11.28
Nevada	13,559	30,044	5,195	- 21,680	2.80
New Mexico	134,581	115,821	62,537	- 43,777	3.29
Oregon	608,268	480,568	190,388	- 62,688	2.42
Utah	31,139	78,093	12,924	- 59,878	4.61
Washington	122,255	143,581	31,259	- 52,585	1.24
Wyoming	165,283	122,279	79,879	- 36,875	7.28
Total	1,429,406	1,831,339	495,697	-897,630	4.50

129

Table 4.2: Continued

[1]From USDI Bureau of Land Management Public Land Statistics, 1978, (Washington: USGPO, 1980) Table 115, pp. 173-4; plus USDA Forest Service "1978 Annual Collection Statement," (unpublished computerized files in each of six Western Forest Service Regional Office).

[2]From U.S. Congress House Committee Appropriations, Department of Interior and Related Agencies Appropriations for 1978. 95th Congress, 1st session, 1977, p. 218 and USDA Forest Service, "Detailed Statement of Obligations by Geographic Location, Fiscal Year 1980," (unpublished internal files) pp. 481-525.

[3]From USDI Bureau of Land Management Public Land Statistics, 1978, (Washington: USGPO, 1980) Table 122, p. 180 and USDA Forest Service, "1978 Payments to States from National Forest Receipts" (unpublished computerized files, Program Development and Budget Staff, Washington Office).

[4]Columns (1 minus 2 minus 3).

[5]Jack L. Gardener, ed., The Book of States: 1980-1 (Lexington, Ky: Council of State Governments, 1980) pp. 282-3.

Table 4.3:   Estimated Land Use and Market Value of
              Selected Forest Service Lands

	Acres (000s)	Market Value ($000,000)	Implied Value per Acre ($)
Timberland			
Sustainable	21,434[1]	6,000[5]	138
Mineable	22,070[2]		
Rangeland	62,330[3]	136[6]	2
Isolated Sites	5,360[4]	2,750[7]	550
Residual	198,838	-	-
Total	315,032	8,900	28

[1]Calculated for commercial forestland above Site Class
V, including all managed by the USFS in W. Oregon and
W. Washington, sixty percent in California, eighty
percent in Idaho and Montana.   USDA Forest Service,
The Outlook for Timber in the United States (Washing-
ton: FRR-20, 1973) Appendix I, Table 5.

[2]Calculated as the remaining USFS land above Site
Class V, plus all of Site Class V in states listed in
fn. 1, plus one-third of all USFS commercial
forestland in the remaining states.   Same source as
above.

[3]Calculated as 0.34 of all rangeland where this share
equals the mineable plus sustainable share of all
forestlands.   From USDA Forest Service, Assessment
of the Forest and Range Land Situation in the United
States (Washington: FRR-22, 1981) Table 2.3.

[4]Calculated as 0.25 of the number of sustainable
timber acres.

[5]Calculated as the present value of the infinite
stream of timber harvest opportunities using a ten
percent discount rate (approximating the market real
borrowing rate) and Clawson's estimate of annual

Table 4.3:   Continued

timber   value (which should be adjusted for inflation
since 1973 and net of both   harvest   costs   and   non-
timber   opportunities on some of the poorer sites) M.
Clawson, "The National Forests", Science, vol.   91
(Feb. 20, 1976) pp. 762-67.

[6]Calculated as 0.34 of the present value of the
infinite   stream   of   livestock grazing opportunities
using a ten percent discount rate.   E.   Orenstein
"Economics   of   Public Rangeland" (unpublished honors
thesis,   Economics Department,   Duke   University,
1982).

[7]Calculated as 0.05 of the value of operative   mines,
which was calculated as one-half the present value of
the infinite stream of gross mineral receipts using a
ten percent discount rate.   USDA Forest Service
(1981) Table 2.10.

5
Divestiture, Harvest Expansion and Economic Efficiency: The National Forests in the Early 1980s

David H. Jackson

Abstract: The focus of this analysis is the divestiture of western public lands and future timber harvests. An assessment is made of the current demand, cost, and price situation for national forest timber. The author concludes that the current situation both nationally and in the northern Rockies is that timber management costs exceed timber management income before receipt sharing. Also, data indicate that the marginal costs of increasing the levels of harvest are rising. Several prospective ways of improving the managerial efficiency of national forest timber management are discussed.

Key words: timber management, federal receipts and expenditures, allowable cut, environmental quality, divestiture.

INTRODUCTION

Current debate over management of national forestland focuses on two issues: (1) timber harvest expansion; and (2) divestiture of western public lands. While essentially political in nature, each issue has important economic aspects. This analysis will focus on several efficiency aspects of both divestiture and harvest expansion.

The Reagan administration proposes expanding federal timber harvests by at least forty percent. The rationale is the belief that recent harvest levels have been unreasonably restricted by environmental concerns and that harvest expansion will help fuel the economy and overcome federal budget deficits.

David H. Jackson is associate professor, School of Forestry, University of Montana.

133

Sagebrush Rebellion supporters also argue that federal management has been too restrictive and insensitive to community issues, particularly local opportunities for economic development. The sagebrush rebels say state management is preferable to federal management of public lands. U.S. Congressmen Kramer and Winn and Senator Percy go a step further. They argue for divestiture of "surplus" federal lands, forecasting gains to both local and federal treasuries as a result.

Krutilla and Haigh (1978) have inquired into the economic justification of the national forest system. It is their view that the national forests exist in order to solve problems of market failure. Wildlife, clean water, and aesthetics won't be supplied optimally under private organization of production because of the difficulties in defining exclusive use rights.

While areas of market failure are important in assessing the overall efficiency of the national forests, this paper focuses on national forest timber production. Are there efficiency or equity reasons for continued national forest timber production aside from multiple use or the joint provision of market and non-market goods and services?

Perhaps the key proponents of divestiture of the national forests are Baden and Stroup (1975). But their arguments are conceptual and lack any reference to empirical fact. This paper bases assessment of the current situation, to the extent possible on reliable data and information, in order to determine the implications of harvest expansion and/or divestiture.

ECONOMIC BACKGROUND

One cornerstone of economic thought is the theory of product demand. Demand theory suggests that if the price of a good is decreased while, at the same time, prices of related goods, tastes and preferences and societal wealth are constant, more of that good will be purchased. Typically, demand functions are plotted with price on the vertical axis and quantity demanded on the horizontal axis, such as in Figure 5.1. In this figure, we see the inverse relationship between the price of a good and the quantity demanded. At price p_1 more quantity is demanded q_1 than is demanded at price p_2 ($p_1 < p_2$) where quantity q_2 is consumed.

The various price quantity pairs indicate another important aspect of demand curves. The shaded rectangle under the curve identifies the total revenue accruing to a firm selling quantity q_1. If the price of timber is p_1 per billion board feet and the quantity demanded is q_1 billion board feet, then total

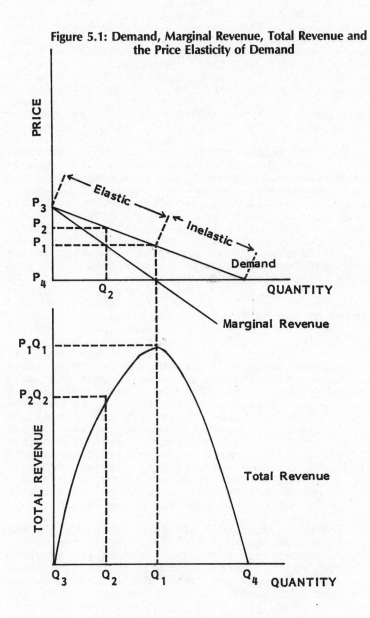

Figure 5.1: Demand, Marginal Revenue, Total Revenue and the Price Elasticity of Demand

timber sales revenue is p_1q_1, or the area of the shaded rectangle in Figure 5.1. In the lower part of Figure 5.1, we chart the total revenue accruing to the firm at various prices. When price is extremely high, as at p_3, quantity demanded is zero, and, since no one buys anything, total revenue is zero. As price declines, more of the good is purchased and total revenue increases. As price decreases and quantity increases, total revenue continues to increase until it reaches its maximum at the price/quantity pair, p_1q_1. Below this point, price is so low that, even though quantity demanded is increasing, total revenue is diminished. This trend reaches its extreme at price $p_4=0$. Although quantity demanded is high, since the price is zero, total revenue, p_4q_4, is zero. Demand is said to be price elastic if a decrease in the product price results in an increase in total revenue. Conversely, demand is said to be price inelastic if a decrease in price results in such a change in quantity demanded that total revenue falls.

Again referring to Figure 5.1, the price elastic and price inelastic ranges of the demand curve are labeled. Elasticity can be estimated for demand curves by the formula $\{(\triangle Q/Q) \div (\triangle P/P)\}$. If one estimates elasticity of demand for timber and the value falls between zero and minus one, timber demand is price inelastic. If, on the other hand, the price elasticity of demand falls between minus one and minus infinity, it can be said that consumption is on the elastic portion of the demand function.

One more function is labeled in Figure 5.1. It is the marginal revenue function (MR). What this curve shows is the change in total revenue for small quantity movements. Note that the value of marginal revenue (the change in total revenue) is positive (negative) where the price elasticity of demand is elastic (inelastic). The relationships between demand functions, total revenue functions, marginal revenue functions, and the price elasticity of demand are specific to a given demand function. If factors such as the prices of related goods or income change, then the demand curve for the good in question will shift to the left or right depending on the nature of the changes.

A second cornerstone of economic thought is the theory of product supply. Briefly stated, the total costs of production rise as the quantity supplied increases. Rising total costs corresponding with larger quantities produced occurs for several reasons. Perhaps most importantly, as producers attempt to eke out more product in a given time, they typically encounter diminishing returns in production. Simply stated, the level of product produced increases less than proportionately when producers use more and more inputs in manufacturing.

For purposes of clarity, Figure 5.2 represents a total cost (TC) function for a firm. Note that TC eventually rises with higher quantities at a faster rate. In the lower part of Figure 5.2 are the average total cost curve (ATC) and the marginal cost curve (MC). By definition, ATC is the total cost divided by the quantity produced. Marginal cost is the change in total cost for a small change in the quantity produced. In short, it is the slope of the total cost (TC) function in Figure 5.2. Under conditions of efficient production, the marginal cost function in Figure 5.2 is synonymous with the firm's supply function. Thus, the idea of supply itself is based upon both production theory and cost theory.

In Figure 5.3, the industry supply function (SS) is the sum of each firm's marginal cost function in Figure 5.2 and the demand function (DD) comes from the demand function in Figure 5.1. Both functions plot quantity as a function of price. They have a common point where they intersect. At this common point, suppliers will offer just enough to fill market demand at price P_e. The supply and demand functions simultaneously determine output and price.

TIMBER DEMAND FUNCTIONS: SOME RECENT EMPIRICAL RESULTS

The demand for timber is derived from the demand for wood products. Timber (logs) are a factor of production in the manufacture of lumber, plywood, wood pulp and other numerous wood products. Since 1930, economists have recognized some important relationships between the demand for such products as wood and the derived demand for factors of production such as timber. Alfred Marshall said that the more inelastic the demand for the products, the more inelastic would be the derived demand for the factors of production. Also, he argued that the more essential the factor of production, the more inelastic will be the derived demand for that factor of production.

Recent empirical work on the demand for timber suggests that Marshall's understanding of derived demand was crystal clear. Economists since McKillop (1967) have understood that the demand for wood products is inelastic, a fact recently reconfirmed by Adams and Haynes (1980). Thus, the derived demand for timber ought to be inelastic because product demand is inelastic. Timber is also, of course, essential in manufacturing wood products.

Again, the empirical results do not refute Marshall's understanding of the nature of derived

Figure 5.2: Total Cost, Average Cost and Marginal Cost

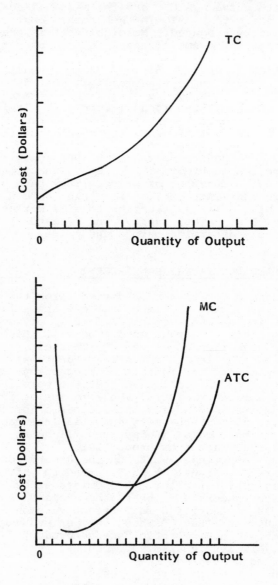

Figure 5.3: Competitive Equilibrium

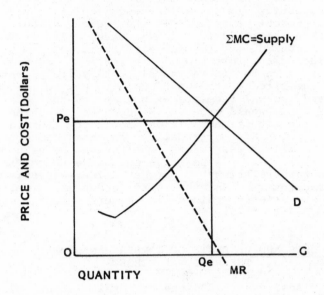

demand. Furthermore, two empirical studies recently
published approach the estimation of timber demand
from very different analytical perspectives.   Haynes,
Connaughton and Adams (1982) develop estimates from
product demand equations.   Majerus (1982), following
an approach outlined by Jackson (1982), estimates
timber supply and demand directly.   Where the two
approaches overlap geographically, the estimates of
the price elasticity of demand for national forest
timber are shockingly similar.   Majerus estimates that
the price elasticity of demand for national forest
timber in Montana is -.333.   Haynes, Connaughton and
Adams estimate the price elasticity of demand for
national forest timber in Montana and northern Idaho
to be -.285.   The latter study finds that national
forest timber demand is price-inelastic in   all
administrative regions of the United States.
    Surprisingly little attention has been given to
the issue of inelastic timber demand in the forest
management and economics literature.   Recall from
Figure 5.1, where demand is inelastic, an increase in
supply will reduced total revenue. This then applies
to the national forests.   The importance of the
statistical estimates of the elasticity properties of
timber demand can be illustrated in the following
example.

Suppose the national forests examine the effect
of a potential wilderness addition on federal timber
sale receipts. The demand for timber in the region is
price-inelastic. If the wilderness addition reduces
national forest supplies in the region, timber sale
receipts on the residual timber base will increase
because timber demand is price-inelastic.
Wilderness creation increases government
receipts. There is a complementary relationship
between the size of the national forest wilderness
system and federal receipts -- not an inverse relation
as most people would expect. Wilderness creation on
national forest timber lands could be termed a
positive pecuniary externality in the economists'
jargon. Wilderness users won't earn the value (an
externality). It is a positive one since there is a
complementary relationship between wilderness size and
timber receipts. As the word pecuniary implies,
wilderness affects things in monetary or value
terms.[1]

COSTS AND BENEFITS OF TIMBER MANAGEMENT:
THE NATIONAL FORESTS

In fiscal year 1980, the national forest system
expended approximately $1.2 billion on timber (Table
5.1). The expenditures combine activities of both a
capital nature (investments) and an operational nature
(sale preparation, sale administration, road maintenance). In the same year, total timber sale receipts
were about $1 billion before receipt-sharing with
state and local governments for roads and schools.
After receipt sharing, net income for the timber management program was roughly a negative $440 million,
the national forest timber management programs' contribution to the federal debt.
The financial picture in Forest Service Region 1
(Montana and northern Idaho) is similar to that of the
rest of the country, but here more detailed budgetary
information allows perhaps a better assessment of
income and expenditure problems. Timber selling
prices are generally lower in the northern Rockies
than they are nationally. This, in turn, tends to
exacerbate the expenditure and receipt scenario. As
per Table 5.2, timber management expenditures were
about $146 million while receipts were approximately
$61 million. Using average timber prices in recent
years, expenditures are about two and one-quarter
times receipts. After sharing receipts with counties
for roads and schools, Region 1 contributed about $100
million to the federal debt. Road construction, an
activity of a capital nature, accounted for some

Table 5.1:   Forest Service Expenditures and Receipts
on Timber Management, Fiscal Year 1980

National Data

($1,000)

Protection and Maintenance	$ 304,349
Fighting Forest Fires	69,190
Road and Trail Maintenance	84,809
Reforestation and TSI	101,865
Timber Sale Betterment	80,579
Brush Disposal	43,730
Timber Salvage Sales	11,899
Constr. Forest Roads	236,577
Purchase Election Road Construction	54,219
Timber Purchases Road Construction	201,656
Restoration of Roads - Highway, Trees	15,262
TOTAL Timber-Related Expenditures	$1,204,135

Timber Receipts

Receipts from Deposits	625,407
Sale Area Betterments	116,576
Timber Salvage Sales	14,530
Brush Disposal	42,374
Restoration of Improvement	198
Cooperative Work	29,895
Est. Value of Roads Built by	
Purchases in Lieu of Cash	164,226
Total Receipts	$ 993,206

SOURCE: USDA Forest Service Annual Report for Fiscal
Year 1980.

Table 5.2: Forest Service Region 1 Expenditures and
Receipts on Timber Management, Fiscal Year
1980

Northern Idaho and Montana

Expenditures   ($1,000)

   Sale Preparation $ 11,181
   Sale Administration   7,029
   Timber Resource Plans   2,208
   Salvage Sales   140
   Fire: Presuppression and Suppression   19,034
   Total Silvicultural Improvement   31,398
   Road Construction
     a. Appropriated Funds and Purchaser
        Election Construction   41,792
     b. Purchaser Road Credits   22,989
   Road and Trail Maintenance   7,722

TOTAL Timber Expenditures $ 146,124

Timber Sale Receipts

   Timber Sale Receipts   25,988
   Sale Deposits
     Sale Area Betterment (KV)   6,179
     Salvage Sale Fund   976
     Brush Disposal   4,624
   Purchaser Road Credits   22,989

TOTAL Timber Sales Receipts $ 60,756

At recent harvest levels of 1.2 mmbf, timber expenditures are $121.77/mbf before deduction of purchaser
road credits. Expenditures net of purchaser road
credits are $102.61/mbf. For the period 1976-80,
average selling price in Montana and Idaho was
45.00/mbf in constant 1980 dollars and net of road
credits (Ruderman). Thus, expenditures are approximately 2 1/4 times receipts in recent years at recent
prices and budgets in Region 1.

SOURCE: Data provided by Fiscal Management Staff,
USDA Forest Service, Region 1, Missoula,
Montana.

forty-four percent of the total timber expenditures in
the northern region.

It is difficult to allocate directly all
expenditures to current activities since investments
are intended to yield future benefits. If the
variable costs are limited to sale preparation, sale
administration and road maintenance, they are
averaging about $23/thousand board feet while timber
prices in recent years have averaged about
$45/thousand feet. Thus, the major way that current
budget levels must be economically justified is on the
basis of future investment returns.

Given the problems associated with combined
capital investments and operating costs in recent
budgets, data from an economic analysis of 1980 RPA
alternatives was used (McQuillan 1979). Using the
capitalized costs of timber management at the discount
rate of four percent, which is preferred by the Forest
Service, the costs of producing different long term
levels of harvest are represented in terms of equal
annual payments.^{2} Thus, as is shown in Figure 5.4,
the average annual and marginal costs of achieving
different long term levels of sustainable harvests in
Region 1 are increasing with higher harvest levels.
The costs depicted in Figure 5.4 are lower than the
current budget in Table 5.2, in part because fire
management costs of perhaps $25/thousand are not
included in the graph.

The diagram does not allow any direct inference
about the efficiency of timber management since the
recently-published regional demand equations were not
available to the Forest Service. Note though that the
annual average and marginal costs of maintaining the
recent harvest level of 1.2 billion board feet in
Region 1 is considerably higher than recent average
stumpage prices.

A few cautions in interpreting national forest
cost data are warranted. Until the passage of the
National Forest Management Act in 1976, national
forest accounting would have to be characterized as
"appropriations" accounting. Since the passage of
NFMA, the national forests have instituted a cost
accounting system. It is difficult if not impossible
to allocate costs to multiple uses. For example,
forest roads are constructed beyond timber extraction
standards so as to safeguard the general public using
the roads as well as the many other resources of the
forests (water and fish come particularly to mind).
Thus, when one examines the direct costs and benefits
of national forest timber production, there is invari-
ably a loss in explaining benefit changes across the
many resource influences.

**Figure 5.4: Region 1 Timber Management Costs
(1980 Dollars)**

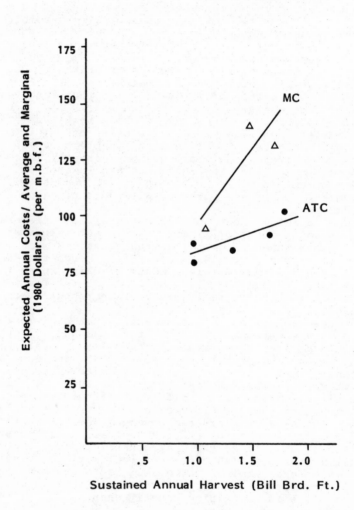

Sustained Annual Harvest (Bill Brd. Ft.)

Roads in the national forests are seldom built
without timber extraction use. Furthermore, increasing the level of harvest will "cause" the construction
of more forest roads to standards specified by the
agency. Thus, the shape and magnitude of the marginal
cost function shown in Figure 5.4 seems appropriate.
The task of developing multiple use interaction with
the gross and net benefits associated with different
harvest levels is not adequately dealt with in the
literature, nor will that problem be solved in this
paper.

The current situation both nationally and in the
northern Rockies is that timber management costs
exceed timber management income before receipt
sharing. Furthermore, the northern Rocky Mountain
data indicate that the marginal costs of increasing
the levels of harvest are rising. The same situation
is expected on a national scale.

Timber prices and price trends are extremely
important in assessing efficiency trends. Figure 5.5
shows some representative price trends for timber in
the northern Rockies. Prices reported are net of
purchaser road credits. Most important, the figure
shows that selling prices for other public ownerships
have increased relative to the national forest timber
prices. In part, this difference must be imputed to
the fact that more national forest lands are roadless
in this area than in other public forest lands. Thus,
the typical national forest sale has more purchaser
credits for construction (and reconstruction) of roads
than do timber sales on other public lands in the
area.

However, not all the difference in sale prices
can be accounted for by differences in purchaser road
credits. Majerus (1982) plotted the following relationship (see Figure 5.6) in Montana between product
price over time, stumpage price on the national
forests, and appraised manufacturing and logging
costs. Quite clearly, production costs have increased
in the northern Rockies relative to lumber prices, and
as a result, stumpage prices have not increased as
much as they have elsewhere.

During the time period shown in Figure 5.6, there
has been a substantial revolution in the style or
quality of national forest timber management in the
northern Rockies. Clearcut size and frequency have
dropped, increased use of cable yarding systems have
been made, and smaller timber of inferior value
increasingly has been utilized on national forest
sales. Each of these factors reduces the selling
price of timber (Jackson and McQuillan 1979). Without
much doubt, these factors, as well as purchaser road
credits, have contributed to the drop in national

Figure 5.5: Average Stumpage Price* of Timber Sold on
Publicly-Owned or Managed Lands in Idaho

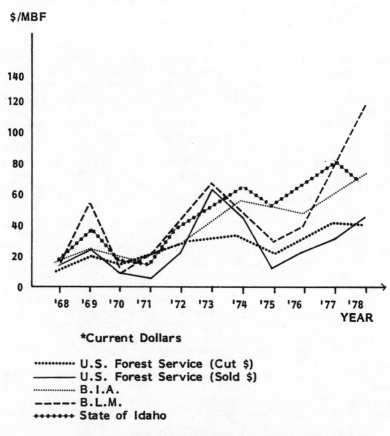

*Current Dollars

············· U.S. Forest Service (Cut $)
————— U.S. Forest Service (Sold $)
················ B.I.A.
————— B.L.M.
✦✦✦✦✦✦ State of Idaho

Source: USDA Forest Service, Production, Prices,
Employment, and Trade in Northwest
Forest Industries (Quarterly) Portland.

Figure 5.6: Historical Lumber and Wood Products Price Index,
Logging Hauling and Manufacturing Costs and Stumpage Price

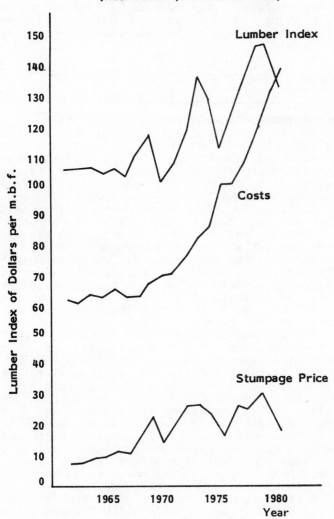

(Real Dollars, 1967 Base Year)

Source: Majerus (1982)

forest timber prices relative to that of other timber suppliers. Each of the public land agencies has somewhat unique management missions. The national forests have become more environmentally-oriented than the others in recent years. The greater environmental orientation of the agency has increased logging costs and reduced stumpage prices. While the data on production costs and relative prices is specific to the northern Rockies, the scenario is expected to be similar in other regions in the national forest system. Unfortunately, data elsewhere are not as readily available.

ECONOMIC ASPECTS OF DIFFERENT LEVELS OF NATIONAL FOREST HARVESTING

Thus far, the following relationships have been found: (1) the price elasticity of demand for national forest timber is inelastic; and (2) the marginal costs of increasing the level of national forest harvesting are rising. Recently, the Reagan administration has argued that the Forest Service should increase its annual cut. Quite clearly, the empirical reality of the proposed harvest increases runs counter to the federal government's announced desire to reduce the federal deficit. An outward shift in the agency's supply function will reduce federal income because the demand for national forest timber is inelastic. Under current cost scenarios, higher harvests require higher agency expenditures. Thus, the administration's direct impact on the budgetary deficit will be even lower receipts and higher expenditures. If the administration wants to directly reduce the national forest system's small share of the federal deficit, a combination of cost and cut reduction seems to be the plausible path.[3]

What then of the privatization of national forest timber lands? No doubt budget costs would fall. Furthermore, there likely would be some short term revenue gain above the administrative costs of privatization. But that does not appear to be the ultimate goal of the privatization interests. Baden and Stroup (1975) argue that there would be significant gains in managerial efficiency and social equity accruing from privatization. But there is no empirical evidence offered to support those claims.

Consider the evidence usually presented in the case for privatization. Table 5.3 below shows the level of growing stock, harvest, and growth as well as harvest as a percentage of stock, and growth as a percentage of stock. As Hirshchleifer (1974) has argued, growth as a percentage of stock is a rate of

Table 5.3: Annual Timber Growth and Removal by Ownership, January 1, 1977

OWNERSHIP	Growing Stock	Net Annual Growth	Annual Removal	Physical Rate of Appreciation[1]	Physical Rate of Liquidation[2]	Net Rate of Change
	(million cubic feet)			(percent)		
National Forests System	228,449	3,116	1,937	1.36	0.87	0.49
Other Public Land	75,503	1,957	982	2.60	1.30	1.30
Forest Industry	106,226	4,073	3,890	3.82	3.67	0.15
Farm and Other	300,750	12,518	5,946	3.80	1.80	2.00

SOURCE: An Assessment of the Forest and Range Lands Situation in the United States, U.S. Department of Agriculture, Forest Service, January, 1980.

1 Physical rate of appreciation is net annual growth divided by growing stock times 100.

2 Physical rate of liquidation is annual removal divided by growing stock times 100.

investment yield, or perhaps better, physical rate of
return on capital. A cursory look at the table
suggests that the national forests are the weak sister
in the ownership classification.

There are two problems with this kind of cursory
analysis. First is the implicit assumption that each
unit of stock has the same worth as the unit of
harvest. Small trees simply are not worth as much as
large ones on a unit volume basis, so all ownerships
no doubt are earning higher rates of return that the
data indicate because inventories have, on the
average, smaller trees than currently are being
harvested. But the proponents of privatization
suggest, with a pass of a mysterious hand, that there
would be a higher overall level of efficiency. As the
data in the table suggests, privatization of the
national forest might double or triple the rate of
harvesting on what now constitutes national forest
stocks. Undoubtedly this would increase the physical
rate of investment yield, but physical yields do not
constitute financial rates of return.

Hirschleifer has clarified the question of how to
calculate what he called the experienced rate of
return on assets such as timber. His point is as
follows:

$$\text{Experienced Rate of Return} = \frac{\text{Income} + \text{Asset Value Change}}{\text{Initial Asset Value}}$$

Thus, the relevant point regarding privatization is
what its impact might be on the rate of return on
timber stocks in the United States. Since the demand
for timber is inelastic, gross income from timber
sales would fall under the privatization alternative.
Asset values would fall, or else increase more
slowly -- at least in the near term. The national
adjustment in the rate of return would be negative.
The only case that privatization enthusiasts can make
is that cost savings after divestiture would be so
great it would offset the income losses that would
occur across all ownership classes.

The remaining efficiency argument left to the
proponents of privatization is nonmarket in nature.
Lower timber prices resulting from increased supply
under divestiture would be transmitted forward to the
ultimate consumers of wood products and produce social
gains to consumers through larger (uncompensated)
consumers surpluses. How large these gains would be
transmitted forward to the product market versus
backward in the forest land market is again unknown.

The political costs of divestiture can perhaps be
more easily enumerated. Private interests currently

hold about fifty-seven percent of the nation's
softwood timber growing stock. Increased harvest
levels through divestiture would unambiguously reduce
the value of the assets which are currently in private
ownership. The rates of return to these individuals
and corporations appears to fall unambiguously with
divestiture. If one chooses to ignore the consumers
surplus argument along with the other social costs of
timber management as do many privatization enthusiasts, there is but one remaining and remote way that
divestiture can lead to improved timber management
efficiency. Here the direct cost savings accrued by
replacing national forest management with private
management would be so great that the rate of return
would increase in spite of lower revenues. To date,
no divestiture enthusiast has made this case. There
is little known about the private costs of timber
management.

Harvest Levels and Receipt Sharing for Roads and
Schools

Under current law, twenty-five percent of timber
sale receipts are turned over to local and state
governments to support roads and schools. The revenue
base for payments include purchaser road construction
credits, Knudsen-Vandenberg timber sale deposits, plus
cash payments for timber. For example, in FY 1980
Forest Service Region 1 paid out roughly $14 million
to counties for roads and schools in northern Idaho
and Montana. The national forests can influence
payments through timber marketing, (i.e., species,
logging systems, silvicultural systems). Perhaps more
basically, the overall level of timber supply in a
region will affect timber receipts and the resulting
level of payments. Since the demand for timber is
price inelastic, higher annual cuts will produce
smaller total receipts and resulting lower payments to
counties for roads and schools. Wilderness reservations which reduce harvest levels will increase
payments to counties within a region or state, although payments emanating from the affected forest
likely will fall (Majerus 1982).

The Allowable Cut Effect

There has been considerable debate concerning the
use of the so called "allowable cut effect" (ACE) by
the national forests in analyzing and justifying
timber investment alternatives (Schweitzer, Sassaman
and Schullau 1972 and Teeguarden 1973). Simply

stated, national forest managers have treated the entire forest property as a whole in determining the
annual allowable cut and the level of timber management investments. Frequently, investments immediately
increase the level of harvest of the overall forest
property, even if the manipulated site won't yield its
product for years to come.

Typically, no price impact is foreseen for the
affected forest property. Owing to immediate harvest
increases, rates of investment return often are
extremely high when ACE is used as a preferred
investment criterion. Usually, old growth timber is
liquidated more rapidly in order to justify the
investment in intensive timber management.

Heretofore, no one has inquired into the implications of using ACE as a national forest system policy
where demand is price inelastic. The blanket or
system-wide effect of adopting ACE as an investment
criterion generally will be a higher level of supply,
and a lower level of sale receipts from the national
forests. Where the use of ACE increases supplies with
an inelastic timber demand function, the rate of return would appear to be unambiguously negative. Using
ACE as a national forest policy will reduce income
whenever the investments justified by ACE increase the
sustained level of harvests.

There are problems and complexities in scheduling
harvests under current legislation. However,
investment returns must be calculated on a project
level first, and then aggregated to a forest level.
Those that can't be justified on a project basis
should be eliminated.

ASPECTS OF CURRENT NATIONAL FOREST TIMBER MANAGEMENT:
A SUMMARY

The current situation is summarized in Figure
5.7. At the current level of national forest
harvesting (SS), the price of timber exceeds the
average operating costs (AOC) of placing timber on the
market. Recall that the costs of sale administration,
sale preparation and basic road maintenance in Region
1 are less than timber sale receipts. The fundamental
reason that expenditures exceed receipts both
nationally and in the northern Rockies is the high
level of investment in roads and future timber stands
(particularly when receipt-sharing is viewed as a cost
to the federal treasury). We also saw that the
average total costs and marginal costs of expanding a
sustainable level of harvests are increasing. Thus,
MC and ATC are shown as exceeding price along the
demand function (DD) at recent demand levels.

Figure 5.7: The Current Demand, Cost and Price Situation
of the National Forest System

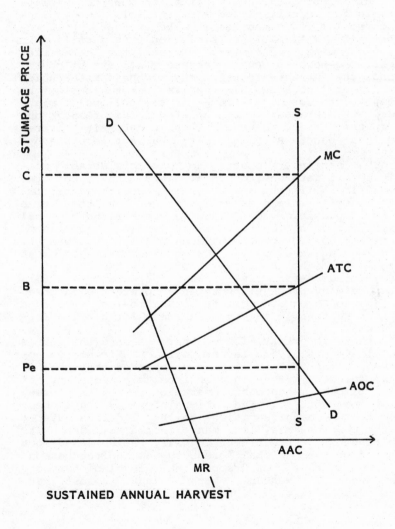

Furthermore, since the demand for timber is price inelastic, current supply (SS) intersects current demand (DD) in a region where marginal revenue is negative. This basic situation, as described in Figure 5.7, has no parallel in the private sector. It can't truly be an equilibrium condition, since private firms could not continue to operate at these levels of loss. It can only exist as an equilibrium condition if our elected representatives are willing to fund the national forests as they have been in the recent past.

Furthermore, the above situation does not violate some larger condition of societal well-being. In a strict social efficiency sense, the excess cost of the amount $(C - P_E).(AAC)$ possibly could be justified in the following contexts. First, the non-market benefits generated could exceed the excess costs. Second, the current situation may be the best choice among several negative alternatives. For example, the unemployment costs of lower harvest levels might exceed the excess costs depicted in Figure 5.7, but the costs of reducing unemployment might rise faster than the benefits gained from harvest levels above AAC.

The national forests do take considerable measures to mitigate environmental disturbances, but the scientific ability to assess precise environmental impacts is still in the formative stages. At this time it is impossible to determine whether the national forests are doing too much or too little in an economic sense to protect the national forest environment, where logging takes place. Currently, national forest management might be characterized by the concept of "safe minimum standards" (Ciriancy-Wantrup 1963). There are many precautions taken to protect endangered species, to safeguard against soil erosion and even provide reasonable safety parameters for citizen forest users.

Other important forces have shaped the curves shown in Figure 5.7 in recent years. Strong components of the U.S. public have demanded that the national forests improve the environmental quality of their timber management operations, and the Forest Service has done it. The national forests have been asked to make major additions to the wilderness system and the Congress has, in many instances, done it. Simultaneously, the timber industry has demanded more timber from the national forest system and the national forests have not dropped their level of harvests precipitously. (Montana, where national forest harvests dropped forty percent within a decade, is a notable exception.)

But now we seem to be at a crossroads. The current administration decidedly is against subsidization of the wood products industry. They want to privatize the national forest lands; they are seemingly anti-wilderness; and they want to cut the federal deficit (at the same time as they cut taxes and propose the largest military spending increase in the nation's history). Thus, faced with the situation described above, they must ask themselves what can be done to alleviate the situation short of privatization?

WHAT THE REAGAN ADMINISTRATION CAN DO
TO SOLVE ITS PROBLEMS

Referring back to Figure 5.7, there are four basic courses of action that can be taken. The administration can: (1) reduce or maintain the level of harvests on the national forests; (2) reduce costs; (3) cross its fingers in anticipation of burgeoning timber demand in the future; and (4) revise its agenda and accept the current situation. In reality, a reasonable policy would incorporate all of these elements to some degree, although they are presented in separate topical order with various degrees of emphasis.

Policies Pertaining to the Annual Allowable Cut

The implications of an inelastic timber demand function have been discussed in detail. Major departures from current harvest levels designed to increase national forest timber supplies will not aid the administration in solving its budgetary problems. But, some regions in the country are experiencing reasonably dramatic reductions in private growing stocks. Stabilization policies through transition periods may be warranted. If private timber stocks are being liquidated rapidly in a region, one should be able to anticipate how the derived demand for national forest timber will behave in that region relative to the nation as a whole. This kind of analysis should be encouraged. Currently, national timber goals are allocated to administrative regions by the Washington office, and these in turn play a role in harvest scheduling on individual forests. Regional supply and demand modeling could play a much stronger role in Forest Service planning than it currently does. This is turn would de-emphasize the national "needs" approach.

Opportunities to Reduce Timber Management Costs

In general, there are considerable opportunities to reduce timber management costs on the national forests and improve overall managerial efficiency. Some very substantial progress in cost reduction already is being made in Region 1.

Forest road and bridge construction comprise at least thirty-two percent of the timber management-related expenditures of the national forest system (Table 5.1). In regions such as the northern Rockies, where road construction costs are higher than average and the national forests are comparatively speaking "undeveloped," about forty-four percent of the timber-related expenditures in recent years have involved construction and reconstruction of forest roads and bridges. (Trail construction in recent years is nil, Table 5.1).

There are several major underlying factors which affect road construction costs. One is the engineering standards to which a road or bridge is designed or built. For instance, design standards such as roadway width or minimum stopping distance affect earthwork quantities, culvert volumes, and gravel surfacing volume. Next is the general terrain through which a transportation system is developed. For example, deep V-shaped canyons typically entail longer bridges and steep side slopes require more earthwork. Economic aspects of the road construction sector also play heavily in determining costs. Not only will wage rates and equipment costs affect road construction costs, but so does the productivity of the construction sector. Important also is the cyclical nature of road construction. During ebbs in the cycle, bidding on Forest Service road contracts reflects intense competition as evidenced by lower contract costs. Finally, road expenditures are affected by policy and management choices which affect the spatial pattern of forest roading and development. If managers choose to build roads to distant versus proximate timber, the time pattern of road expenditures will be affected.

The design standards currently in place are well above those of simple timber extraction. Roads are designed to meet federal safety standards in terms of stopping distance and sight (seeing) distance. Design standards are elevated to reduce soil erosion and water pollution by specifying more frequent culverts, bridges, ditches, and surfacing of the roadway itself. It is difficult if not impossible to impute incremental benefits to such engineering decisions, although the cost savings of reduced design standards are more easily documented. We found that the Forest

Service considers itself liable for negligence in the public safety aspects of forest road design. Recently, there has been substantial progress in more cost effective road standards.[4] Much more can probably be done in this vein.

Perhaps the most useful avenue to investigate for national forest budgetary savings involves the issue of "advance roading." From the standpoint of managing a developed forest property, there is little doubt about the efficacy of a road or transportation network. But, when man inherited the naturally endowed forest wealth, the lack of roads was perhaps the only flaw in God's design. The concept of advance roading seeks to rectify this omission as rapidly as possible. Timber is sold at distant places in preference to proximate ones. Roads are built with a combination of appropriated funds and timber purchaser obligations or credits. Sales which are located within these funding constraints, but distant to currently roaded areas, are preferred since the "advance" road opens other sites and stands for fire protection, and other cultural treatments. There are other strategic aspects to the advance roading issue which are quite obvious. Advance roads claim more national forest acreage for development in a shorter period of time than would a more prudent time and space progressive entry into a roadless area.

No doubt, there are instances wherein advance roading is an optimal choice. However, determining whether this would be the efficient course of action appears to lie outside the current analytical scope of national forest planning (Jackson 1982). Right now there are forest plans and project plans. Probably the largest savings to the Forest Service would be found in intermediate transportation planning where sales are planned in a network context, as outlined by McQuillan (1981a) and applied by Merzenich, et al. (1981). This kind of planning would allow more prudent development by avoiding roads into areas where the development costs are excessive in respect to timber values. It would also identify an optimum order of road and rate of development in an area.

Currently, forest planning models include the scheduling of both positively and negatively valued timber. Some timber has a negative value because of stand quality, logging, and road construction costs. Other things equal, the negatively valued timber is included in the forest harvesting schedule due to an allowable cut effect, although the negatively valued timber usually is not scheduled for harvest until the end of the planning horizon. Forest plans normally are updated every ten or so years. McQuillan (1981b) concludes that each updating of the forest plan will

produce a lower annual allowable cut than the previous
plan since the negatively valued timber looms closer
in the planning horizon.
   Current state-of-the-art forest planning may
stand in conflict with both Section 6 and Section 13
of NFMA. Section 6 limits harvesting to lands economically suitable for timber production and Section
13 calls for sustained yield. Constraining forest
plans so that timber is only available for harvesting
when it has a positive value (based in part on price
expectations) seemingly would improve the implementation of the law. And by likely reducing Forest
Service expenditures for road construction and cultural treatments both now and in the future, it offers
a substantial opportunity for cost reduction.
   Other opportunities to reduce expenditures
already are recognized by the Forest Service. For
example, a major research project designed to improve
the efficiency of forest fire suppression activities
currently is underway.[5] Forest Service Region 1 now
is investigating a new timber appraisal procedure
which could save millions of dollars if applied
nationally.[6] In addition, some training programs
which are designed to improve the efficiency of timber
sale layout and design are underway.[7]

Opportunities to Increase Timber Market Benefits

   Since the 1970s logging and manufacturing costs
in the northern Rockies have increased substantially
relative to wood product and stumpage prices. As
Jackson and Flowers (1982) have observed, changing
tree size and management style in the national forests
apparently has helped stabilize employment in the face
of lower harvest levels. Obviously, any management
choices made by the national forests which curtail
increases in logging and manufacturing costs in the
future will increase timber sale receipts, since
timber prices are a rent or value residual above and
beyond the costs of logging and product conversion.
   The style of national forest timber management
(including standards for merchantibility) must be
re-examined continually in terms of the following key
factors:
   1. Sale location relative to markets. Sales
      proximate to mills command higher prices due
      to lower haul costs and also require lower
      initial road investments.
   2. Partial cutting versus clearcutting. Holding
      tree size and logging systems constant, the
      empirical evidence indicates that timber
      prices are lower where shelterwood and

selection systems are employed over clearcutting and seed tree cutting (Jackson and
McQuillan 1979).
3. Tractor yarding versus skyline and helicopter
yarding. Again logging systems which are
generally more advantageous in terms of site
protection reduce stumpage prices.

I realize how controversial these points are, but
I believe that one economic aspect of the decade-old
clearcutting controversy was a reduction in national
forest receipts as the national forests moved toward
fewer and smaller clearcuts and more costly logging
systems. As a result, it is recommended that the
Forest Service carefully re-examine the use of these
systems since their costs are opportunity costs in
terms of foregone public revenues. As one observer
once said, we are faced with the question of the mix
of environmental quality over space. For example, we
can have areas of very high water quality in some
areas and low quality elsewhere, or we can have
mediocre water quality over larger areas. In the
latter instance, more partial cuttings (with more
frequent logging on an area) along with more costly
logging systems may partially mitigate sediment
yields.

National forest timber sales typically are
complex in terms of a mosaic of species, logging
techniques and cultural treatments used. An
individual sale often is broken into units comprising
unique combinations of these variables. When timber
is sold, the sale itself is the package for valuation,
and bidding reflects the averaging of high and
low-valued sale units. In many instances, profitable
sale units in effect cross subsidize unprofitable
ones; the result is a lower average selling price or,
on occasion, the offering which receives no bids.

In any timber sale, there often are many
compelling reasons to include inferior or unprofitable
timber. Sometimes the larger trees are left on the
site to provide a superior seed source for the next
crop, to provide superior aesthetic values, or to
provide habitat for certain wildlife species.
Additionally, decadent stands often are included in
sales in order to improve the productivity or future
growth of a forest site.

However, the tradeoffs in benefits accruing from
these kinds of decisions are not examined seriously in
the preparation of timber sales. While the NFMA
required an economic analysis of each proposed sale, I
am unaware of any implementation of this portion of
the legislation. An appraisal is done, but it is one
of the last steps in timber sale preparation prior to
bidding. Furthermore, the appraisal does not analyze

the costs and benefits of project alternatives (the
value analysis mentioned in note 7 is a partial step
in the right direction). Keep in mind that the most
marginal stands under recent market conditions likely
will increase in value relative to superior ones in
the future. This is a fundamental reason to hold them
in stock.

Considerable attention has been given to the
implications of the price elasticity of demand for
timber. The general assessment shown before in Figure
5.7 suggests that the national forests currently are
operating where marginal costs exceed price (demand).
We have suggested many ways to help alleviate this
problem short of harvest reduction. On balance, any
policy analysis which ignores one of the obvious
solutions to the problem is simply inadequate. The
national forests never have addressed the question of
pricing policy. Multiple use or sustained yield are
neither supply nor pricing policies. The level of
sustainable yield depends upon the budget over time as
much as upon any biological growth coefficients. The
substantial issues, of course, are the relationship
between output, cost and price -- in both the near and
distant term. Exerting price influence is unavoidable
when the national forests control roughly half the
nation's total timber inventory and operate currently
at a capacity where receipts are insufficient to cover
the out-of-pocket costs to prepare and administer many
timber sales.

Policies Pertaining to Efficient Utilization

One of the major means of conserving timber
resources is to use a greater portion of the available
biomass at harvest. The advantages of increased
utilization seemingly are endless, and the history of
improved utilization no doubt is a major conservation
success story. However, there is a major impediment
to efficient timber resource utilization on the
national forests, and the solution to the problem
involves the basic nature of most national forest
timber sales contracts.

Currently, there are two basic contract formats
widely used in timber sales. One is referred to as a
lump-sum contract and the other, which is of primary
importance to western national forests, is a scaled
sales contract. Under contracts specifying scaled
sales, the timber purchaser pays for wood on the basis
of each unit of volume removed (scaled) at an agreed
upon (bid) price. Typically buyers bid different
prices for different species classes included in the
sale. Thus, for example, if a buyer bid $200.00 per

thousand for the Douglas-fir included in a sale, the total amount paid would depend upon the amount of Douglas-fir removed and scaled or measured from that sale as well as the bid prices and volumes of other species scaled.

In contrast, a lump-sum sale involves a single payment for the entire lot of timber included in the sale. Thus the payment obligation does not vary with the actual volume of logs removed from the sale.

Each alternative sale contract implies a different incentive to utilize wood included in the timber sale because each affects the marginal costs of wood procurement. Under a lump-sum sales contract, the marginal cost of wood procurement is limited essentially to the costs of harvesting and hauling to a mill site. Under lump-sum sales the timber payment becomes a sunk cost. The marginal costs of wood procurement are higher under scaled sales contracts because the timber purchaser pays the stumpage price for each unit of timber removed from the sale as well as the costs of harvesting and hauling to a mill site. The difference in marginal costs between the two contract stipulations affect the incentives to utilize inferior logs included in the sale.

Figure 5.8 summarizes these points in a graph. The delivered value line shows the value of various log grades delivered to a mill site. The delivered value is net of the costs of logging standing timber and transporting the logs to the mill. Under a lump sum sale, all five grades of logs would be utilized since their respective values are positive.

Suppose instead now that a scaled sale is used in place of the lump-sum sale and that the timber buyer has bid X dollars/thousand for the timber. Notice now that two log grades are worth less than the winning bid price in the example. Thus if the timber purchaser can avoid utilizing these lower grade logs, his profit can increase.

Specification of scaled sales contracts creates unnecessary conflicts between the Forest Service and timber purchasers. While buyers can increase their profits by avoiding the use of log grades four and five in the diagram, national forest timber receipts will fall if all the valued material isn't used. Conflict between buyer and seller arises in the enforcement of utilization standars. Actually avoiding the utilization of these inferior logs is frequently a simple matter.

Contracts usually require that felled trees be cut into standard log lengths of 32', 16', 12', 10', and 8'. These coincide with the various lengths of lumber found in the U.S. Contracts also stipulate a minimum top diameter that trees should be utilized to.

162

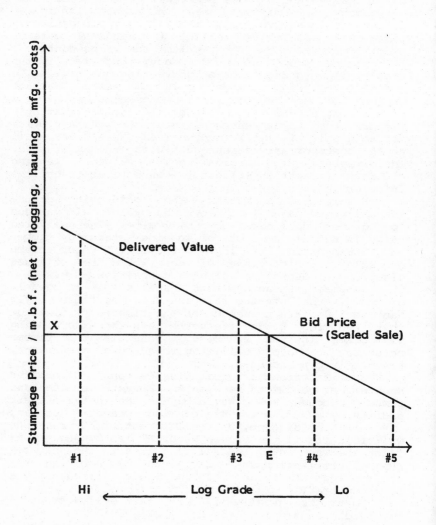

Figure 5.8: Utilization Incentives-Scaled Sales

Suppose that a logger can cut one more 12' log from
the top portion of a tree before reaching the minimum
top diameter limit. If instead he cuts an 8' log
length, a 4' nonmerchantible length is left in the
woods, is unscaled and as a result not a financial
liability under a scaled sale contract where the bid
price exceeds the value of the 12' foot log that could
be removed under a lump-sum sale contract.

No doubt, many readers may find the discussion of
the economic logic of cutting logs into different
lengths to be somewhat boring or trivial. It is a
well known fact, however, that post-logging wood
residues on national forest lands in the west far
exceed logging residues on private industrial forest
lands. One factor which no doubt contributes to the
situation is the use of scaled sales contracts by the
Forest Service. (In logging industrial lands there is
typically a paper transaction between woodlands and
mill profit centers primarily for tax purposes.) Thus
there are significant differences in the out-of-pocket
costs of wood procurement which in turn help in
explaining the differences in utilization.

Unfortunately, the difference in utilization
incentives set in motion by scaled sales contracts
over those in lump-sum sales is reasonably well known
in the forest economics literature. The President's
Report on Timber and the Environment (1973) of a few
years back recommended broad adoption of lump-sum
sales. Beuter and Arney (1972) and Nautiyal and Love
(1971) had discussed the implications earlier.

It is difficult to explain the survival of scaled
sales on the national forests in the light of a blue
ribbon commission's recommendation that they be
discontinued. Lump-sum sales would increase the
nation's timber supply without increasing the acres
logged. The costs of sale preparation, sales
administration, road construction and maintenance
would drop on a per-thousand basis. With lower
volumes of logging slash, slash disposal and site
preparation costs would also fall, and the increased
ability to utilize timber efficiently would contribute
positively to the national forest receipts. Lump-sum
sales should be the order of the day in national
forest timber sales and they should be adopted without
further hesitation.

Improving the Cost-Benefit Situation: Contract
Specifications

Virtually all of the road construction and
logging along with major portions of reforestation and
timber stand improvement work on the national forests

is done by contracting with firms in the private
sector. As a result, the specifications of these
contracts affect the costs of work to be completed and
resulting bids. Perhaps half or more of the timber
management budget is spent on contracts. There is a
need then to recognize the important relationship
between contract specifications and project costs.
The following represents an illustrative example.

Merzenich (1978) found in a statistical
examination of pre-commercial thinning contracts that
contract specifications significantly affected the
winning low bid. The contractor "is required to
remove excess trees only when they exceed a specified
height." In order to improve the quality of
pre-commercial thinning work, the Forest Service had
lowered the minimum height specifications for a
counted "leave" tree from twenty-four inches to six
inches. Of course on many contracts that meant a
considerable increase in thinning work. Costs
increased about $21/acre in current dollars when
thinnings had to include trees down to a six-inch
height.

The question is the extent to which incremental
project benefits resulting from alternative contract
specifications can be warranted. Careful scrutiny of
contract specifications could result in eliminating or
changing some contract clauses which are simply too
costly. Contracts can be "packaged" more effectively.
For instance, combining several small planting
contracts on different sites into a larger one which
would occupy a crew for one planting season would also
likely result in budgetary savings (Merzenich 1978).
The examples are specific in nature, although the
situation may be somewhat more general. Contract
clauses throughout major areas of work such as road
construction, logging and silvicultural improvements
could be sources of significant cost reduction and/or
market benefit increases.

On Becoming More Economical

It was not until 1976 that the Congress required
the national forest system to develop a cost
accounting procedure as a basis for resource planning.
Some seventy years after the inauguration of the
nation's forests, the Congress seemed to want the
Forest Service to become cost and benefit conscious.
Like many new thrusts in public administration,
developing a greater economics consciousness does not
just happen. It requires an assessment of the current
analytical decision support methods for making
day-to-day project level decisions as well as the

economics   skills and knowledge of the line management
of the organization.   Finally, an assessment of the
employee   rewards   and   sanctions which can be used to
improve national forest efficiency is required so that
a system commensurate with the economic mission can be
devised (Krutilla and Haigh 1978 discuss the mission
of the national forests). When these things are done,
forest economics will cease to be limited to national
forest plans and instead become the context for
day-to-day management. Our progress along these lines
will be marked with language.   In recent times,
controversial projects have been curtailed because of
"bad economics."   Perhaps the day will come when
managers simply state that "the roads were too costly
so we didn't advertise the sale" or "the project
simply wasn't beneficial enough to warrant further
consideration."
    Since economics often is defined as the study of
the allocation of scarce resources, it is hard to use
the adjectives "good" or "bad." Rather, economics can
be a way of thinking about resource allocation. When
managers have learned the "economics" way of thinking,
their language and their choices will reflect it.

CONCLUDING REMARKS

    This paper attempted to address two major issues
confronting current national forest timber management.
First, the federal government must find ways to manage
more efficiently any and all of its programs. Second,
the federal government must determine what programs it
wants to encourage and what it wants to eliminate.
    While there are many arguments of a non-market
nature that can be made for preserving the national
forest system, this one is based on market grounds.
Since the demand for timber is price inelastic,
privatization schemes which increase the nation's
timber harvests will unambiguously reduce the rate of
return on timber currently held by other interests.
The rate of return on what is currently held by the
national forests can only increase if the cost savings
from private management exceeds the revenue losses and
losses in the rate of price appreciation.
    There are many substantial ways to improve the
earnings of the national forest timber management
program.   Some of them stand in conflict with high
levels of environmental quality and others do not.
Wilderness preservation improves the rate of return on
timber stocks, as does more clearcutting, less
expensive roads, and less expensive logging.
    If there is major public support to increase the
direct efficiency of the national forest timber

management program, the first avenue to take lies in cost reduction. That will entail the development of analytical decision support methods, the training and reward of line managers, and the establishment of cost reduction targets. Major harvest expansion should not be carried out in the near term. Long term harvest changes should be efficient and keyed to the accomplishment of cost reduction targets. In part, the current timber management situation on the national forests is the result of a post-Earth Day cultural awareness in the United States. Rather than denigrate the Forest Service, it is constructive to note its accomplishments in the past decade. The environmental quality of national forest management has increased substantially. Harvests have been maintained on a land base which has been reduced substantially. The time is ripe to improve the overall efficiency of national forest timber management. It can be done.

NOTES

1. Assistant Secretary of Agriculture John B. Crowell apparently failed to recognize the implications of an inelastic timber demand function in a recent address. Crowell stated that the timber opportunity cost of maintaining old growth habitat for spotted owls "is more than $100,000 per pair annually." At a four percent discount rate, Crowell implies that the capitalized cost of maintaining owls is $2,500,000 per pair. Had he recognized that timber demand is price inelastic, he would have found that owls complement government timber receipts. (Crowell 1982).

2. The RPA plan is of a forty-five-year duration. The annual equivalent costs were calculated for each alternative with the well-known formula for the present value of fixed term annuity of equal annual payments.

3. The case might be made that the increase in national forest harvests would result in higher taxable income in related sectors. This issue is beyond the scope of our paper, although it is difficult to make this case because of the great substitutability between taxable private supplies and non-taxable Forest Service timber.

4. Interview with William Gourney, U.S. Forest Service Region 1, Forest Engineering Staff, October 18, 1982. The costs of public works contracts roads

(new construction only) have dropped between twenty percent and thirty percent in the past three years due to a combination of changes in design standards and higher bidding competition in the slumping economy.

5. The FEES project at the Riverside, California, Forest Fire Laboratory is moving in this direction.

6. Interview with John Combes, USFS Region 1, Forest Management Staff, October 18, 1982.

7. Region 1 has developed a training program called "value analysis." The thrust of this program is to produce cost effective timber sales. The program may expand toward more comprehensive benefit-cost analysis.

8. Logs are frequently bucked into various standards lengths. If the logger could take one more sixteen foot log from the top of a tree and choose to take a twelve foot one instead, a four foot non-merchantible top is left in the woods. It is extremely expensive to police bucking, particularly when lump sum sales solve the problem.

BIBLIOGRAPHY

Adams, D.M. and R.W. Haynes. 1980. "The softwood timber assessment and market model: Structure, Projections and Policy Simulations." For. Sci. Monograph 22. 64 p.

Baden, John and Richard Stroup. 1975. "Private rights, public choices and the management of the national forests." Western Wildlands. 2,4:5-13.

Beuter, John and James O. Arney. 1972. "Lump-sum bidding on federal lands in western Oregon." Research paper 12. Oregon State University, Corvallis.

Ciriancy-Wantrup. 1963. "Resource Conservation Economics and Policy." Rev. Ed. University of California Agri. Expt. Station. Berkeley.

Crowell, John B. 1982. "Fish and wildlife: a fuller dimension to improve resource management." Remarks to the 47th North American Wildlife and Natural Resources Conference. Portland, Oregon. March 29. Mimeo.

Haynes, R.W., K.P. Connaughton and D.M. Adams. 1981. "Projections of the demand for stumpage by region: 1980-2030." USDA Research Paper PNW-282. Fac. N.W. Forest and Range Expt. Sta., Portland, Or. 13 p.

168

Hirschleifer, Jack. 1974. Title unknown. Paper presented to a symposium on the economics of sustained yield forestry. November 24, Univ. of Wash., Seattle.

Jackson, D.H. and A.G. McQuillan, 1979. "A technique for estimating timber selling value based upon...." For. Sci. 25 No. 4 620-626.

Jackson, D.H. 1982. "An integrated management approach to determining operable timber stocks." Proceedings of Management of Second-growth Forests: The State of Knowledge and Research Needs. University of Montana, Missoula.

Jackson, D.H. and P. Flowers. 1982. "The national forests and stabilization: a look at the factual record." Western Wildlands. 8,4.

Jackson, D.H. Forthcoming. "Subregional timber demand: remarks and an approach for prediction." For. Ecol. and Mgt.

Krutilla, J.V. and J.A. Haigh. 1978. "An integrated approach to national forest management." Envir. Law 8:373-415.

Majerus, G.A. 1982. "Econometric estimation of demand and supply curves for timber in Montana, 1962-1980." Masters Thesis. University of Montana, Missoula. 52 p.

Marshall, A. 1930. Principles of Economics. London: MacMillan.

McKillop, W.M. 1967. "Supply and demand for forest products -- an econometric study." Hilgardia 38. U. of California, Berkeley.

McQuillan, A. 1979. "Report of economic analysis of Forest Service Region 1: 1980 RPA data." Mimeo. 21 p.

_____. 1981a. "Evaluating timberland allocation and management intensity." Ph.D. Thesis. University of Montana, Missoula 271 p.

_____. 1981b. "Harvest schedules as seen by federal, state, private and industrial foresters." Paper presented to Western Forestry and Conservation Assoc. Meeting. Sun Valley, Idaho.

Merzenich, James P. 1979. Classifying Timberland Based Upon Its Timber Management Investment Potential. Bull. 42. Mont. Forest and Conservation Expt. Sta. Missoula, MT.

Merzenich, J.P. et al. 1981. Economic analysis of the Montana Wilderness Study Areas. USDA Forest Service Region 1, Missoula.

Nautiyal, J.C. and D.V. Love. 1971. "Some economic implications of changing stumpage." For. Chron. 47:1-4.

President's Advisory Panel on Timber and the Environment. 1973. Report. USGPO. 540 p.

Schweitzer, D.L., R.W. Sassaman, and C.H. Schallau.
    1972. "Allowable cut effect." J. of For.
    70,7:415-418.
Teeguarden, D.E. 1973. "The allowable cut effect: a
    comment." J. of For. 71, 4:2240226.

Community Stability
and the Federal Lands

George M. Johnston

INTRODUCTION

Suggested changes in Forest Service timber management based upon economic efficiency criteria, or decisions to commit currently roadless areas to wilderness designation, ineluctably lead to distributional issues associated with timber resource dependent community stability, as well as environmental concerns. This presentation will review major themes in the literature, including policy prescriptions and their potential impact upon resource dependent communities. The discussion is analytical and non-normative. There is no effort to justify decisions based solely on community stability issues, but rather to ascertain those values in the context of other values. Specific attention is paid to the relevance of the analysis and issues to eastern Oregon. Policy and management options which suggest the dynamic results and implications of proposed changes in federal timber management strategy will be reviewed.

REVIEW OF THE LITERATURE

According to Marion Clawson (1976), a truly comprehensive analysis of the economics of national forest management would necessarily include a consideration of localized impacts. This need arises

---

George M. Johnston is associate professor of natural resource economics, Eastern Oregon State College. Valuable comments were received from Bob Weinberger, forester, Boise Cascade Corporation and Tom Quigley, economist, USFS Range and Wildlife Lab.

171

because of the application of neo-classic economics at
the national level. Implementation of the prescriptions suggested by Hyde and Jackson would reduce or
eliminate timber management in some regions like
eastern Oregon, where costs of timber management are
high. Clawson (1976) has also suggested the
"uneconomic" operation of a national forest would
represent a subsidy to local communities. Hyde (1980)
has also recognized the issue. Cutler (1980) noted
that 80,000 workers directly depend upon national
forest timber.

However, the degree to which community stability
issues should be considered in timber management
decisions is the subject of some controversy in the
literature (Waggener, 1977; Kromm, 1972). Waggener
(1977) noted that definitions of community and
stability are difficult and somewhat arbitrary.
Different empirical definitions of community will
produce different analytical results. The same
problem arises when defining other concepts, such as
rural or urban. Geography, political organization and
population size can separately and together help
define a community. Stability also will include a
wide range of variables, including income and
employment, or specifically, the rate of change of
each. Both conceptual and measurement problems are
obviously important in an area where little empirical
work has been done. These problems are, nevertheless,
not insurmountable. Any specific effect will,
perforce, require analysis of the particular community
or region.

In eastern Oregon, National Forests represent
sixty-five percent of total commercial forest land,
other public (BLM) five percent, private forests
thirty percent. Boise Cascade Corporation, the
largest timber firm in eastern Oregon, depends upon
the Forest Service for roughly sixty percent of its
supply. It purchases approximately ten percent from
nonindustrial private sources. The remainder comes
from Boise Cascade land. O'Toole (1979a) has argued
that forests in eastern Oregon, specifically in the
Wallowa and Whitman National Forests (1979b), are
inefficiently managed because costs exceed the price
paid for stumpage. This argument in a broader
national context is articulated with more sophistication by Hyde (1980 and 1981). Work by Helfand (1981)
also supports this conclusion. Prescriptive
implications of these analyses suggest curtailing
forestry in eastern Oregon. Indeed, it is estimated
that eighty percent of sales in the past year in
northeastern Oregon were below cost of managing the
sale, though this percent is inflated by bark beetle

salvage. Both the efficiency and community stability issues are relevant within the eastern Oregon context. It is argued by Helfand (1981) and implied in Coggins and Wilkinson (1981) that Forest Service sustained-yield, even flow management is justified using the community stability argument. The two issues are often related. Sustained-yield even flow is a biological rather than an economic approach to timber management. Community stability, then, is analyzed as a regional issue, unrelated to national efficiency calculations. Controversy surrounds the role of regional issues in benefit cost analysis (Randall 1981). The U.S. Water Resources Council (1973) resolved the issue somewhat by suggesting a separate regional account, but the relationship to the national account remains undefined. Often regional economic changes from national policies are considered as "merely" transfers, should certain assumptions on employment be met (Mishan, 1973). Obviously, either continuation or discontinuation of sustained-yield practices based on sales below cost arguments will affect both the multiple use, community, timber and environmental values in many regions. Local economic structure and some of these local costs to eastern Oregon communities were discussed by Obermiller (1977, 1980) though in an input-output framework. Krutilla and Haigh noted that:

> For instance, a decision that would de-stabilize the existing community and its facilities by reducing the flow of timber should be carefully examined, because efficiency criteria, if carelessly applied, would overlook the real social costs of idle capacity and unemployed workers. (1978, p. 382)

Supply restricting Forest Service policies are neither the only nor primary cause of community instability. Demand related macroeconomic policies of the Federal Reserve Board affecting interest and mortgage rates have had a tremendous influence on the current state of the Pacific northwest economy and on resource-dependent community stability in particular. The Forest Service may help create community instability by adding wilderness areas or decreasing timber supply but it cannot assure community stability because of demand-related factors (Krutilla and Haigh, 1978). Inversely, the Forest Service could increase instability by increasing timber supply, hence dependence, and exposing communities to demand factor shifts.

Nevertheless, with an anticipated high demand for Forest Service softwood (Conservation Foundation, 1982), potential efficiency criteria management changes could lead to destabilization. It should be noted, however, that high demand and hence stumpage prices will affect the number of sales below cost.

Land withdrawn from timber management because of sales below cost could be managed directly for other multiple uses or could be considered, as is the case for many roadless areas, for inclusion in the National Wilderness system. Exclusion of much of the roadless areas from timber production might very well have a minimal effect on timber supply (Irland, 1979). Regional and community implications will depend on alternative sources from either public or private lands. Increased recreational income might also help local community adjustment. Nevertheless, as Emerson has noted, "cumulative withdrawals of publicly-owned commodities may ultimately become sufficient to push market prices and consumer expenditures upward." (1982, p. 6) Substitutes -- either in the form of increased Canadian imports or alternatives to wood use -- might then be feasible.

Those interested in wilderness or environmental values which are interdependent with timber management will need to consider effects on timber dependent communities. Given the current state of the economy, proposals for changes in the outputs of federal lands which could adversely affect employment in a given region are likely to meet considerable resistance regardless of how well they pass rigorous cost-benefit tests. (Peskin, 1981)

SALES BELOW COST

Forest Service sales management does not consider costs. Pricing is explained in Gregory (1972) and O'Toole (1979a). Many National Forests in all regions of the country have sales below cost. (Helfand, 1981) Oregon was not listed as having such sales in Helfand's results but this result could be explained by old growth sales and higher prices in general. Nevertheless, evidence does exist that sales below cost are frequent in eastern Oregon. (O'Toole, 1979b) As mentioned earlier, approximately eighty percent of recent sales can be put into the sales below cost category, due in part to salvage sales.

Market prices could account for cyclical variations in the number of sales below cost. Care will be required in land use decisions on a regional, forest, and even site basis. Short run calculations of efficiency can, therefore, either help or hinder provision for either environmental or local economic values, depending upon prices. Higher prices lead to fewer sales below cost, though the evidence does suggest that some regions seldom cover costs. (Helfand, 1981)

Analyzing the cost side of the controversy typically involves the cost, quality, and ultimate use of roads. (Hyde, 1980) The degree to which roads are constructed for other multiple uses, such as recreation, will require consideration of cost allocation. Costs associated with archaeologists, sociologists, biologists, engineers, public information specialists, overhead, and other administration reasonably could be attributed to other goals, as well as to timber sales management. This is, of course, a difficult issue in public expenditure analysis. One could argue that the non-timber uses should cover some of these costs or, on the other hand, require that the costs be covered by timber uses. The decision is one of value trade-offs. Oregon has asked for at least some of these costs to be incurred in management of private land through the Oregon Forest Practices Act. To the degree that the costs above receipts represent costs associated with multiple outputs, other cost allocations could be argued. Environmental arguments of bias against wilderness in current sales below cost must then recognize that, while granting real environmental losses, other complementary values are gained by some of the mandated costs.

COMMUNITY STABILITY ISSUES

Whether one then refers, often pejoratively, to such sales as subsidies may then be reexamined in the face of different cost allocations relative to benefits. The incidence of either costs or benefits, monetary or non-monetary, of a change of policy, as with the original policy, will vary according to individuals and groups. For example, small timber firms receive a small business set-aside portion of timber sales. The price in those sales is not bid up as much as is the case with larger timber firms. A large share of the sales below cost go to these smaller businesses, and this is often very important to a local economy. Should alternative sources of local timber not exist, these firms will have more difficulty in reacting to regional shifts in supply. In this case a national level calculation of efficiency would relegate the loss of these fixed assets as simply sunk costs. The incidence of these costs, though, are localized, affecting some of the performance variables related to community stability.

In addition, cutting sales below costs could drive out
small businesses and increase monopoly conditions in
regional economies. Monopoly costs of this policy
change could be estimated and considered in the
analyses.
    Again, adequate supply will not guarantee local
community stability. But are there any benefits to
maintaining resource-dependent community stability?
Certainly secondary benefits do occur. As Hyde noted:

> Beneficial secondary impacts occur as part
> of all investments -- including timber,
> recreation, and all alternative uses of
> any public agency budget. Part of any
> argument about the beneficial secondary
> impacts of public timber management must
> be a demonstration that these impacts are
> greater than would occur with alternative
> investments (in short, the secondary
> opportunity costs). (1980, p. 168)

While input-output analysis might capture small
changes in an economy over the short run and, perhaps,
provide valuable information on market structure, it
will not be very useful for large changes in the
resource base over longer periods.
    Non-monetary benefits of resource-dependent
communities seem not to have been often analyzed
explicitly. Kromm (1972) did review variations in
employment structure suggesting often low-paying jobs.
Because of (or in spite of) the small community
employment, social, and environmental situation, a
different individual with often different mores comes
out of these communities. Without expounding a
forestry version of rural or agricultural fundamental-
ism, there may be non-monetary benefits to maintaining
cultural diversity in the nation. Expressions of
demand for that diversity could be evidenced by
current urban population interest in living in rural
areas. Much of this kind of analysis could parallel
Krutilla and Fisher's (1975) analysis of natural
environments. Maintenance of cultural diversity or
the availability of a life style will represent an
option value for some of the present and future
generations. Vicarious demand for the existence of
these communities might also exist. There may be
diminished opportunities for such a life style. The
diminution of the cultural base might be analogous to
loss of the genetic base, with the same problem of
uncertainty. Such an analysis or such values may seem
trivial, but economists who don't consider such values
are producing normatively biased analyses proportion-
ate to their incidence.

Some government policies have specifically
supported other kinds of rural communities, market
structure, and agricultural firm size with, for
example, provision of rural infra-structure and
schools. Forest Service policies designed to enhance
community stability may possibly provide for values
held by many. It is, of course, up to the democratic
decision-making process to determine whose preferences
are to count. But measurement in a monetary or other
quantified form will be at least as difficult for
community stability issues as they are for environmental values. (Randall, 1981) Perhaps the best
input into the decision making process is to list, as
best as possible, the monetary and non-monetary
effects and the incidence of same. Reliance on a
monetary benefit cost analysis will certainly not
account for many values held significant by a large
number of people.

Beyond these difficult operational problems,
political and legal issues abound. Samuels and Schmid
noted that the "Rendering of property totally useless
for economic purposes may or may not be perceived as a
legal injury requiring compensation." (1981, p. 218)
Nevertheless, the so-called taking issue and the
obligations of the government or rights of local
communities become a central issue. While large
businesses can adjust to supply restricting wilderness
designations, smaller firms -- such as local loggers
-- will bear a proportionately larger cost. Property
values might also decline. These effects are apparent
in today's demand related problems. (McKillop, 1978)
In-lieu-of-tax payments to local counties will be cut
back in either demand or supply-related destabilization. Because of the depressed timber economy, some
counties in Oregon are severely affected by reductions
in these payments. But recall, as Hyde (1980)
mentioned, that secondary opportunity costs associated
with community continuation also would need to be
considered.

Local community "rights" were partially recognized in the case of the Redwood National Park
expansion. Much of the Park Expansion Act dealt with
provisions for mitigating regional economic impacts.
(Irland, 1979) The act assumes causality between park
expansion and unemployment, which might be difficult
where intensive management or non-industrial private
timber provide options. Employment projects, potential output increases from other National Forests, and
expanded unemployment benefits were in the act. However, employment problems still exist in the affected
region. The Reagan administration attempted to cut
some of these benefits. The precedent of the Park
Expansion Act will have to be considered pragmatically

when harvest reduction decisions are considered for implementation. As Irland noted, "One of the major challenges of land-use policy in the future will be to provide for preservation of viable community economics-based wildlands, while protecting environmentally significant resources." (1979, p. 130)

POSSIBLE RESPONSES TO MANAGEMENT CHANGES IN EASTERN OREGON

There are management or market alternatives to decreased Forest Service timber supply based upon the efficiency criteria. These alternatives include increased management on the same national forest, increased demand for and supply from nonindustrial forests, selling timber land to private companies, and more intensive management in other regions.

Reductions in potential forest lands due to wilderness expansion or sales below cost could be balanced by increased management of the remaining parts of the same National Forest. Money saved from more common extensive management (Chapman, 1980) could be used. Some communities will not have this option. The Umatilla National Forest in northeast Oregon and extreme southeast Washington has "virtually no opportunity to offset any of the reduction in programmed harvest through reallocation of funds to more intensive management of the remaining land." (Fight, 1978, p. 29) Financial and employment effects of this strategy are relatively significant. There will also be constraints on intensive timber management because of other multiple use goals.

Another potential strategy, and one often proposed as a result of elimination of sales below cost "subsidy," is an increase in production, because of the price mechanism, on nonindustrial private forests. (Clawson, 1977, 1979) Success of this strategy will depend upon the management objectives and price sensitivity of these owners, and the market structure they face. Fifteen percent of the forest land in eastern Oregon is non-industrial private land. In eastern Oregon these lands have been extensively cut but are projected to double their potential supply between 1970 and 2000. (Gedney, 1975) It is likely that significant public timber withdrawals will not be balanced by this increase given the predominant role of federal timber in the region.

While some increase in demand for nonindustrial private timber can be expected, the market structure may impede the price signal. The relatively large number of small land owners sell timber to just a few mills. This lack of competition is likely to keep prices down. So in periods of high demand, non-industrial private land will not be paid the market value because of monopoly. In periods of low demand their reservation price will likely be sticky downwards and they will not be able to sell the timber. The obvious cycles in timber prices and inherent uncertainty will dampen the influence of the price signal.

Should Forest Service lands be sold to the timber industry, then management goals will exclude provision of some of the other uses: recreation, wildlife preservation measure, erosion, etc. However, the Oregon Forest Practices Act does control for some of these goods. Costs of management are generally lower because of different goals, i.e., roads are of a poorer quality. Timber mining would increase and most of the stands now considered sales below cost will be harvested. Obviously some other multiple use values will be sacrificed. Private management of these lands would not lead to community stability. Indeed, increased timber industry community dependence is likely to lead to demand-induced instability. Also, different timber firms, because of their financial management (i.e., being highly leveraged), may cut timber much faster than other companies. This ultimately could lead to long run community economic decline.

Finally, in Oregon the most productive timber lands are in the western and not the eastern part of the state. There are likely no sales below cost in western Oregon, partially because of the large stands of old growth. Diminution of timber sales in eastern Oregon, based upon a criteria of producing trees on better sites, is likely to increase efforts to harvest old growth stands. Timber in western Oregon is also undergoing competition from other uses so that increased prices for timber land might keep the land in timber use. Obviously, increased production from these lands will increase regional employment and income. Nevertheless, there are important potential wilderness areas which would become targets for timber harvesting as a result of increased demand and the need for more land for intensive management.

Should a particular region consistently have sales below cost, regardless of prices, and cost allocation issues do not seem important, then a determination to cut back timber sales likely will have to consider and help mitigate local economic effects. Certainly the transition is likely to be slow. "Length of the period could be tied to local labor mobility and the remaining life of fixed capital investments. Alternatively, we might consider the costs of retraining or moving the labor force and purchasing the fixed capital." (Hyde, 1980, p. 188) Suggestions to reduce timber supply, which may significantly affect a local region, are going to encounter political opposition. While there is no economic rationale which would suggest that a politically created externality should be mitigated, anymore than a market created externality, successful implementation of such a plan designed to provide for other environmental values will, of need, have to consider such mitigation. The form of economic mitigation will depend on local circumstances as was the case with the Redwood National Forest.

CONCLUSION

Demand and technology in the present economy assumes the major role in community economic stability. There is currently a three year backlog of harvesting Forest Service timber sales. The relationship of price on sales below cost and sales below cost on price needs further empirical investigation. Nevertheless, Forest Service policies can affect community stability when demand is high. The nature of costs and benefits could well be more complicated than simply referring to that cost as a subsidy to local communities. Other multiple use goals are also met by the assignment of costs to timber. Cost allocation would then have to be examined within the context of other non-timber multiple use benefits. Several other categories of benefits include possible gains from maintaining a more competitive local market structure and providing for cultural (life-style) option values.

There clearly are going to be trade-offs with various environmental and wilderness goals and, indeed, many people both within and without these regions will need to make decisions between strongly held values. Selective perception of any given set of values will only make final resolution of the conflict more difficult. An inappropriate or incomplete application of economic efficiency criteria will lead to biased analysis favoring one group's values over another's. This paper has examined but one issue related to those value trade-offs.

BIBLIOGRAPHY

Brodie, J. Douglas, McMahon, Robert O. and Gavelis,
    William H. (1978). Oregon's Forest Resources:
    Their Contribution in the State's Economy.
    Corvallis, OR: Oregon State University, School
    of Forestry.
Chapman, Roger C., LeMaster, Dennis C. and
    Weatherhead, Donald J. (1980). "Forestry in the
    Inland Empire." Journal of Forestry. September.
Clawson, Marion. (1975) Forests For Whom and For
    What? Baltimore, MD: Johns Hopkins University
    Press.
Clawson, Marion. (1976). The Economics of National
    Forest Management. Baltimore, MD: Johns Hopkins
    University Press.
Clawson, Marion. (1977). Decision Making in Timber
    Production, Harvest, and Marketing. Washington,
    D.C.: Resources for the Future.
Clawson, Marion. (1979). The Economics of U.S.
    Nonindustrial Private Forests. Washington, D.C.:
    Resources for the Future.
Coggins, George Cameron and Wilkenson, Charles F.
    (1981). Federal Public Land and Resources Law.
    Mineola, N.Y.: The Foundation Press, Inc.
Cutler, M. Rupert. (1980). "Timber Giveaway--A
    Dialogue." The Living Wilderness. 44:34. (June.)
Emerson, Peter M. (1982). "Remarks presented at
    Resources for the Future Seminar Series."
Fight, Roger D., Johnson, K. Norman, Connaughton, Kent
    P., and Sassman, Robert W. (1978). Roadless
    Area-Intensive Management Tradeoffs on Western
    National Forests. Washington, D.C.: USDA Forest
    Service, Western Resource Policy Economics
    Research.
Gedney, Donald R., Oswald, Daniel D. and Fight, Roger
    D. Two Projections of Timber Supply in the
    Pacific Coast States. Portland, OR: USDA Forest
    Service, Pacific Northwest Forest and Range
    Experiment Station, PNW-60.
Gregory, G. Robinson. (1972). Forest Resource
    Economics. New York: John Wiley and Sons.
Helfand, Gloria Ellen. (1981). An Analysis of the
    Costs and Receipts of National Forest Timber
    Sales. St. Louis, MO: Washington University
    Masters Thesis.
Hyde, William F. (1980). Timber Supply, Land
    Allocation, and Economic Efficiency. Baltimore:
    The Johns Hopkins University Press.
Hyde, William F. (1981). "Timber Economics in the
    Rockies: Efficiency and Management Options."
    Land Economics. Vol. 57, No. 4 (November.)

Irland, Lloyd C. (1979). Wilderness Economics and Policy. Lexington, Mass.: Lexington Books.

Kromm, David E. (1972). "Limitations on the Role of Forestry in Regional Economic Development." Journal of Forestry. (October.)

Krutilla, John V. and Fisher, Antony C. (1975). The Economics of Natural Environments. Baltimore, MD: Johns Hopkins University Press.

Krutilla, John V. and Haigh, John A. (1978). "An Integrated Approach to National Forest Management." Environmental Law. Vol. 8, No. 2.

McKillop, William. (1978). "Economic Costs of Withdrawing Timber and Timberland from Commercial Production". Journal of Forestry. (July.)

Mishan, E.J. (1973). Economics for Social Decisions. New York: Praeger Publishers.

Obermiller, Frederick W., Miller, Lester F., and Gilmore, Gary D. (1977). Profile of a Rural Growth Center: Union County, Oregon. Oregon Alternative Futures Growth Center Project: Project working paper No. 5 (March.)

Obermilller, Frederick W. (1980). "The Local Costs of Public Land Use Restrictions". (Unpublished manuscript.)

O'Toole, Randal. (1979a). A New Reality: Timber Land Suitability in Oregon National Forests. Eugene, OR: Cascade Holistic Economic Consultants.

O'Toole, Randal. (1979b). Timber Productivity in the Wallowa and Whitman National Forests. Eugene, OR: Cascade Holistic Economic Consultants.

Peskin, Henry M., Portney, Paul R., and Kneese, Allen V. (1981). Environmental Regulations and the U.S. Economy. Baltimore: The Johns Hopkins University Press.

Randall, Alan. (1981). Resource Economics. Columbia, Ohio: Grid Publishing, Inc.

Samuels, Warren J. and Schmid, A. Allan. (1981). Law and Economics: An Institutional Perspective. Boston: Martinus Nijhoff Publishing.

The Conservation Foundation. (1982). State of the Environment 1982. Washington, D.C.: The Conservation Foundation.

U.S. Water Resource Council. (1973). Water and Related Land Resources. Establishment of Principles and Standards for Planning. Washington, D.C.: Fed. Reg. 38(4).

Waggener, Thomas R. (1977). "Community Stability as a Forest Management Objective." Journal of Forestry. (November.)

Walker, John L. (1977). "Economic Efficiency and the National Forest Management Act of 1976." Journal of Forestry. (November.)

Some Historical Trends
in Timber Management

Thomas J. Barlow

Go to the west, the southwest, the Rocky Mountain states and stand in grazing land territory. You then realize that for 50 or 100 miles in every direction the government is the owner. But ever since the area was settled, ranchers have been able to lease that land for sheep and cattle grazing. There probably are strong arguments for eventually transferring some of that grazing land to the private sector.

When we're talking about national forests, we're talking about a wholly different animal. The feelings and the political history going into the national forests will determine what happens there. Further, the western national forests have an entirely different history than the eastern national forests. The failure to recognize these differences or the failure to appreciate them -- even by people closest to them in a management status -- has led to some of the problems in policy-making of the last ten and twenty years.

Virtually the whole western U.S. was government land at one time, either through purchase or treaty. Then chunks of it were transferred out for various purposes to various individual or corporate entities until transfer was halted in the 1890s by an executive fiat. What you had left is today's public domain, a large part of which is the national forest.

In the eastern states, the lands had been out of the public domain until the early part of the 20th century. All of the eastern national forests were purchased back from the private sector under various acts of Congress in the '20s and '30s. For the most part, they were tracts that timber companies owned and had logged entirely and they probably saw a way to

---

Thomas J. Barlow is an environmental consultant.

make one final killing by selling it back to the
federal government. In some cases, the federal government actually moved very aggressively on some of
the areas that had been cut out, were washing out,
blowing out, in the Appalachian region particularly
and down through Texas.

After the turn of the century, and into the
first, second, and even the third decade of this
century, most of that eastern land was pretty barren.
So the custodial arrangement that evolved there was
this: The government sent foresters in to protect the
land, to restore it, to help the forests come back.
The reason Congress passed those land purchase bills
was that the land was not going to produce harvestable
timber. It was land that, once restored, was going to
protect the watersheds.

You had foresters and you had people in the local
communities, older people now, who were intent on
seeing that land recovered. Then, in the '60s, you
had a management attitude come into the Forest Service
that saw the west and the east as the same. The forests were treated as mature resource whether they were
the virgin forests of the west or the revitalized
forests of the east, and that caused lots of problems.

I agree that there has been a lot of progress
made in management approaches by the Forest Service in
the last ten years -- approaches that would provide
timber and yet be more sensitive to the various needs
of users of the forest, of recreation and non-timber
users of the forest. I remember that when I started
working on forestry back in the early '70s there were
growth trends showing in recreation usage even then,
and some of the old timers in timber management were
concerned about it. I went over to the Forest Service
shortly after the Arab oil embargo, and there were
people in the service who were overjoyed at the prospect that recreation was going to trend down now. Oil
was going to be two or three or four times as expensive so it was going to be more difficult for people
to pay for driving their cars out to the furthest
reaches of the National Forest system. History has
not borne that out, of course. Recreation use increases every year, and I don't see it trending down
for quite some time.

So I think that places more pressure on managers
to get the trees out in a manner that is coordinated
with people's desires and feelings and values. We
need to know more about the dollar costs of the selective logging v. clearcut logging. If it's true that
there are more expenses in clearcut logging, are they
expenses to the logger or expenses to the land manager? The reason that I bring out expenses to the land
manager is this: If we're going to operate our

national forests in a manner that is fair to the
private forest sector, we've got to recognize that
management expenses are significant and the private
forester needs a proper return on his investment. So
the public forests can't undersell the private
forester.

A year and a half ago I went into an Agricultural
Stabilization and Conservation Service office in Mis-
sissippi. The ASCS, as some of you know, runs the
Forest Incentives Program (FIP). Their bulletin board
was covered with posters and they had brochures there
on the lower expense to the land owner of operating a
selective cutting system in his forest. He could keep
his costs down this way; he didn't have the costs of
intensive management; he could get a steady flow of
timber out and didn't have to cut it and wait for
twenty or thirty years for the next round of logging.
There were valid arguments that this was the least
costly way -- selective logging or group selection or
shelterwood -- less intensive logging than clearcutting would save him money and make more net profit in
the short and the long run.

Not enough has been said here about whether
timber use or timber demand projections for the next
decade are valid. Some people, including myself, poke
away at the Forest Service's projections of a doubling
in demand by the year 2030 as based on some unlikely
assumptions in certain areas. For example, the Forest
Service sees a large number of the existing housing
inventory in the U.S. as simply falling to pieces.
Therefore this housing will have to be replaced and
this translates into a portion of that projected
doubling in demand. I don't see people, even if
they're in a house that's starting to crumble around
them, walking out and letting it collapse. I see them
getting into a "fix-up-mode" very quickly and we are
seeing a growth industry in home remodeling centers,
such as we now have around Washington, D.C. The
"fix-up" attitude prevails across the country, and
industry recognizes it with its move into the lumber
yard and home remodeling center business.

However we come out on projections for the
future, it is essential for the Forest Service to
recognize that we've got a private forestry sector out
there in all stages of growth and inventory condition
and all types of management approaches and management
desire by the private forest sectors. I would just
say that when you're considering the point about
harvest and community stability in national forest
areas, we've got to look at the potential income to
rural areas in the southeast where national forests
are not located. Look at the income and the viability
of the local timber industry and the local timber

growers of the private forest sector, just as much as
you would in the northwest region where public forests
predominate.

Why isn't the private forest sector looked at
more carefully? This is something that has not been
done in the past; I think it's not been done for
structural reasons within the forestry profession in
this country. We didn't have scientific forestry or
scientific management approaches in the timber establishment in this country until the latter part of the
19th century. And then these approaches came in
through government foresters. The forestry schools
that were developed at various land grant schools
flowed out of this federal structure. Then there was
a flow into state forestry agencies of federal approaches but the tremendous federal timber inventory
led to state forestry really being a stepchild to the
federal government structure. It's a stepchild when
it comes to budget considerations, and I'm just not
sure how you can remedy that situation with the
present national forest structure. The state foresters only come to Washington once a year, or send their
representatives to town once a year, to ask for some
money from the federal treasury for fire protection or
forestry incentives. We need to get both horses,
public and private forestry, pulling in the traces
equally and sharing their fair measure of the load of
timber supply.

Part 3

Nonfuel Mineral Issues

6
Better Management of Nonfuel Minerals on Federal Land: A Look at the Issues

Bruce C. Netschert

Abstract: The Mining Law of 1872 claim/patent system and proposed revisions opens the author's discussion. The patchwork administrative system for mineral activities is criticized. The extent to which withdrawal of public lands hinders mining access is reviewed from the point of view of both mining and environmental positions. Lack of statistically reliable information compounds the problem. The national security perspective on mineral policy is evaluated and found to be unpersuasive.

Key Words: claim/patent system, leasing, Mining Law of 1872, withdrawal of public land, national security.

INTRODUCTION

The purpose of this conference is "to encourage an open and balanced discussion of ways in which the federal lands can be 'better managed.'" In this session we are concerned with the nonfuel mineral resources.

Environmentalists believe the preservation of environmental values should take precedence in the management of federal lands. The mining industry believes it is in both its own interest and the national interest not to have the exploitation of the mineral resources of the federal lands unnecessarily curtailed or interfered with. Representatives of the federal government face the task of reconciling these conflicting positions in legislation if they are members of Congress and in regulations and administrative

Bruce C. Netschert is vice president, National Economic Research Associates, Inc.

decisions if they are in the executive branch. State
administrators and legislators must preserve the
interests of the states as well. Our goal is to
determine what common ground can be established
between widely divergent and strongly held opinions.
I believe it should be possible to arrive at agreement
on at least some elements that would constitute better
management of the nonfuel mineral resources of the
federal lands from both points of view.

Obviously, it is possible to categorize the many
issues involved in more than one way. I have distinguished between four broad issues which, I think,
among them subsume all the others.

REVISION OF THE MINING LAW

Administration of the federal lands for nonfuel
mineral exploitation takes place under a statutory
dichotomy. All hardrock minerals are covered by the
Mining Law of 1872 which established the claim/patent
system. All nonmetallic minerals other than construction materials are covered by several other laws, all
of which use the leasing system. The construction
materials (sand, gravel, pumice, clay, etc.) are
handled through competitive sale under still another
law.

It has been suggested that there is neither a
geologic nor an economic reason to distinguish between
leasable and locatable minerals.[1] The existence of
the two parallel systems applying to different minerals, moreover, has led to definitional and administrative problems. Logically, therefore, all minerals
should be covered by a unified system.

This subissue, however, is overwhelmed by
another. Whether or not there should be uniform
treatment of all minerals, there is wide agreement
that the Mining Law of 1872 is anachronistic and
inadequate. Its provisions are geared to the nature
and philosophy of nineteenth century mining in the
west: individual prospectors and small mines working
vein and lode deposits, and the proposition that
"mining is the highest and best use of public
lands."[2] Now, in contrast, "...exploration for
hardrock minerals is increasingly focusing on low-
grade disseminated deposits as a result of improved
technology and the growing scarcity of high-grade
discrete deposits,"[3] and both exploration and mining,
as a consequence, have become large-scale operations
undertaken by large corporations. As for the philosophy, "{s}ocial and economic values that have evolved
over the years no longer warrant development of
domestic resources regardless of consequences...."[4]

Specific criticisms of the Mining Law focus on access, acquisition of title, and payments. Critics contend that the law is totally incompatible with the modern philosophy of public land management as expressed in many other statutes and general public attitudes. It reflects the nineteenth century view that public lands were there for the taking, so to speak, and that the government's role in this activity should be minimal. Today, on the contrary, public lands are viewed as a public trust; any use or disposition of them should take into account environmental preservation and should require payment to the government that truly reflects the value that is being obtained. To those most indignant about the payment provisions, the whole procedure under the law is nothing more than a giveaway. As Shakespeare put it (Henry IV, Part I), "You may buy land now as cheap as stinking mackerel."

The general opinion among the critics appears to be that the 1872 Mining Law should be repealed in toto and replaced by a leasing system that covers hardrock minerals in the same fashion as all other minerals, both fuel and nonfuel, are covered. Entry for prospecting would be controlled, leases would be subject to competitive bidding, title would always remain with the government (since ownership of the land is not necessary for mining), and as owner, the government would receive fair royalties on what is produced.

Although the American Mining Congress agrees that the Mining Law needs revision, state mining associations are unanimously opposed.[5] All elements of the mining industry, however, are united in opposing the adoption of a leasing system for hardrock minerals. Among the several arguments advanced by the industry are the following:[6]

1. Leasing is basically inappropriate to the nature of the exploration for hardrock minerals and to the technologies employed. The individual prospector, moreover, is still a significant source of discoveries.

2. Competitive bidding for leases against large corporations would freeze out the small miner, who still contributes to domestic mineral production and who remains important to local economies in the west.

3. The transition from the claim/patent to the leasing system would have a serious adverse effect on all existing hardrock mining on federal land. It is not clear how a claim could be converted into a lease.

4. Administration of hardrock mining under the lease system is an invitation to litigation.

5. The administration of a leasing system involves excess costs.

The first four of these arguments seem to me to be valid in the application of the present nonmetallic mineral leasing laws to hardrock minerals. There is an undeniably large difference between the nature and costs of prospecting for the former compared with the latter. Some distinction, such as that in the current leasing laws, clearly has to be made between prospecting leases and production leases. But the distinction in present law rests on areas with known deposits and those without, with competitive bidding required in the former instance and noncompetitive leasing permitted in the latter. Yet it is far more difficult to identify new areas of hardrock mineral occurrence without extensive exploration work.

The problem, then, is to design a leasing system that recognizes the different nature of occurrence of the hardrock minerals, and the position of the individual prospector and small mine operator in the industry on the one hand, and at the same time is satisfactory to the environmentalists and the government on the other. I cannot believe that this problem is insoluble.

The objection that leasing involves excessive costs would seem to be refuted by the data in a Department of Interior study. According to this study, the costs of administering the lease system for nonfuel minerals in 1978 were $8.4 million (versus revenues of $37.8 million). The costs of administering the claim/patent system for "nonleasable minerals," on the other hand, were $19.6 million (versus revenues of $1.8 million). Yet the leasing involved far more administrative activity than did keeping track of assessment work on claims and patenting them.

In addition to the foregoing, the mining industry makes a purely economic argument, namely, that the imposition of royalties has adverse economic consequences. It moves marginal mineral deposits to submarginal status, and it raises the cut-off grade in every deposit that is worked. This objection is not easily answered. One can, I think, dismiss the notion that there should be no royalty at all as incompatible with the prevailing philosophy on the use of publicly available resources for private gain. The area in which the use of such resources is permitted with no charge has narrowed progressively with time. To my knowledge, the only other instance that remains is the electromagnetic spectrum. License fees for radio and TV stations are nominal and there is no fee whatever for the use of the frequency.

But the determination of an appropriate royalty is difficult. As MacDonnell has noted, royalties should at least reflect the opportunity costs, but

such costs may include nonmeasurable scenic values.
This suggests that they should be taxed ex ante --
that is, before production -- which means they would
not necessarily bear any relation to the value of the
discovery. MacDonnell concludes that royalties should
be kept modest, with the government forgoing capture
of some of the economic rent rather than precluding
the exploitation of what would otherwise be clearly
economic deposits.[8]

I would add that a royalty system for hardrock
minerals should also include provisions for administrative flexibility, with wide latitude in the
establishment of royalty levels for different metals
and, indeed, for a given mine over time. I would even
suggest considering some means of tying the royalty to
price (averaged over a suitable time period), through
either an ad valorem rate or a schedule of royalty
levels.

Finally, in the context of this conference, I
suggest that putting all nonfuel minerals on a leasing
basis would go a long way toward solving the conflict
between the interests of the mining industry and those
of the environmentalists.

IMPROVED ADMINISTRATION

In its comprehensive study of management of the
mineral resources on federal lands, the Office of
Technology Assessment (OTA) has called attention to
the welter of governing statutes, the inconsistencies
among them, the divided and overlapping administrative
responsibilities of the agencies concerned, and the
lack of coordination among them. As OTA puts it,
"Mineral activities continue to be governed by a
patchwork system developed over more than a century in
response to various goals, problems, and pressures."[9]
Purely as a matter of governmental efficiency, this
would constitute a problem even in the absence of the
conflicting positions of the environmentalists and the
mining industry. Clearly, "better management" of the
federal lands in the nonfuel mineral field includes
improved consistency and coordination.

The nature of the problem is illustrated by the
following examples given in the OTA report:

> ...[S]ulfur on acquired land in any State
> is leased. But sulfur in the public
> domain is leased in Louisiana and New
> Mexico only; it is disposed of by entry
> under the Mining Law in almost all other
> States; and it is not available under law
> in a few States. Similarly, copper is

disposed of by lease on most acquired
land, and by entry under the Mining Law on
most of the public domain. Yet copper on
public domain national forest in Minnesota
is leased. Copper on acquired land
outside the national forests, on the
public domain in Wisconsin, Missouri,
Michigan, Kansas, Alabama, or Oklahoma, or
on the public domain outside the national
forests in Minnesota is not available
under any law.[10]

Such inconsistency is logically repugnant, and is, I
am sure, highly frustrating for the mining industry.

The first question raised by this statutory and
administrative hodgepodge is whether a consolidation
of all the relevant statutes is desirable. It seems
to me the answer clearly is yes, especially if the
Mining Law is replaced with a leasing system. If all
nonfuel minerals are to be under leasing, why not on a
uniform basis?

By "uniform basis" I do not mean a basis that
ignores differences in that nature of different
minerals and their occurrence. Allowance could be
made for the differences between hardrock deposits,
sulfur, fertilizer minerals and sodium minerals, but
that allowance would be within an overall framework of
provisions that were themselves consistent. I can see
no reason, for example, for different treatment of the
public domain and acquired lands.

The second question is the extent to which
overlapping and competing agency jurisdictions can and
should be reduced. In the OTA's view, the major
problem exists between BLM and the USGS.[11] As it
stands, it could be fully resolved by secretarial
order. If a bill for the complete consolidation of
statutes governing the administration of the mineral
resources on federal lands were before the Congress,
perhaps the mere threat of the loss of secretarial
discretion in this regard through the pending legislation would be sufficient to get the needed remedial
action by the secretary.

As for the coordination problems created by the
establishment of the Department of Energy, the resolution depends on the fate of that department. If the
present administration is successful in abolishing it,
those problems would presumably disappear. If DOE
lives on, however, it would seem necessary to handle
them in the consolidation legislation.

There remains the matter of federal-state coordination. In the last analysis this has been, and I
believe must remain, a matter of intent and willingness by the federal administrators to consult and work

with state officials in the administrative process.
Over time, the lack (or perceived lack) of such
readiness is corrected by the political process --
witness the Sagebrush Rebellion. Whether the present
administration has gone too far in accommodating state
desires and interests is something the next presidential election may decide.

ACCESS AND WITHDRAWALS

The issue of the extent to which withdrawal of
public lands from access for mining purposes is
desirable and justified is probably the one on which
conflict of interest, opinions and positions is
sharpest.
Generally speaking, the environmentalists want
withdrawals maximized. In the extreme view, mining on
the federal lands should be prevented in this manner.
The mining industry wants withdrawals minimized, and
the extreme view is illustrated by the following:

In preparing for the future...it makes no
sense to deny exploration activities in
wilderness areas. Unlike many other natural resources, such as water, timber and
pastureland, the mineral endowment of...
land cannot be determined at the surface.
The potential for minerals can be estimated, but these estimates have historically
been grossly in error (e.g. southern
Arizona), and have varied dramatically as
geologic theory, economic conditions and
exploration technology have changed. For
this reason, the mineral rights of federal
land have historically always taken precedence over all surface rights. Ore
deposits are accidents of the earth's
crust, formed under special circumstances,
and their value to society far outweighs
that of the small amount of surface over-
lying them. It will become increasingly
important for our society to capitalize on
these assets, wherever they occur, and to
let the wilderness areas assume a secondary priority.[12]

The mining industry argues that the Wilderness
Act, RARE II (Roadless Area Review and Evaluation II)
and the BLM Wilderness Study and establishment of
"Primitive Areas,"[13] together with the sharp upturn in
withdrawals for all reasons in recent years[14] all constitute an unjustified limitation on the industry's

ability and right to search for and develop the mineral resources of the federal lands. Industry argues that these withdrawals reflect more the extreme position that mining on those lands should be eliminated than a reasonable position based on clear instances of preeminence of nonmineral values over mineral values.

The environmentalists retort that withdrawals have increased because of the continuing failure to revise or repeal the 1872 Mining Law, with its provision for unrestricted entry and uncontrolled mining on patented claims. As Secretary Andrus has put it, "...land managing agencies turn to withdrawal as a means of land management, especially when private surface ownership conflicts with the land uses or management objectives of the land administering agency or when surface disturbances impact on surrounding areas."[15] Environmentalists also argue that the areas in which there is total prohibition of mineral activity are much smaller than they appear at first glance. They contend that prospecting is not necessarily prohibited, existing rights are grandfathered, leasing is allowed in many instances, and there is a variety of exceptions in many statutes and programs.

Clarification of the issue is hindered by the lack of any authoritative, unambiguous statistics. Given the divided jurisdictions and responsibilities, there is no mechanism for compiling comprehensive statistics. Table 6.1 shows the results of two such efforts. According to the Interior and OTA figures, roughly half of all federal lands are either closed to mineral activity or highly restricted. This suggests that the mining industry has a point. According to the figures compiled by the environmental organizations, on the other hand:

> In total, 40 percent of the federal lands are closed to hard rock mineral location and leasing; 27 percent are closed to leasable mineral activity only. Because much of that 40 percent is withdrawn for the national petroleum reserve, oil shale lands, powersites, military use, and native selections, less than 28 percent of the federal lands are closed to hard rock location as a result of environmentally protective withdrawals. Twenty-two percent, at most, may be closed for environmental reasons to development of leasable minerals.[16]

The difficulty of resolving the withdrawal issue is further compounded by still another statistical

Table 6.1: Comparison of Federal Land Inventories Prepared by the Department of Interior (DOI) and the Office of Technology Assessment (OTA)

(Percent of total federal lands)

Law	Closed		Highly Restricted		Moderately Restricted		Slight or no Restriction		Total	
	DOI	OTA	DOI	OTA	DOI	OTA	DOI	OTA	DOI	OTA
Mining Law:[1]										
Non-ANCSA[2]	14.7	13.1	2.3	5.3	10.4	12.8	30.0	32.6	57.4	63.8
ANSCA	27.2	26.8	13.9	1.2	--	6.8	1.8	1.4	42.9	36.2
Total . . .	41.9	39.9	16.2	6.5	10.4	19.6	31.8	34.0	100.0	100.0
Mineral Leasing Laws:[3]										
Non-ANSCA	8.2	10.9	15.8	9.3	5.0	12.7	32.1	36.6	61.1	69.5
ANSCA	30.4	27.4	6.9	1.0	1.6	1.0	--	1.2	38.9	30.6
Total . . .	38.6	38.3	22.7	10.3	6.6	13.7	32.1	37.8	100.0	100.0

[1] OTA study included acquired lands in the closed category and Indian reservations in the no restrictions category. DOI study did not include these lands.

[2] Federal lands affected by Alaska Native Claims Settlement Act.

[3] OTA study included Indian reservations with federal lands. DOI study considered them private lands.

SOURCE: U.S. Department of the Interior, Report on the Issues in the Nonfuel Minerals Policy Review, Draft for Public Review and Comment, August 1979, Table C-5.

deficiency. If withdrawn or restricted acreage has little or no mineral potential, such acreage is irrelevant to the argument over the impact of withdrawal on the mining industry. Moreover, "{w}ithout competent mineral land classification, prospecting permits themselves become unfairly branded as 'giveaways.'"[17]

The Geological Survey is charged with the responsibility of identifying those areas of the federal lands containing potentially valuable leasable minerals and so classifying them for leasing purposes. Yet,

> {d}espite the importance of such assessments, we found that the Geological Survey will need 50 years or more to complete them. In the meantime, decisions could be made that would convert these lands into other uses, such as recreation and wilderness areas. Once these decision are made, lawsuits and protests from affected interests make it difficult, if not impossible, to resolve them. In view of such problems, GAO has recommended that the Geological Survey accelerate these programs to complete them in the shortest time possible -- 20 years or less.[18]

With respect to the withdrawal issue, there is simply no way of knowing the true significance of the withdrawal data. Nor would improvement of those data make any difference in this regard. The OTA study to which I referred included an attempt to make an estimate of the potential of federal lands for selected minerals, ten of which are nonfuel minerals. Of the ten, conclusions could be drawn for five as to the rough percentage of estimated resources for the nation as a whole that exist on federal lands. For the other five the data were deemed insufficient to draw any conclusion. But even this exercise is a far cry from identifying the potential of specific tracts.

The only specific data to my knowledge are contained in the investigations by the Geological Survey. The results of these studies of wilderness and primitive areas, wilderness study areas, and one or more national monuments, national parks, national recreation areas and wildlife refuges have been collected by a private association of mineral exploration geologists. They show the following: of 101 areas, fourteen were found to be highly mineralized, twenty-five to have a favorable mineral potential, and the remaining sixty-two to have little or no potential.[19]

Where does all this leave us? I submit that even
the figures I have just recited really tell us very
little about the significance of withdrawals. How do
we measure the implications of fourteen highly
mineralized areas?   By size of area? By estimated
resource content? By the value of the resource? As I
see it, there is not and never will be any way of
quantifying the effect or significance of withdrawals.
Reasonable judgment must be applied in (as Secretary
Andrus puts it), "...a compromise between simply
closing Federal lands to mineral development, on the
one hand [sic], or leaving them completely open to
uncontrolled mineral development, on the other
hand."[20]   To which I would add, the compromise would
take the mineral potential into account to the extent
it can be estimated.

NATIONAL SECURITY AND MINERALS ON FEDERAL LANDS

The linking of national security to federal land
policy with respect to mineral exploitation is a
recent phenomenon.   The mining industry has always
stressed the role of domestic mineral production as a
means of lessening our dependence on foreign mineral
supply, but it is only in recent years that the issue
of access to the public lands has been raised in this
regard.   It has been brought to a head by the present
administration, notably in the pronouncements and
actions of Secretary Watt and in the pending National
Mineral Security Act of 1981.[21]
The argument, in brief, is as follows: Our
dependence on overseas sources of minerals is increasing.   Imports of several mineral commodities
supply a very high percentage (ninety percent or more)
of consumption. These commodities are essential in
many high technology applications, especially for
military purposes. The source of these imports is in
countries, especially those in Africa, that are
presently or potentially politically unstable.   The
Soviet Union is taking advantage of this situation by
waging a "resource war" to promote instability in
those countries or bring them under Soviet influence,
thereby giving the Soviets the ability to cut off our
supply if they so choose. Our strategic vulnerability
on this score is therefore far greater than it has
been in the past and will worsen in the future.
Most of our known domestic resources of hardrock
minerals are in the western states and Alaska, where
sixty-four percent of the total acreage is federal
land.   Much if not most of that land has not been
explored with modern techniques nor the application of
the new theories of ore genesis based on the revolu-

tionary new concept of plate tectonics. For national
security reasons (including both the preservation of
economic strength and the lessening of strategic
vulnerability), says the argument, it is therefore
essential that the mining industry be given the maximum opportunity to explore for and develop the
remaining mineral resources on the federal lands.

The significance of this argument in the present
context is that it introduces a new aspect -- national
security -- into the issue of use versus preservation
of federal lands. Access to the lands for mineral
exploitation is not justified as a legal right or an
economic benefit, but as a matter of overriding
national interest of the highest priority.

The opponents of this new argument attack it at
every point. The "resource war" is a chimera. Imports as a percentage of consumption is not necessarily a valid measure of vulnerability. There are other
ways of providing for national security, notably the
strategic stockpile, but also such things as improved
conservation and recycling, redesign and substitution
(and research and development therefor). For our
purposes here, however, we can pass over these points
of difference and focus on the federal lands element
of the argument. The question, as I see it, is this:
Assuming the United States is seriously vulnerable on
the score of mineral import dependence, and assuming
further that the strategic stockpile and the various
means of reducing consumption of the metals in question cannot adequately reduce that vulnerability, to
what extent can recourse to the federal lands accomplish the task?

At first glance, the answer would seem to be
positive and unambiguous. Almost all mining districts
in the west and Alaska are on federal lands. The west
and Alaska are among the world's most highly
mineralized regions. Therefore, further exploration
should turn up new deposits.

But let's look at the metals that have been
mentioned most frequently as instances of alarming
vulnerability -- chromium, cobalt, columbium, manganese, platinum, and tantalum. In all these instances,
imports are eighty percent or more of consumption,
Africa is an important source, and (with the exception
of manganese, which is essential in blast furnace
operations) all have high technology and military applications. Domestic production of all these metals
to date can be characterized as minor, sporadic and
marginal. Known domestic reserves are either minor,
submarginal or both.

The argument of the administration and the mining
industry implies that maximizing the percentage of
federal lands open to exploration would result in the

discovery of sufficient resources of these metals to make a significant difference in our degree of import dependence for their supply. But what constitutes a significant difference? Is it five percent or fifty percent? It would, of course, be different for each metal, depending on the degree to which there are no substitutes for its use in products which are themselves of vital industrial and military importance. Platinum in catalysts would be one such use, whereas the use of chromium for plating household appliances would not.

Suppose now that significant resources (however defined) were discovered. To take an example at one extreme, assume discovery of a large, high-grade cobalt deposit with production costs equal to or lower than those of the African sources and a potential capacity to supply, say, more than half of U.S. consumption for twenty years. The national security argument for exploitation would then carry great weight, even if the deposit were in the heart of a wilderness area and exploitation inevitably would involve extensive despoliation.

Suppose, at the other extreme, that discoveries consisted of small, submarginal deposits that could at best provide only a modest reduction in the degree of import dependence. This would, I presume, settle the question, but at the cost of unjustified exploration activity on presently withdrawn land. As the cartoon puts it, "Back to the old drawing board."

The middle result would raise another problem. Suppose the discoveries were of large, submarginal deposits that could make a significant difference in import dependence. The national security argument would then hold that the lessened strategic vulnerability would be worth the cost of the subsidization, and development should proceed on that basis. But this would not be sufficient. Before it could actually be applied in a decision to subsidize production it would have to be shown that the cost of the security gain by this means was less than that of alternative means, such as stockpiling.

As I see it, the proponents of the national security argument have not yet made a convincing case for the existence of sufficient resources of the "proper" metals on the federal lands to warrant wholesale removal of the restrictions to entry. The answer to this, I realize, is that there can be no absolute proof short of actual drilling. The explorationists must get onto the land, so it is a Catch-22.

Is it, really? Let's forget about absolute proof and ask only that the industry provide better substantiation than it now offers that the "proper" resources exist, and that the proposed wholesale opening up of the federal lands would not result in merely more copper, lead, zinc, molybdenum and silver. Geophysical investigations involve minimal intrusion on the land, and none at all when done aerially. From the geophysical data, pick especially promising sites. Drill those sites with equipment brought in by helicopter. If something really good is found, then put the issue squarely to the land authorities. As I see it, up to this point there has been no intrusion worth getting excited about.[22]

I find the national security argument unpersuasive when used in broad brush fashion. But there is, I think, a place for the issue. Industry is entitled to consideration of that argument on its merits when applied to specific circumstances. To revert to my earlier example of a superb cobalt discovery, I would find it difficult in my own mind to say that it should not be exploited merely because it was in a wilderness area. If, on the other hand, the deposits were along Bright Angel Trail in the Grand Canyon (to be decidedly hypothetical), national security would be irrelevant. In the end, judgment on this, as in all public policy issues, must be reasonable. National security cannot be used as an absolute that overrides all other considerations, but neither can environmental preservation.

In conclusion, I suggest some questions for consideration:

1. Can a leasing system for hardrock minerals be fashioned that would be acceptable to both environmentalists and industry? Can the small prospector/miner be taken care of in such a system? Should all nonfuel minerals be under a single system that takes into account differences in the form and nature of occurrence of different minerals?

2. Is legislation necessary to achieve better administration of nonfuel minerals on the federal lands, or is it a matter of good administration and interagency coordination? What changes in agency structure, regulations and administration of those regulations would represent improvement from the state point of view?

3. What would constitute a compromise on the access/withdrawal issue acceptable to both sides? Is there a feasible way for the industry to engage in exploratory surface operations subject to limitations that would satisfy reasonable environmental criteria?

4. Would it be possible to rank wilderness areas, or portions thereof, in some kind or order or classification that would permit a trade-off

between environmental values (however estimated) and the value of a discovered deposit?
5. Are the results of USGS investigations helpful
in the resolution of the access/withdrawal
issue?   If so, should there be a massive increase and acceleration in such work by the
Survey?
6. Is there any way in which the mining industry
or the government can obtain sufficient information on the probability of occurrence of
specific minerals on the federal lands so that
the national security issue can be property
weighed in individual administrative decisions?

NOTES

1. Office of Technology Assessment (OTA), Management of Fuel and Nonfuel Minerals in Federal Land,
Current Status and Issues (Government Printing Office,
Washington: April 1979), p. 105.
2. General Accounting Office (GAO), Mining Law
Reform and Balanced Resource Management, EMD-78-93,
February 27, 1979, p. 7.
3. OTA, op.cit., p. 109.
4. GAO, op.cit., p. iii.
5. See, for example, Mining Law Reform, Hearings
before the Subcommittee on Mines and Mining, House
Committee on Interior and Insular Affairs, 95th
Congress, 1st Session, 1978, p. 141 and passim.
6. See GAO, op.cit., pp. 31f.
7. R. H. Nelson, "An Analysis of 1978 Revenues
and Costs of Public Land Management by the Interior
Department in 13 Western States," (Department of the
Interior, unpublished, December 1979), Table 4.
8. L. J. MacDonnell, "Public Policy for Hard-
Rock Minerals Access on Federal Lands: A Legal-
Economic Analysis," Quarterly of the Colorado School
of Mines, Vol. 71, No. 2, April 1976, p. 104.
9. OTA, op.cit., p. 99.
10. Idem.
11. Ibid., pp. 232-237.
12. Minerals Exploration Coalition, Mineral
Resources in Wilderness (Denver: May 1982), p. 6.
13. For a discussion of Primitive Areas, see J.
D. Foster, "Bureau of Land Management Primitive Areas
-- Are They Counterfeit Wilderness?" Natural Resources Journal, Vol. 16, No. 3, July 1976, pp.
621-663.

204

14. "At one time, 90 percent of all Federal lands were available for mineral exploration development. However, beginning with the passage of the Wilderness Act of 1964, which created 9.1 million acres of federally-protected wilderness area, successively more and more public land throughout the United States has been declared off-limits to mining. In the past decade, numerous withdrawals have been carried out, under a variety of authorities, and as a result, two-thirds of all federal lands now have moderate to prohibitive restrictions on mineral exploration and development." GAO, Learning to Look Ahead: The Need for a National Materials Policy and Planning Process, EMD-79-30, April 19, 1979, pp. 29f.
15. Mining Law Reform, Hearings before the Subcommittee on Mines and Mining, op.cit., p. 110.
16. Environmental Policy Center, et al., Minerals and the Public Lands, October 1981, p. 67.
17. L. C. Lee and D. C. Russell, "Perspective: Where Do We Go From Here?" Mining Engineering, May 1977, p. 33.
18. GAO, Learning to Look Ahead, op.cit., p. 16.
19. Minerals Exploration Coalition, op.cit., pp. 41-324.
20. Mining Law Reform, Hearings, op.cit., p. 110.
21. See, also, the National Materials and Minerals Program Plan and Report to Congress, submitted by the President on April 5, 1982, pp. 2-4.
22. Perhaps the decision as to whether a specific site is worth drilling could be aided by the application of computer technology to the assessment of the prospect. This is suggested by the recent report of the successful use of an artificial intelligence program to identify previously unknown ore-grade molybdenum mineralization in eastern Washington. See A. N. Campbell, et al., "Recognition of a Hidden Mineral Deposit by an Artificial Intelligence Program," Science, Vol. 217, September 3, 1982, pp. 927-929.

The Economic Significance
of Mineral Resources

Harold J. Barnett

A central question is the economic significance
of mineral resources on U.S. public lands which are
withdrawn from access by industry. I have been doing
research on availability of non-fuel minerals in
international markets -- on whether they have been
becoming increasingly scarce in an economic sense to
the U.S. and other countries. Certainly the mineral
resources on the withdrawn lands are substantial, but
the magnitudes available for the marketplace are very
much larger. It is not at all clear that the international price trends of non-fuel minerals relative to
prices of other goods and services have been much
affected by the withdrawals. For the U.S., relative
prices did not increase from the Civil War to 1970,
and the increases during the past decade are primarily
related to economic turbulence -- the effects of OPEC,
inflation, productivity, pollution and safety regulation, etc. Worldwide, relative prices of non-fuel
minerals generally have not increased in the 1970's
decade.[1] Worldwide, the new findings, substitutions,
and innovations appear to have offset depletions and
withdrawals. If these trends continue, then we should
not feel coerced generally to invade reserved wilderness lands for minerals.

However, trends could change as economic needs
grow. The Third World efforts to cartelize the
world's mineral resources in the sea could sharply
restrict development of the vast, potential ocean
supplies, in efforts to increase mineral prices.
Thus, economic pressure to find and extract minerals
on U.S. reserved lands could increase. And this
pressure could be reinforced by a further argument

Harold J. Barnett is professor of economics, Washington University, St. Louis.

that minerals development of withdrawn lands is necessary for national security. These are legitimate
challenges to denying access to minerals on reserved.
How should they be answered?

The defect of the economic need or national
security argument as a <u>generalization</u> is that it is
impossible to prove or support. It cannot be true
that every other value in the society -- economic,
social, aesthetic, moral -- must give way to an assertion of economic or national security need. The case
for invasion of reserved lands must be argued in terms
of social benefits and costs of <u>specific</u> proposals:
Which minerals? Are there alternative reserves or
supplies elsewhere? Would not stockpiles of the
specific mineral be better or cheaper? And, further,
what are the details of the specific proposal? How
would exploration be carried out? Where and when?
How much damage would be done? What are the probabil-
ities of success?

When the economic and national security cases are
thus specifically argued, then they may not be coun-
tered with a generalized assertion that reserved lands
are untouchable. I cannot believe that every square
mile of wilderness, perimeters as well as interiors,
irrespective of size of the reservation, is precious
beyond all competing claims; or that every exploration
or development is destructive of great values.

Reservation and area specifics should be characterized by types of restrictions. Processes for
review and evidence should be established. The burdens of proof can be heavy and the times for review
infrequent. But there must be a way of accommodating
diverse needs and changing circumstances and views in
the society. Of course, preservationists would prefer
omnibus, absolute restrictions forever. But this is
no more reasonable than a Pentagon or mining association claim of absolute privilege.

I offer a comment concerning marginalism, markets, and incentives. In each specific case, our
society can choose to make a decision either in a rel-
tively free economic market or by government regulaion
or arrangement. A single, overall solution is not
possible, for it has long been clear that the U.S.
public chooses that we should have a mixed economy.
The choices between economic market and political
process, therefore, have to be <u>specific</u> as to time,
place, product, participants, and degree. And the
choices will change, as we observe the results from
previous choices and as circumstances and public
preferences change.

As we look over the world, it is clear that,
while neither the free market or government choice
gives great results, we should lean toward free

economic markets, where possible. The empirical evidence is quite favorable for market decisions from World War II to about 1970. In further support of the market, the economic evidence of the 1970s is rather unfavorable for government decision-making. It appears that we tend to overload government economic and regulatory decision-making beyond capabilities.

Whichever we choose in any particular case, we should emphasize "process efficiency." A great virtue of our U.S. society, in markets and in government, is that it is experimental and evolving -- and can learn from mistakes. This is because there are many markets, many governments, many choices by consumers, and many incentives to productivity in most cases. And the less able economic units -- private or public -- tend to fail and disappear. The essentials of good markets are not necessarily the terms "private" and "profit." The essentials are diverse: free suppliers who compete; who cannot control consumers or users; who are permitted or forced to bankruptcy or collapse if they do not perform well; and who have incentives which drive them to be productive and efficient. In such situations, each generation, led by entrepreneurial agents, makes its own decisions and perhaps revises former ones.

NOTE

1. H.J. Barnett and C. Morse, Scarcity and Growth (Johns Hopkins Press, 1963); H.J. Barnett, "Scarcity and Growth Revisited," in Scarcity and Growth Reconsidered, ed. V.K. Smith (Johns Hopkins Press, 1979); H.J. Barnett, G. van Muiswinkel, and M. Shechter, "Are Minerals Costing More?" in Perspectives on Resource Policy Modeling, ed. R. Amit and M. Avriel (Ballinger Publishing, 1982); H.E. Goeller and A.M. Weinberg, "The Age of Substitutability," American Economic Review, V, no. 68:6.

Management of Non-fuel Minerals:
A Mining Industry Perspective

Thomas C. Nelson

Some facts and figures illustrate the seriousness of the mining situation.

From July, 1981 to July, 1982, mining employment decreased by 380,000, or thirty-two percent. Metal mining employment declined by 60,000, or fifty-seven percent. In August, 1982, the U.S. unemployment rate was 9.6 percent, but it was 14.7 percent in the mining sector and 21.8 percent in the primary metal manufacturing industries. Comparing those percentages to the widely publicized 16.3 percent unemployment figure for the depressed construction industry reveals the depths of this problem.

In terms of production, bulk ferroalloys production declined from over two million short tons in 1970 to less than 1.3 million tons in 1981; 1982 production is estimated at .8 million tons, or less than thirty percent of capacity. Domestic raw steel production exceeded eighty-five percent of capacity in early 1981 but currently hovers around thirty-seven percent. Current ouput of domestic usable iron ore is less than ten percent of the industry's approximately 100 million long tons per year capacity. Titanium production is currently at about fifty percent of capacity. Domestic tungsten production is about thirty-five percent of the 1981 rate.

In terms of net profit, primary nonferrous metals net profit is less than twelve percent and primary iron and steel less than four percent of 1980 profits. The total iron and steel industry profit, based on first quarter figures, is $100 million dollars.

Setting aside the issue of "how much" should be open to access for mining, I think that it is fair to.

Thomas C. Nelson is assistant to the president, American Mining Congress.

conclude that neither environmentalists nor the mining industry know the real status of withdrawals in terms of acreages or purpose.

The mining industry quotes the Office of Technology Assessment (OTA) and the Department of the Interior for its information on withdrawals. (1,2) The environmentalists use their own pronouncements.(3) None of these reports, by and large, deal with the issue of "de facto" withdrawals that constitute an ever increasing acreage of substantial magnitude.(4)

The only review of withdrawn areas now underway is subject to review under Section 204(1) of the Federal Land Policy and Management Act of 1976. The subject acreage is sixty-three million acres; 623 million acres of federal land are excluded from the review.

True, various interest groups interpret data in different manners and with differing conclusions. But let us start from an accurate and accepted data base. There is no such base available.

It would help if the environmental groups, the oil and gas industry, and the mining industry joined hands and pressed for an accurate, definitive inventory of lands withdrawn from mining and mineral leasing, both de jure and de facto, by land managing agencies.

The door is open. In his "National Materials and Minerals Program Plan and Report to Congress" of April 5, 1982, the president said that the administration will examine this issue.

In our judgment, what is needed is a straightforward, simple inventory approach. Given adequate authority to obtain cooperation and data from the various bureaus, a good person and two "gofers" could get the job done in a year, and all groups could then make their interpretations from sound data.

Dr. Netschert's discussion of national security and mineral lands should be considered, where applicable, in tandem with Dr. Landsberg's dissertation on U.S. minerals policy in last month's "Resources."(5)

The point is made that almost all mining districts in the west and Alaska are upon federal lands; therefore, further exploration should turn up new deposits.

Alaska Mining Association President David Heatwole gave an interesting presentation on Alaska exploration during a technical session on Alaska lands at the American Mining Congress convention October 13, 1982. (6) Through a series of slides, Mr. Heatwole showed that the Canadian Yukon, Alaska, and Siberia share the same harsh climates, lack of transportation, and the same geological formations. He then overlaid these maps with producing mines. The Canadian Yukon and Siberia had a plethora of base metal and strategic

mineral mines, but Alaska has only one producing mine
(other than gold) and it is coal.
Heatwole concluded that restrictive land classi-
fications played a significant role in the ability of
Alaska to provide for our nation's mineral needs.
The paper further points to those metals of
alarming vulnerability. It is interesting to note
that Alaska has active exploration underway for four
of the six metals listed, even with the severe restrictions upon access.(7)
If maximizing the percentage of federal lands
open to exploration would result in discoveries, Dr.
Netschert asks what constitutes a significant difference in our degree of import dependence? In response,
let me elaborate on the position of the American
Mining Congress.
In view of the supply data which are widely
accepted and the record on access to foreign resources
that it is more important than ever, we contend that
where there is the possibility of viable domestic
mineral production it be given every opportunity to
succeed. And further, quoting Dr. Simon Strauss:(8)

I again emphasize that the American
Mining Congress is not now suggesting that
the government set up some program of
paying high prices or above-market prices
for minerals.
We want the creation of an atmosphere
of encouragement for the domestic miner,
an atmosphere which in recent years has
been absent.

For hardrock minerals, huge acreages are necessary for
exploration. For example, in its gold exploration
program, which resulted in the discovery of a single
new major deposit, Homestake made 1,111 reconnaissance
examinations. Those examinations carefully eliminated
prospects as a result of more intense exploration,
but, in all cases with no or a minimum of surface
disturbance.(9)
But the area actually mined is small. In the
entire history of our nation, less than three-fourths
of one percent of our lands have been disturbed by
mineral development, including strip mining in the
east and oil and gas development in the south. Most
of the disturbed lands have been rehabilitated, either
by reclamation programs or naturally.(10)
Finally, I share Dr. Netschert's feeling that if
a mineral deposit were along Bright Angel Trail in
Grand Canyon, national security be damned. But that
is not the case for which national policy was ever --
or should be -- intended. I hope that we are discuss-

ing the other hundreds of millions of acres of public lands. They are beautiful, yes, but they are areas in which rational choices can and should be made.

Sure, there is a difference in treatment of public domain and acquired lands, but there are other differences between the two -- differences in congressional committee jurisdiction, what amounts to differences in wilderness acquisition, and other anomalies.

The bulk of acquired lands that we talk about in relation to mining are eastern national forests. And the acreage of western acquired lands or eastern public domain is so small that it is inconsequential to miners. So the acreages of public domain in Wisconsin (10,143) acres, Missouri (2,647 acres) (11) or acquired land outside the national forest open to mining really isn't worth the effort of getting the law changed.

The statutory hodgepodge and consequently the administrative hodgepodge was really cleared up for all users of federal land and for the land administrator by the passage of the Federal Land Policy and Management Act of 1976. This cleared state claims, overlapping general land laws, withdrawals, rights-of-ways and a whole host of incongruities for the miner.

There has been a problem in function within the Department of the Interior concerning jurisdiction. Bureaus come and bureaus go. But the job gets done with a little prodding from the environmentalists here and the miners there. Even when there is interdepartmental jurisdiction, e.g., Forest Service lands, the job gets done. In fact, the number of administrative appeals and law suits concerning mining per se in relation to the population of hard rock operating plans has been small to none over the years. Rather the complaints concerning mining have related to NEPA, Endangered Species Act, rights-of-way and the like.

The last of the four issues -- the General Mining Law -- has been the subject of a great deal of controversy. I speak to the general mining law because to use the "Mining Law of 1872" is a misnomer. The law has been so modified by amendments and so interpreted by court decisions that it is no longer a simplistic law passed over 100 years ago.

First, regardless of OTA's conclusions, there is a geological difference between the public domain leasables and locatables. The leasables usually occur in beds of rather large acreage, varying in depth of body, overburden, and quality. The locatables, in spite of advances in extraction methodology, still are mined as veins, lodes, or discrete deposits covering relatively small geographic areas, and the exploration strategies differ. Dr. Netschert agrees that the differences are real.

The specific criticisms cited are access, acquisition of title, and payments. I do not understand the access problem; it is not explained. As far as acquisition of title is concerned, there were only thirty-one claims involving 4,333 acres patented in 1980, the latest year of record available to me. A spot sampling indicates that this figure is higher than most recent years. This is hardly a problem of large magnitude.

Payments and leasing are two separate issues and should be addressed separately. Leasing involves pre-discovery and exploration activities. Payments on royalty are primarily a production phenomenon. The arguments of inappropriateness to hard rock exploration, freezeout of the small miner (who still prevails in exploration), transition from a claim/patent system, and litigation, are all valid reasons for not adopting a leasing scheme.

There are other reasons for opposing changes in the location system by the mining industry. In a nutshell, the reasons all focus on the inability of the administrative agencies and bureaus to initiate and administer a workable, predictable system that will allow for continuing operations. We have had miserable experience with geothermal leasing, coal leasing, oil shale leasing to name a few.

We think that there are five concepts which are basic to any realistic and effective mining legal regime and regulations:

1. Prospecting for minerals should be encouraged by allowing maximum and non-exclusive access to the public lands to search for mineralization.

2. A prospector should be given exclusive exploration rights for any particular area for the time he is focusing detailed exploration attention on it.

3. A person who discovers a valuable mineral deposit should have an exclusive right to develop and mine it, including the right to defer such development for a reasonable period of years until economic or technical conditions justify production.

4. The law must provide a mining venture with security for the duration of mining, on terms reasonably set in advance.

5. There is a need to protect our public lands from environmental abuses.

One note of warning. When I speak of time, I am talking of decades. At present, it takes from eight to thirty-four and a half years from discovery on public land until the first penny of return to the investor.

As far as a royalty system is concerned, Caesar will be given that which is Caesar's, whether it be through the corporate tax structure, severance taxes, royalty or combination. State severance taxes seem to be the order of the day.

With reference to royalty, I think the argument that it is an anti-conservation move deserves further explanation.

Royalty decreases the amount of ore that is commercially mineable. A royalty is a fixed cost and for each additional cost that is added to a mining operation, the effect is to raise the cutoff grade of ore that can be economically mined. The addition of fixed costs forces a mine operator to high-grade the mining operation and leave in the ground lower grade materials that, if mined and processed, could not pay for the fixed costs of the operation. In the nonferrous industry, the minerals produced are sold on the international market where market prices are determined by supply and demand. The producers have no control over prices. Instead of being able to pass on to consumer the cost of paying the royalty, the net revenue to the operator is reduced. If the operation is marginal it would force curtailment or cessation of operations.

Although a royalty system may not be insoluble, I suggest that the serious student study the work that Dr. O'Neil carried out recently for the Department of the Interior.(12) For individual situations, Dr. O'Neil points out that individual systems have evolved representing unique, negotiated agreements. Unfortunately, this is hardly the way in which the federal government could or should approach the issue.

Finally, of all the lands in the United States, the greatest overall mineral resource potential exists on the federal lands. The federal lands are generally the harsh, inhospitable mountainous areas left over after the choice agricultural lands were appropriated in the settlement of the west during the last century. The more mountainous areas were not of interest for agriculture and thus were more likely to be retained in federal ownership. In our century there has been continued interest in retaining the mountainous areas in federal ownership for their scenic and recreational values. The same geologic forces that created the mountains and their scenic beauty -- the volcanic action, faulting, uplifts, the movements of tectonic plates, and other forces -- are also the forces that account for the migration and deposition of minerals in the concentrations adquate to permit extraction. For these reasons the retained federal lands constitute our national treasure house of minerals.

We have only scratched the surface in mineral exploration of the federal lands. There are vast unexplored areas. Alluvium, volcanic flows, layers of barren sedimentary rock and other materials likely conceal vast mineralized zones. Therefore, if federal lands are declared off limits to mineral exploration there is a significant impact on the ability of our nation to find and develop mineral resources. Mineralization is widely dispersed throughout the federal lands and it is safe to conclude that the withdrawal or segregation of half of the federal lands from exploration and development reduces the potential of mineral development from federal lands in the same proportion.

NOTES

1. Office of Technology Assessment. Management of Fuel and Nonfuel Minerals in Federal Land, Current Status and Issues: G.P.O., Washington, D.C. 1979, 105 pp.
2. U.S. Department of the Interior. Final Report of the Task Force on the Availability of Federally Owned Minerals Lands, Volume 1. G.P.O., Washington, D.C., 103 pp.
3. Environmental Policy Center, et al. Minerals and the Public Lands, October 1981, 67 pp.
4. Comptroller General. Interior's Program to Review Withdrawn Federal Lands -- Limited Progress and Results. GAO/RCED-83-26, October 7, 1982, 58 pp.
5. Landsberg, Hans H. What next for U.S. minerals policy? Resources, 71:9-10. Resources for the Future, October, 1982.
6. Heatwole, David A. An Objectives View of Mining in Alaska. Presented to the American Mining Congress, Las Vegas, Nevada. October 11, 1982.
7. Bundtzen, T.K., C.R. Eakins, and C.N. Crowell. Review of Alaska's Mineral Resources, 1982. Division of Geological and Geophysical Surveys, State of Alaska, 52 pp.
8. Strauss, Simon D. National Mining Policy hearings before the Senate Subcommittee on Energy and Mineral Resources, April 7, 1981. Mining Congress Journal, June 1981: 38-39.
9. Anderson, James A. Gold -- its history and role in the U.S. economy and the U.S. exploration program of Homestake Mining Co., Mining Congress Journal, January, 1982: 51-58.

216

10. Edwards, Howard L. Hearings on H.R. 3364 before the House Subcommittee on Mines and Mining, October 20, 1981.

11. Bureau of Land Management. Public Land Statistics, 1980, 191 pp.

12. O'Neil, Thomas: Alternative Royalty Systems for Hard-Rock Minerals. Prepared for the Office of Minerals Policy and Research Analysis, U.S. Department of the Interior, March 31, 1980, 79 pp.

Mineral Facts and Fictions

Richard W. Wright

I shall focus my comments on several facts and fictions that are often confused in discussions on hardrock mining and that are important to sort out if there is to be any progress in resolving the debate. Most of my comments are condensed from the study that I authored for the U.S. Congress' Office of Technology Assessment, Management of Fuel and Nonfuel Minerals in Federal Land (1979), to which I refer you for a more complete discussion.

Two major facts make it difficult, but not impossible, to achieve optimum coordination of mineral and nonmineral activities: first, most mineral deposits are not easily identified; second, many nonmineral resources are not easily valued (OTA pp. 184-185).

Mineral deposits, especially in long-explored areas such as the lower forty-eight states, generally are hidden beneath the surface and can be found only through costly and risky exploration. Moreover, changing geologic concepts, economics and exploration, mining and processing techniques can make areas attractive that once were thought to have little or no economic mineral potential. This has occurred for copper in southern Arizona, taconite in Minnesota and the Carlin-type gold deposits. Identification of mineral deposits depends on continuing access for exploration and cannot be satisfied by one-time surveys by the government or by industry. Modern exploration uses sophisticated techniques that cost hundreds of thousands or millions of dollars, with only about a ten percent chance of success. Thus, mineral firms are not likely to explore a given area unless they are assured of the right to develop and produce whatever they may find. (OTA pp. 46-67.)

Richard W. Wright is associate professor of law, Benjamin N. Cardozo School of Law, Yeshiva University.

217

On the other hand, it is difficult to place a
value on many nonmineral resources -- scenic beauty,
endangered wildlife and plant species, air and water
quality, ecosystem functions, wilderness and local
lifestyles -- and also to predict what impact mineral
exploration and possible subsequent development will
have on these resources.

How, then, do you make a decision on whether to
allow exploration, with the right to develop, in an
area with important but difficult-to-value nonmineral
resources, when there is at best a ten to twenty percent chance of finding an economic mineral deposit of
unknown value? (OTA pp. 189-190.)

Historically, an absolute preference was given to
mineral activity, based on two fictions which continue
to enjoy widespread currency in the mining industry
today. They are, first, that economic concentrations
of minerals, unlike other resources, are "where you
find them," and, second, that these economic mineral
deposits are always the most valuable resource
wherever they are found. (OTA pp. 185-189.)

It is true that economic concentrations of the
more valuable minerals are rare (they are more valuable precisely because they are rare). Subeconomic
concentrations are more widespread, and often become
economic as higher-grade deposits are depleted, or as
improvements are made in technology. Moreover, many
minerals, especially the hardrock minerals, are recy-
clable and can be substituted for by other minerals or
synthetics.

Many nonmineral resources are similarly rare or
"where you find them" and are subject to the same
economics of more expensive, lower quality alternatives: watersheds, acquifers, hydroelectric power-
sites, old-growth hardwood timber, prime agricultural
land, white-water rivers, etc. Some nonmineral resources are, even more than mineral resources, "where
you find them" since there are no alternatives at any
cost: unique landforms (the Grand Canyon), cultural
sites (Mesa Verde), endangered species, etc.

The premise that mineral activity is always the
most valuable use of a tract of land was based originally on the high net value of high-grade surface or
near-surface mineral deposits in contrast to the
generally low or minimal commercial land values of the
arid, remote and unpopulated western regions. Little
thought was given to noncommercial land values.
Today, many if not most mineral deposits are of much
lower grade and are located at greater depth than
mineral deposits discovered in the past. They are
most expensive to find and mine, and their net value
thus is often much lower than in the past. On the
other hand, many of the commercial nonmineral

resources (timber, forage, game, water) have become
scarce and hence much more valuable due to growth in
the population and the economy. In addition, there is
growing appreciation of many noncommercial nonmineral
resource values: recreational, esthetic, ecological,
scientific, cultural, option preservation, etc. It is
far from clear that in every instance these nonmineral
resource values would be outweighed by any possible
mineral deposit, no matter how common the mineral or
how marginal the deposit.

A third argument is often made by the mining
industry that we shouldn't be concerned about mining's
effect on nonmineral resources since mineral activities disturb such a miniscule fraction of the nation's
land -- only one-quarter of one percent. This is also
a fiction, derived from a failure to appreciate the
limits of the U.S Bureau of Mines (USBM) studies on
which it is based. USBM Circular 8642, published in
1974, concluded from a survey of the mineral industry
that only 0.16 percent (3.65 million acres) of the
nation's land had been utilized by the mining industry
between 1930 and 1971. A partial update, USBM
Circular 8862 (1982), raised the figure to 0.25 percent (5.7 million acres) for the period 1930-1980.
But the bureau's figures do not include land explored
and worked for oil and gas, although oil and gas
activity is the most extensive mineral activity (approximately 130 million federal acres were leased in
1982, but probably only one-tenth of this was being
actively worked). They do not include land affected
by exploration, although much larger areas are affected by exploration than by development and production.
For each operating mine, there are exploration pits,
drill sites, roads and other impacts scattered over an
area much larger than the mine area, as well as similar impacts from the ten to 100 unsuccessful exploration projects that occur for each successful project.
The figures do not even include most of the land
affected by development and production. They include
only the areas actually excavated or used for waste
disposal. They do not include areas used by mills,
processing plants, roads, powerlines, pipelines and so
forth and the much larger areas affected by these
ancillary facilities, especially the roads. They do
not include the surrounding areas, often very extensive, in which wildlife, scenic viewing and recreation
may be affected as the result of the physical, visual
and aural impact of the mine, its road network and
other facilities. (OTA pp. 180-181.)

The USBM figures themselves demonstrate an accel-
erating magnitude of surface disturbance as mining
moves increasingly from underground to open-pit and
surface mining. Half again as much disturbance

occurred between 1972 and 1980 (2.05 million acres) as occurred in the previous forty-two years (3.65 million). Finally, as industry itself has often stated, mineral activity in the United States is concentrated in federal land areas, which contain almost all of the nation's most significant natural and recreational resources (OTA pp. 41-45, 176-178). Figures on aggregate land disturbance in the nation as a whole do not help resolve specific problems of proposed mineral activity in federal land areas with important nonmineral resource values.

I hope I have demonstrated that an absolute preference for mineral activity is not justifiable. But that does not mean that there should be an absolute preference against mineral activity, which is what the land withdrawal process represents. Why not allow carefully limited exploration and development, with restrictions scaled to the importance and sensitivity of the nonmineral resource values? Such restrictions could be stricter during the exploration stage to protect nonmineral resource values from being destroyed when there is only a ten percent chance of finding an economic deposit (e.g., nonroad access, with certain sensitive areas off-limits), but some of which (e.g., nonroad access) could be relaxed if an economic deposit were found. Distinctions based upon the type of deposit being sought (and found) -- e.g., platinum versus gypsum -- could also be made.

The problem is that the Mining Law of 1872 does not allow such a balanced approach. If land is open to activities under the Mining Law, there is no authority to prohibit certain impacts. There is only authority to mitigate those impacts as much as possible consistent with the preferred mining use. Moreover, the land is open for development of any hardrock mineral, no matter how common, and no matter how valuable the nonmineral resources that will be affected. It is open not just for gold or copper, but also for vermiculite for kitty litter or gypsum for wallboard. It is open for development no matter how marginal the economics of the deposit may be, and the right to explore and develop overrides any nonmineral resource value. It is open for anyone to come in to explore whenever and for whatever, without any weighing beforehand of relative values by the federal land manager. There is no control over entry, except such mitigating conditions as the overworked land manager may be able to devise. There is no requirement of any payment for destruction of surface resource values that may occur during exploration or development -- not even for a dam or ranger station. The law perversely requires unnecessary and damaging "assessment" work to maintain claims. If an economic deposit is found, the discoverer may obtain title to the surface as well as the mineral deposit, thereby creating a private "inholding" that may be used for any purpose without even mining the deposit. Such inholdings can make it much more difficult to manage the surrounding federal land, especially if they are in critical locations. (OTA pp. 190-206, 214-215.)

Leasing, or a modified claim system with some control over access and with the right to impose restrictions to prohibit impacts, would allow a more balanced approach. Until recently, the leasing laws were administered in the same fashion as the Mining Law: an all-or-nothing approach, either open with an absolute preference given to mineral activities under each lease or withdrawn (officially or through no-leasing decisions). But the authority has always existed to adopt an in-between position along the lines of the one outlined above, and recent administrations, until the current one, had made considerable progress.

None of the objections to leasing seem persuasive to me. First, leasing is not "basically inappropriate" for hardrock minerals. It is used by many countries and most of the western states for hardrock as well as non-hardrock minerals. It is used for hardrock minerals on federal acquired land, including the major lead-zinc deposits in Missouri. There is not a large difference between the nature and costs of exploring for and developing hardrock versus nonhardrock minerals. The geologic configurations for many of them are very similar. Exploration for oil and gas in the western Overthrust Belt is not so dissimilar from exploration for copper or uranium in Arizona. Development of leasable synfuels is not so dissimilar from development of molybdenum. (OTA pp. 52-55, 65-66, 104-106.)

Second, leasing of hardrocks need be no more competitive than it is now for the nonhardrocks. Competitive leasing generally exists only for known deposits or structures, which means that only very rarely would hardrocks be leased competitively. Prospectors and small miners would not be shut out. They would, as is now the case for almost all leases of non-hardrock minerals (other than coal and oil shale, the locations of which are known), receive leases on a first-come, first-served basis, exactly as occurs under the Mining Law, but without needless location and "discovery" work, and with much more secure tenure for exploration. (OTA pp. 108-112, 116-124.) It should also be noted that the greatly increased expense and sophistication of modern exploration has reduced the role of the individual prospector as a significant source of discoveries. (OTA pp. 49-52, 67-75.)

Third, the transition from the claim/patent to the leasing system could be accomplished as easily as it was in 1920 when the non-hardrocks were converted from the claim/patent to the leasing system: all valid claims would simply be converted to prospecting permits or leases.

Fourth, administration of hardrock mining under the Mining Law provides many more opportunities for litigation than under the leasing laws -- e.g., lode versus placer, location requirements, extralateral rights, millsites, pedis possessio, assessment work, discovery of a valuable mineral deposit on each twenty-acre claim, and so forth. (OTA pp. 116-134.) Finally, given all these archaic provisions in the Mining Law, plus the presence of environmental challenges similar to those under the leasing laws, it is extremely doubtful that a properly enforced Mining Law would involve less administrative costs than a leasing system.

Certain features of the current leasing systems are not as centrally important as some people in industry and the environmental community would have us believe. For example, a leasing system need not require payment of royalties on the value of the mineral produced. From the standpoint of the federal taxpayer, such payments are a bogus issue, since they almost all are turned over to the western states rather than to the general treasury. Moreover, the western states can and do take care of themselves through severance, property and sales taxes. (OTA pp. 260-282.) Much more important than royalties are rentals to cover the unavoidable "opportunity costs" associated with damage to or preclusion of nonmineral resource values and activities as a result of mineral operations. (Royalties comparable to those on state and private lands might be needed to avoid making the federal lands artificially attractive.) (OTA pp. 147-150.)

One last issue with respect to which fiction is often substituted for fact concerns the extent and significance of withdrawals of federal land from mining. The important question is not how much total land is withdrawn, but rather what are the reasons for each particular withdrawal and are the reasons sound in each case? But much mileage has been given to claims that two-thirds of the federal land is closed or "locked up" to mineral activity. These claims stem from Bennethum and Lee's article "Is Our Account Overdrawn?" in the September 1975 issue of the Mining Congress Journal. That article, although useful in focusing attention on the withdrawal issue, contained many significant flaws. It treated land as closed which was actually open with slight or moderate

restrictions.   It used incorrect acreage figures and
double-counted.   It failed to separate out the effects
of the massive but temporary land selection process in
Alaska.   It treated land as closed to mineral activity
simply   because   it was not available under the Mining
Law, even though it was available under   some   special
leasing law or from a state or the Alaskan natives.

The   OTA   study   carefully   compiled   and   cross-
checked   all   the   available data to correct for these
and other flaws in other analyses,   and   the   analysis
was   fully   explained   in   a lengthy appendix (OTA pp.
331-369).   Authors of   the   other   withdrawal   studies
agree   that   the OTA analysis is the most thorough and
accurate.   Unfortunately, however,   the   OTA   analysis
itself   is   often   misquoted   and   misunderstood.   A
common example is the reference   and   table   in   Bruce
Netschert's paper, which is taken from a Department of
the Interior publication.   The table cites OTA figures
from   an   early draft, rather than the final corrected
figures in the official published   report.   It   also
states that OTA included Indian reservations as federal land; OTA did not.   It   states   that   OTA   included
federal   acquired   lands   in   the closed category, but
this is true only with respect to the Mining Law.   OTA
noted   correctly   that   hardrock   minerals on much acquired land are available through leases, although not
under the Mining Law.

The figures from the final OTA report were:

	Formally closed	Highly restricted	Moderately or slightly restricted
Due to usual actions	16%	6%	44%
Due to Alaska land selections	18%	--	16%
Total	34%	6%	60%

These   figures   were   for the availability of hardrock
minerals in federal land from   any   source,   not   just
under   the   Mining   Law, in 1975.   They show that less
than one-fourth of the federal land was unavailable or
highly   restricted   for   hardrock   mineral   activity in
1975 because of usual types of   land   withdrawal   actions.   The percentage rose to forty percent when the
withdrawals related to the massive but temporary   land
selection   process   in   Alaska were included.   (OTA p.
217.)

In testimony before Congress in 1980, I estimated
that the total amount of federal land   unavailable   or
highly   restricted for hardrock mineral activity might

have risen by then to forty-five to fifty percent
since the Alaska land withdrawals were still in effect
and the RARE II and BLM wilderness review programs
were underway (although substantial amounts of acreage
in both programs had already been released). I also
estimated that the percentage would drop to thirty-
three percent or less when these programs were
completed. (Hearings on H.R. 2743 Before the Subcommittee on Energy Resources and Materials Production of
the Senate Committee on Energy and Natural Resources,
July 29 & 31, 1980, pp. 153-169.) I believe these
estimates are still fairly accurate, and that we have
moved down to or below thirty-three percent as the
Alaska land selections and the RARE II and BLM wilderness review programs have wound down in the last
several years. Although there has not been any new,
thorough analysis of the hardrock situation, that
situation probably is comparable to the oil and gas
situation. For the latter, a new analysis, similar in
approach to the OTA study, recently has been completed
by an industry-environmental task force brought
together by the Scientists' Institute for Public
Information (SIPI).

The SIPI task force, on which I served, estimated
the availability of federal onshore land for oil and
gas leasing, drilling and production in 1981 to have
been:

	Closed	Rarely leased	Varying leasing policy	Open with varying mitigation conditions
Alaska	35%	28%	3%	34%
Lower 48	7%	11%	12%	70%
Total Onshore	16%	16%	9%	58%

The task force also estimated the percentages of
federal undiscovered recoverable oil and gas resources
affected, which is of course more relevant than the
percentages of land affected. We found that most of
the closed or rarely leased land in onshore Alaska is
thought to have very little oil and gas potential.
Over ninety percent of the undiscovered recoverable
resources in federal land in onshore Alaska is thought
be in the National Petroleum Reserve, which is being
leased, and the coastal plain of the Arctic National
Wildlife Refuge, which will be available for geophysical exploration in 1983. A congressional decision on
possible development is due in 1988. In the lower

forty-eight states, most of the federal land with good oil and gas potential has been leased (120 to 130 million acres). This includes almost all of the federal land in the western Overthrust Belt below Montana. About eighty to ninety-five percent of the RARE II and BLM wilderness study areas with significant oil and gas potential have been made available for leasing and actual activity. The data indicate that, at least with respect to oil and gas, there has been no lockup of the resources in federal land.

Of course, the picture for the hardrock minerals is much less clear. But it bears repeating that the significant question is not the aggregate availability of federal land or resources, but the reasonableness of individual withdrawal actions. Given the role of the federal lands as a treasure house of nationally and internationally significant surface resources, and the inability to protect those resources adequately on any tract of land that is open to activities under the Mining Law, withdrawal may often be the only reasonable option.

The situation looks like that which occurred during the first two decades of this century. At that time increasing amounts of land being withdrawn from mineral entry forced a reappraisal of the federal mining laws that eventually resulted in the adoption of a leasing system for the fuel and fertilizer minerals. Withdrawals were made then due to concerns about competition, mineral conservation and a fair return to the government. Today's concerns are protection of and compensation for the nonmineral resources affected by mining on federal land. As before, it is unlikely that the "withdrawal problem" will be resolved until the underlying concerns are resolved by major modifications or replacement of the Mining Law itself. (OTA pp. 79-99, 215-220.)

Part 4

Rangeland Issues

7
The Distribution of Benefits and Costs Associated with Public Rangelands

William E. Martin

Abstract: The paper begins with a description of the western rangeland resource, its place in the national and regional economies and its contribution to meat production and outdoor recreation. The specific costs and returns of federal management of the range are presented, and set in the context of the larger federal budget. Rangeland privatization is analyzed relative to the national debt, economic efficiency, and the distribution of benefits and losses. The author concludes that neither the issue of economic efficiency nor welfare distribution is as simple as many proponents of privatization have maintained. A management system much like the current system is suggested.

Key words: economic efficiency, welfare distribution, livestock production, privatization, recreation.

INTRODUCTION

The effects of any economic policy may be examined within the context of economic efficiency and welfare distribution. Economic efficiency focuses on how to generate the largest quantity of net benefits from a given set of resources, regardless of who receives the benefits. Welfare distribution concerns questions of who gets the benefits and who pays the costs whether or not total net benefits are maximized. Almost any policy will benefit some people only at the expense of others, and it is rarely clear whether a social welfare gain has been achieved.

William E. Martin is professor of agricultural economics at the University of Arizona, Tucson.

In this paper, these issues of efficiency and distribution are discussed in the context of U.S. public rangeland policy.

THE RANGELANDS

The federal government owns forty-eight percent of the land in the eleven contiguous western states, not including trust properties (Figure 7.1). In Alaska, ninety-six percent of the land is federally owned, but Alaska is excluded from this discussion because it is a different case. It is the eleven contiguous western states that have the history of providing grazing and recreational opportunities, and have the history of management by the Bureau of Land Management (BLM) and the U.S. Forest Service (USFS). These also are the states where the Sagebrush Rebellion erupted and the states targeted by current range privatization proposals.

A lesser quantity of federal land is used for range. Grazing is allowed on most lands managed by the BLM and the USFS. These are the lands under discussion in this paper. In the eleven western states, Bureau of Land Management lands total 171.9 million acres or twenty-three percent of the total area. The U.S. Forest Service manages 135.3 million acres or eighteen percent of the total area. Thus, this paper considers 307.2 million acres or forty-one percent of the area of the eleven western states (Table 7.1).

Use and Value for Grazing Livestock

Estimates of the quantity of forage consumed by livestock on BLM and USFS ranges are give in Table 7.2 for the years 1935, 1966, and 1972. Examination of more recent statistics for the BLM and USFS for 1980 suggests that current use has declined to about sixteen million Animal Unit Months (AUMs), but it is not clear that the data are comparable (USDI, 1981; USFS, 1981). While annual forage consumed has declined over time, the percent provided by the BLM and the Forest Service has remained almost constant. Of the BLM AUMs, about eighty-two percent were for cattle, 17.5 percent for sheep, and goats, and 0.5 percent for horses, burros and mules (USDI, 1981). Thus, a current consumption estimate of about 1.1 million Animal Unit Years (AUYs) of cattle production on BLM and Forest Service lands might be reasonable. But what does any given quantity of forage mean to those of us making policy decisions? The quantity of forage consumed must be converted to some marketable

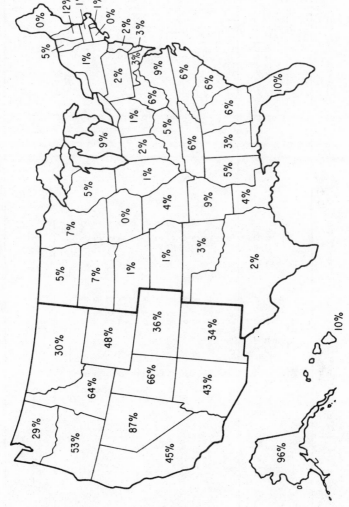

Figure 7.1: Percentage of Land by State in Federal Ownership or Control

Table 7.1: Bureau of Land Management and Forest Service Lands in Eleven Western States

States	Land Area				Share of Total State		
	BLM	Forest Service	All Federal	Total State	BLM	Forest Service	All Federal
	(million Acres)				(percent)		
Arizona	12.6	11.4	31.9	72.7	17	16	44
California	15.6	19.7	45.1	100.2	16	20	45
Colorado	8.3	13.7	20.0	66.5	12	21	36
Idaho	11.9	19.9	33.7	52.9	22	38	64
Montana	6.3	16.7	27.7	93.3	7	18	30
Nevada	48.4	5.1	60.8	70.3	69	7	87
New Mexico	12.7	8.7	26.1	77.8	16	11	34
Oregon	15.7	14.6	32.2	61.6	25	24	52
Utah	22.6	7.8	34.9	52.7	43	15	66
Washington	0.3	8.8	12.6	42.7	1	21	29
Wyoming	17.5	8.9	29.9	62.3	28	14	48
Total	171.9	135.3	358.9	753.1	23	18	48

SOURCE: Nelson (1981).

Table 7.2: Animal Unit Months of Forage Consumed by
            Livestock on Bureau of Land Management and
            Forest Service Rangeland

	BLM	USFS	TOTAL	Percent BLM	Percent USFS
	--------1,000 AUMS----------				
1935	21,648	11,925	33,573	64	36
1966	13,275	7,989	21,264	62	38
1972	11,999	6,390	18,308	65	35

SOURCE: Nelson (1980, p. 20)

consumer good in order to make any judgment about its
usefulness to people. An estimate of beef production
would be more useful.

The total beef calf crop in the eleven western
states in 1981 was 6,872,000 head or 19.8 percent of
the total U.S. beef calf crop (Table 7.3). Western
beef calves are produced on state and private lands as
well as on public lands, so in Arizona nineteen
percent of the AUMs are from BLM lands, thirty-four
percent from USFS lands, thirty-seven percent from
state lands and ten percent from private lands. The
federal portion totals fifty-three percent (Mayes,
1982). Thus, as a rough estimate, perhaps about ten
percent of U.S. feeder beef calves come from the
public range. Of course, in some areas the public
range is supplemental to private lands during particular times of the year, so because of its crucial
importance at that particular time more than ten percent of the calves would rely on the public range
during some part of the year. On the other hand,
total U.S. beef output includes other livestock (such
as dairy calves), and western beef calves are only
fifteen percent of the total calf crop. Therefore,
the estimate of ten percent of U.S. beef output originating on the western public ranges might still be a
good compromise estimate.

One of the crucial issues in range policy is
whether permitted use on the ranges should be reduced
in order to prevent range deterioration and to bring
about future range improvement. Obviously livestock
producers have a personal interest in this policy, but
the aggregate impact on consumers could be much larger
(Martin, 1981). The impact on consumers may be
thought of either as the maximum amount that they
would be willing to pay to avoid increasing beef

Table 7.3:   Total Calf Crop, 1981.

	Beef Calf Crop		Total Calf Crop	
	1,000 head	percent	1,000 head	percent
Arizona	222	0.6	280	0.6
California	894	2.6	1,710	3.8
Colorado	841	2.4	900	2.0
Idaho	606	1.7	750	1.7
Montana	1,549	4.5	1,580	3.5
Nevada	277	0.8	290	0.6
New Mexico	551	1.6	600	1.3
Oregon	645	1.9	730	1.6
Utah	304	0.9	375	0.8
Washington	345	1.0	530	1.2
Wyoming	638	1.8	650	1.5
Eleven Western States	6,872	19.8	8,395	18.8
Rest of U.S.	27,894	80.2	36,319	81.2
TOTAL	34,766	100.0	44,714	100.0

SOURCE: Western Livestock Marketing Information
Project (1982).

prices resulting from less beef on the range, or the minimum amount that would compensate them for that same price increase. What percent reduction in calf production might occur in the eleven western states from permit reductions aimed at improving the range? The 1980 Resources Planning Act Assessment (USFS, 1980) estimates that forty-six percent of the ranges in the eleven western states are in good or fair condition. Thus about fifty-four percent of the range may need improvement. These ranges would not be producing fifty-four percent of the calves. Perhaps they are producing thirty to thirty-five percent. Permits on these ranges will be reduced but not eliminated. Assume they are reduced by as much as fifty percent (University of Nevada, 1980) creating a fifteen to eighteen percent drop in western range calves. The implied annual per capita loss to consumers would be in the range of $10.00 to $11.00 in 1982 prices.

One must conclude that public range improvement policy is not a crucial economic issue to the individual consumer. To the extent the consumers support such a policy, the motive must be a love of grass -- good and excellent range simply looks better. On the other hand, the public could afford to pay as much as $11.00 per capita per year as an investment in range improvement in order to avoid increases in beef prices. That would come to an aggregate amount of over $2 billion per year.

Use and Value for Recreation and Wildlife

A great deal of effort has been expended in the past decade in developing estimates of value for the outdoor recreation experience. Since recreation is not a market good, special techniques have been developed to obtain an equivalent market price (for example see Gum and Martin, 1975). While the effort to estimate experience values has been relatively successful, there remains the question of how to relate the value of a recreational experience (value of a trip or a recreational day) to the value of the wildlife itself or to the productivity of the range resource. Does more wildlife and/or better range provide a higher valued experience? And what is the production relationship between livestock and wildlife? Presumably there may be some complementary relationship between cattle and wildlife over some range of use (e.g., the development of water for cattle benefits wildlife), but in cases where the range may be overgrazed we would expect cattle and wildlife to be competitive. However, as with the technical data on range improvement production functions in general, data on the trade offs between domestic animals and wildlife do not exist.

Still, if one believes that poorer ranges produce less wildlife, that more wildlife is preferred to less wildlife by recreationists, and that overgrazing by domestic animals is a cause of poorer ranges, it is possible to develop some rough estimates of outdoor recreationists' economic interest in range policy.

Martin, Tinney and Gum (1978) estimated that all hunting activities on Arizona forest and rangelands generated $34.4 million of value to consumers in 1970. This estimate compared to $178.3 million of value to consumers generated by beef production on the same lands. If all access to hunters were eliminated, $34.4 million of value would be lost. But since the loss would occur only to Arizona hunters, rather than to the total U.S. population as would be the case for a decrease in beef, the average annual per capita loss of hunters was estimated as $195 per year. Richards (1980) has estimated losses of similar magnitudes for nonconsumptive users (birdwatchers). In 1982 prices, this potential annual per capita loss in consumer benefits becomes nearly $500.

The hunting population in Arizona is about ten percent of the total population and twenty-two percent of all households (Gum, et al., 1973), a significant segment of the regional population. If an investment to avoid range deterioration was required to maintain a hunting experience of equal quality to their current experience, or simply to retain access to the range, perhaps an average willingness to pay off half of their hunting value of $250 per hunter would not be unreasonable. In the aggregate, $250 per hunter would be an enormous investment. If, as in Arizona, ten percent of the population of the eleven western states are hunters, 3.92 million hunters are implied for a total potential annual investment of $980 million. Since we are speaking of range improvement of about fifteen percent of total western AUYs, the annual value of an additional AUY would be about $1,050 for hunters. Further, this is the value for only hunters. The values for other recreationists and wildlife enthusiasts are in addition.

The Public Interest

Ranchers produce livestock on the rangelands in order to produce a living. The BLM issues grazing permits to approximately 22,000 livestock operators (USDI, 1982). The Forest Service has 16,000 permittees in the U.S. but only 13,000 in the eleven western states (USFS, 1981). Even if there were no overlap between BLM and FS permittees, the total number of permittees on both BLM and forest lands in the west is not more than 38,000 families.[2] It is these 38,000 or fewer families that traditionally have most influenced public range policy. Clearly, they do have good personal reasons to do so.

Yet, as shown by the estimates of consumer benefits given above, the population at large has more to gain or lose from range policy than does the ranching community itself. Every individual consumer of beef could gain or lose an average $10 to $11 per year as a result of recently suggested range improvement policy. The aggregate value is over $2 billion per year. Individual hunters could lose an average of $500 per year if access to the land was lost. Other recreationists and wildlife enthusiasts would have losses of similar magnitudes. Conversely, benefit values of these magnitudes illustrate how much recreationists might pay for the privilege of access if they were required to do so.

COSTS AND RETURNS FROM PUBLIC RANGELAND MANAGEMENT

The values of the rangelands to consumers of livestock and recreation have had little relationship to the costs and returns generated from either the public or the private management of the lands. Generally the costs to recreationalists have been much less than the public costs of management for recreation. But, in fact, consumers of beef also have been subsidized in the sense that livestock ranchers tend to produce such large quantities of beef that beef prices generally remain low. They remain so low that ranchers receive a lower return on their investment than they could obtain in the nonranch economy (Smith and Martin, 1968). Ranchers have tended to be utility maximizers rather than profit maximizers. Ironically, the ranchers, who receive a subsidy from the public through grazing fees lower than the market value for grazing land, have capitalized the value of that subsidy into high ranch sale prices. Thus, during the period of ranch operation, they are no better off than if no subsidy existed. Of course, upon sale of the ranch, the seller will capture any capital gains.

But what of the measurable costs and returns to the federal government resulting from public management of the range? Nelson (1979) developed a detailed analysis of the 1978 revenues and costs of public land management by the Interior Department in thirteen western states, classified by type of commodity.[3] The rangelands of the Forest Service are not included, but the analysis provides a basis for comparing relative

magnitudes of cost and return categories for the
rangeland portions of public lands.
   In 1978 the BLM spent $91.4 million on rangeland
forage production (direct and indirect cost) and
received $16.2 million in revenues. BLM expenditures
on recreation and wildlife on rangelands (excluding
the National Wildlife Refuge System and the National
Park System) were $61.1 million and receipts were
$400,000.
   Nelson (1979, p. 10) comments: "Based on recent
typical forage allocations, more than 75 percent of
available public land forage is presently being used
by domestic livestock and the remainder either used by
wildlife or not directly consumed. Domestic livestock
production thus receives substantial public support at
present." I would note, that if this public support
is, in fact, marginally increasing forage for either
livestock or wildlife use, it is well worth the expenditure as shown in the earlier section of beef and
recreation values. The question, of course, is
whether the subsidy really is doing so. As Nelson
(1980, p. 77) comments in another Department of
Interior Office of Policy Analysis paper, while discussing the bureau's rangeland management program,
"The... basic problem is an absence of any true scientific agreement under the current state of scientific
knowledge."
   Total BLM costs were $512.7 million in 1978. Of
this, rangeland forage production and recreation costs
came to $152.5 million or thirty percent. Revenues
from forage production and recreation were $16.6 mil-
lion, or only 2.6 percent of the total $638.4 million.
Because of revenues on timber, oil and gas, and mineral lands, total revenues of the BLM exceed costs by
$147.4 million.
   The 1978 estimates of Nelson (1979) are presented
because he was able to allocate indirect costs to each
direct output. He noted that grazing fees would be
increased significantly from 1978 levels under the fee
formula contained in the Public Rangeland Improvement
Act of 1978. However, the resulting increased
revenues would likely be more than equalled by added
costs for range improvements mandated by the act and
by required environmental impact statements. The
total 1982 BLM budget has risen to $1.2 billion, 2.3
times that of 1978 (USDI, 1982), but is it not clear
exactly how much is related to rangelands. Decreases
in expenditures on range improvements relative to
recent years are planned, with the responsibility for
maintenance of the improvements being transferred to
the livestock permittees (USDI, 1982, p. 53). While
total revenues exceed total costs, and grazing fees
have risen by about a factor of 1.7, revenues from

forage still remain substantially below forage production and management costs. Increases in BLM
recreation fees are proposed for the 1983 budget, but
revenues would increase only from $.3 million in 1982
to $.9 million in 1983 (USDI, 1982 p. 10).

As an overall point of reference, 1978 rangeland
costs for both forage and recreation of $152 million
were 0.03 percent of total government outlays of $451
billion and 0.3 percent of the 1978 deficit of $48.8
billion (SDC, 1981 p. 258). The total BLM budget for
fiscal 1982 -- $1.2 billion -- was 0.16 percent of
total government spending of $728.4 billion and 1.1
percent of the 1982 deficit of $110.7 billion (Arizona
Daily Star, 1982).

PRIVATIZATION OF THE RANGES

Virtually no one is satisfied with current public
management of the rangelands. Ranchers do not like
bureaucratic interference on what they perceive to be
their lands. Others claim that public lands have been
mismanaged so that range forage conditions have deteriorated. Recreationalists often feel that ranchers
receive priority. Finally, there is a current movement to get the government out of the land management
business and "privatize" the range. This movement
seems to be based on two premises. The first is that
the sale of government property could be used to
reduce the national debt. The second is based on the
ideological belief that private ownership and enterprise inherently is more efficient than government
ownership, with the additional unstated premise that
economic efficiency, without regard to distribution,
is the proper goal of any society.

Steve Hanke, recently on the President's Council
of Economic Advisors, has been a leading proponent of
privatization of public lands, particularly the rangelands. The following quotes from Hanke give the
privatization arguments:

> Balzac, the remarkable nineteenth-
> century French author, finished writing
> The Village Curate in 1845. It contains
> the following passage: "Many lands, which
> could feed entire villages and be immense-
> ly productive, are publicly owned by
> towns. They refuse to sell these lands to
> private owners, in order to preserve their
> right to allow some 100 cows to graze. On
> all these public lands is carved one word:
> incompetence."

In that one word, <u>incompetence</u>, the author characterized the management and use of publicly owned resources. Pertaining to that subject, he observed and studied two general laws: (1) public ownership necessarily leads to an unproductive and inefficient use of resources; and (2) private ownership is a necessary condition for the productive and efficient use of resources.

What makes these laws general? The answer is quite simple. Private property rights make the individual property owner solely responsible for the consequences of his decisions. This gives the owner an incentive to use his property in a productive and efficient manner. On the other hand, with public ownership, politicians and bureaucrats are never directly and solely responsible for the consequences of their decisions.

A property owner, in order to reap financial rewards must successfully anticipate the wishes of consumers and satisfy them in an efficient manner. If he is unsuccessful in accomplishing these tasks, he will be penalized by losses. This process which includes information feedback to property owners, provides an incentive for good performance. Moreover, it provides a mechanism that reallocates property to those who are most competent to satisfy consumers' wants efficiently.

As for bureaucrats and politicians, the market's rewards and penalties are irrelevant. They do not face incentives that foster good performance. The results are clear: publicly owned resources are not used to accommodate consumers' wants efficiently, and public resources are not reallocated to those who are most competent to satisfy the wishes of consumers (Hanke, March, 1982).

In another articles in the same journal, Hanke argues by quoting Adam Smith.

In every great monarchy of Europe the sale of the crown lands would provide a very large sum of money, which if applied to the payment of the public debts, would deliver from mortgage a much greater revenue than any which those lands have

> ever afforded the crown .... When the
> crown lands had become private property,
> they would, in the course of a few years,
> become well-improved and well cultivated
> .... It would, in all cases, be for the
> interest of society to ... divide the
> lands among the people, which could not
> well be done better, perhaps, than by
> exposing them to public sale (Hanke, July
> 1982).

Both quotations give the impression that if these publicly owned lands were transferred to private ownership, their productivity would be increased enormously, possibly by changing to intensive crop agriculture. One also gets the impression that Hanke has not seen these lands, although clearly other writers of his persuasion, such as Baden and Stroup (1982) of Montana State University, must have viewed the property.

These lands are used for grazing livestock because they are not suited for intensive crop production. If the great majority of this surface estate was not used for livestock it would not be used at all, except for recreation. It is possible that individual ranchers would manage the lands in a more productive manner under private ownership but that outcome is not guaranteed. The scientific basis of range management is not developed sufficiently for either public management agencies or private individuals to know with certainty what is the "proper" action (Nelson, 1980, p. 77). But in any case, private individuals would continue to produce livestock on these lands, and regardless of whether they would reduce or increase livestock production in response to market signals, the change in output would be a marginal small percent of total U.S. livestock output.

Reducing the National Debt

Since the surface of most rangeland is suitable only for livestock production or recreation, most of the ranges would be sold for livestock production. Since much of the public land is intermingled with private land and is already an integral part of the ranchers' operations, the land would be of use only to current ranchers or those wishing to buy the whole ranch.[4] Total Animal Unit Years (AUYs) of forage on public ranges are less than 1.5 million. My estimate is about 1.3 million. At $1,000 per animal unit, the total one-time sale value would be between $1.3 and

$1.5 billion. The latter amount has been quoted by Hanke and others as a reasonable expectation for the government.
Ranches do sell for $1,000 or more per AUY, though rationally an investor could not afford to pay that amount for the purposes of making money by raising livestock. But that sale price is with a restricted supply -- not with all public land available on the market. Further, the $1,000 or more is for the capitalized value of the land in excess of the annual grazing fee. Thus, the current ranchers already have partially paid for these public lands and could not afford to do so all over again.[5] Hanke (July 1982, p. 44) suggests charging for "only that portion of the grazing pursuit that has not already been paid for through premiums for private land." My colleagues and I have examined ranch sale prices and found that typically this portion of the ranch price has been about twenty to thirty percent of the sale price actually paid (Martin and Jefferies, 1966). Therefore, I would estimate the maximum value of the uncapitalized portion of the grazing permits at closer to $530 million. This amount would not go far toward retiring the national debt.[6]
The other monetary value to the federal government from selling public lands would be reducing the annual costs of management. These costs were estimated as $152.5 million for both forage and recreation production in 1978. However, that estimate included indirect costs which clearly would not be reduced in direct proportion to the reduction in property. In fact, it is reasonable to assume that management costs of sales could keep annual costs at current rates for many years to come.

Economic Efficiency and Private Ownership

The second premise behind privatization is the belief that private ownership and enterprise inherently is more efficient than government ownership. The argument, and it is a good one, is that if an owner has to take the final financial consequences of his decisions, he will attempt to use his resources in an economically efficient manner. But there are at least two problems with this argument. First, the concept of economic efficiency is prescriptive, not positive. Second, the concept says nothing about the distribution of gains created by "economically efficient" management.

Prescriptive versus Positive Knowledge. Prescriptive knowledge is about how one should act if

they wish to achieve some goal. The goal of an
economically efficient firm is to maximize profit.
Positive knowledge is about what is, not what should
be. Advocates of privatization basically argue that
ranchers would act in an economically efficient manner
under conditions of private ownership. Further, since
it can be shown that -- under certain restrictive conditions of pure competition -- firms operating in an
economically efficient manner will enlarge the total
quantity of goods produced relative to resource cost,
then private ownership is "good" -- a normative
judgment.

But there is no evidence that ranchers do or
would act in an economically efficient manner. In
fact, the evidence is just the opposite. Smith and
Martin (1972) found that ranchers' behavior was based
as much on cultural values as on economics. Ranchers
ranch because they like to, the ranch is as much a
consumption good as it is a productive firm, and the
ranchers often work at another job, or must have
outside income, in order to support a low-return
enterprise.

Further, while livestock production approaches
the competitive model on the output market side, it
would be hard to argue that the limited range resource
allows free entry and exit -- a necessary condition
for a fully competitive economic equilibrium.

The Problem of Distribution. To argue that public ranges should be sold to the highest bidder, one
must also argue that the initial distribution of income and relative prices is socially acceptable. Free
market solutions will always capitulate to effective
demand, and effective demand is governed by income
distribution and relative prices. To say that the
free market solution is better than any other solution
is an ethical judgment, not a positive fact.

It has been suggested that ranchers who currently
hold the grazing permits on the public rangeland be
given first refusal to buy. In my opinion, most
ranchers would be unable to buy at any price acceptable to the general public. As Gray (1979, p. 58)
documented for New Mexico ranches, "The investment per
animal unit is astronomical and bears no relationship
to income regardless of ranch size ... ranches are
carrying a heavy burden of debt in total dollars ...
interest and principal payments ... alone are about a
third of total operating costs on ranches." Gray
figures that a calf price of about $1.40 per pound
would be required to repay current debt, operating
costs, and give a return to labor and management.
Under these conditions, ranchers might be able to pay
the capitalized value of the current grazing fee, if

the fee were capitalized at the current rate of interest on borrowed money. As an example, $2.30 per AUM times twelve months capitalized at twelve percent equals $230. But if the land sale is to raise a billion or more dollars, the ranchers themselves certainly could not afford to buy.

It has been suggested that recreationalists and environmentally-minded groups purchase the lands in which they are interested. I see no effective demand from these groups either -- certainly not for more than a small fraction of the land. In fact, we can be almost certain that effective demand would not be generated regardless of the potential total aggregate value, because, "...rational self-interested individuals will not act to achieve their common or group interest" (Olson, 1965, p. 2).

We are left, then, with those individuals or corporations of great wealth who can afford to hold a low yielding property for speculative purposes. Privatization may be efficient, but the question is for whose welfare?

A CONCEPTUAL ANALYSIS OF THE DISTRIBUTION OF BENEFITS AND LOSSES

The major rangeland issues come down to: (1) should forage production be managed privately or by the public? and (2) would private ownership and management of the land provide adequate access to quality recreational experiences? Since the marginal change in beef production is likely to be minimal under either public or private management, both issues are most important to recreationalists and wildlife enthusiasts. Will forage be provided for wildlife and will access to the areas by provided?

Recreation and Wildlife

The demand for access by recreationalists to any given area is a downward sloping curve D (Figure 7.2). Each area is different from the other, and is spacially separated from its potential consumers. Persons will visit more only at a lower cost.

The marginal cost of providing for an additional recreational opportunity is MC and the average cost per visit is AC. Under public ownership, the government pays these marginal and average costs. Costs would be almost zero if only a limited number of visits occurred, but eventually rise as more and more recreational opportunities are provided. Currently, minimal recreational fees are charged so returns to

Figure 7.2: Demand and Supply of Rangeland Recreation

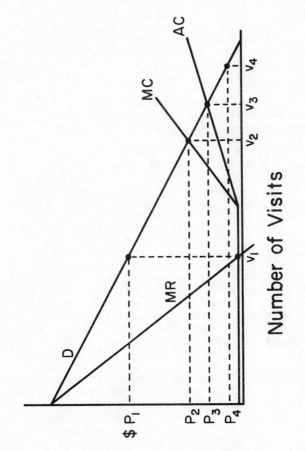

the government are below recreational management
costs. This situation is represented by fee p_4 and the
number of visits, v_4.

Now assume that this area is privately owned.
Further, assume that the private variable costs of
providing recreation are about the same as are the
public variable costs. Access may be controlled by
the owner. Assume that the owner is operating in an
economically efficient manner, as the advocates of
privatization assert they should and will. Under
these conditions, the private owner would equate the
marginal revenue (MR) to the marginal cost (MC),
charging p_1 per visit and causing only v_1 visits to be
taken. It would clearly be in the owners' rational
self interest to severely restrict recreational opportunities. In fact, if the demand curve for any
given area is linear, as drawn in Figure 7.2, and if
marginal costs are close to zero over a significant
range of use, as hypothesized, recreational use would
be cut nearly in half.

If the private owner is a rancher, and is a
utility maximizer rather than a profit maximizer, as I
hypothesize the majority of ranchers are, the owner
would be willing to accept a smaller net revenue,
setting even a higher price or limiting access altogether.

It is just as clear that the current public
solution of low prices and high visits is not an
economically rational solution from the government's
(public's) point of view. The government has no need
to maximize net revenues, but could argue that additional recreation should be worth its marginal cost to
create. This is the standard solution proposed by
economists for providing public services. An example
is the pricing of municipal water. Hanke (1978), an
advocate of privatization, has been a leading proponent of this solution in that context. To charge
less than the marginal cost is to subsidize services
for which the public would otherwise by unwilling to
pay. Thus, the rational public solution would be
price p_2, limiting visits to v_2.

Because the marginal cost solution does create
positive net revenues, the typical public solution to
providing services is simply to try to break even.
Under this solution, services are priced at their
average costs AC with price p_3 creating visits v_3.
This is a reasonable solution if the public believes
that recreation should be provided to as many people
as possible (that is, if they are interested in equity
for the poor) but wish the program to be
self-supporting.

The cost curves in Figure 7.2 are drawn so that
MC is constant and zero, or close to zero, over a

significant range of visits. I believe this is likely to be true for many rangeland recreation areas. But that specific configuration need not hold for the general analysis to be true. It is a specific case of the general case shown in Figure 7.3.

The demand curve D may be viewed as the marginal social benefit curve of the public. Thus, the optimum solution from the general public's view (accepting the distribution of income and offering no subsidies) would be p^*q^*. By restricting output to qp, net social benefits equal to area A are lost. That would be the private monopoly solution. On the other hand, by increasing output to q_b and using average cost pricing, net social losses of B occur. Marginal costs are greater than marginal social benefits. Under the current situation of pricing below the average cost of production, the net social losses are B plus C.

The difficulty with this general analysis, however, is that achieving marginal cost pricing through a public agency is not a costless activity. Marginal costs include only the variable costs of production. The fixed costs of the bureaucracy that do not vary in response to changed output will be incurred regardless of whether the agency is pricing its output efficiently.

Thus, as with most economic policy decisions, we must face a trade-off between efficiency and equity. If the lands are privately owned, we may expect them to be operated efficiently from the owners' point of view. Social losses will be incurred. These social losses may or may not be larger than the costs of running a public agency, whether or not that agency is run in an economically efficient manner. A strict economic efficiency view would require comparing the value of the net social loss (area A in Figure 7.3) occurring because of privatization with the fixed costs of achieving marginal cost pricing by a public agency. But, then one should ask if the economically efficient solution appears equitable, and what the costs of achieving equity would be? The situation is not as clear as the advocates of privatization make it out to be.

Forage Production for Livestock

In contrast to the demand for recreation, the individual livestock producer faces an infinitely elastic demand (Figure 7.4). One rangeland calf is much like any other calf, and beef is distributed to the consumer at their local supermarket. Thus, the public and private solution would be the same if the marginal cost of production were the same under the

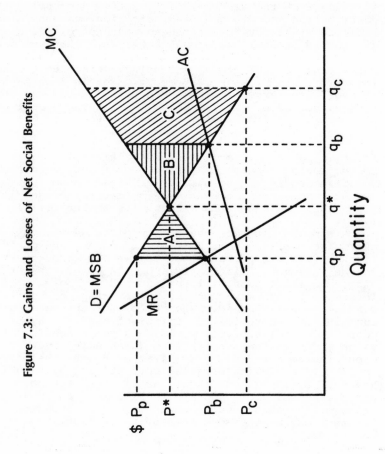

Figure 7.3: Gains and Losses of Net Social Benefits

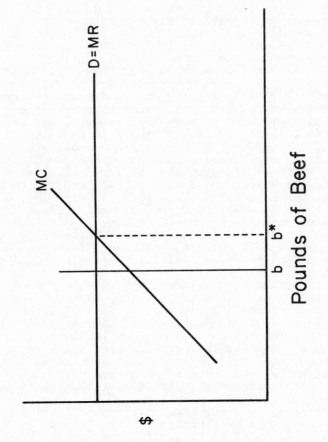

Figure 7.4: Demand for and Supply of Beef at Ranch Level

two conditions. However, under current public ownership and management, much of the range forage
improvement costs have been subsidized by the public.
This subsidy tends to lower the private costs of
production to the ranchers and move the MC curve to
the right, encouraging more production. As a counter
balance, the public agencies then restrict grazing
through the permit system, yielding b quantity of beef
rather than b*. The situation is not economically
efficient and a public bureaucracy is required to
administer the regulations. It is partially for these
reasons that privatization is suggested in order to
internalize all costs.

Advocates of public ownership argue that ranchers
have tended to take a myopic short-run view. They
maintain that by running too many livestock in an
effort to maximize short-run profits, ranchers have
neglected the long-run condition of the range.
Advocates of private ownership reply that ranchers
would not do so if they had security of tenure and
thus a reason to protect their long-run interests.

I tend to believe that the myopic view is almost
forced on ranchers because of the competitive nature
of the beef industry and the very inelastic nature of
aggregate demand for beef. Net profits in the range
livestock industry tend to be very low because a
relatively small increase in total production brings a
large decrease in price. Ranchers get caught in a
cycle of trying to increase short-run production in
order to meet current debt, and this keeps the pressure on beef prices. Privatization would not solve
this dilemma.

In addition, since ranchers sell livestock -- not
wildlife and recreation -- they have no incentive to
maintain and allocate forage for the latter uses. In
some cases, a range that is adequate for livestock
production need not be hospitable for wildlife.
Again, advocates of privatization would argue that if
recreation could be sold, the rancher-owner would look
after that use. But we have seen that this solution
is not necessarily in the interests of the larger
public.

Finally, the strong interest of the aggregate of
consumers in beef production should be reemphasized.
As illustrated in Figure 7.5, because of the inelasti-
city of demand for beef, a small increase or decrease
in the quantity of beef will have large price effects,
creating or destroying large amounts of consumers'
surplus (consumer value), that is, the area p_1abp_2.
The public can well afford to encourage range improvement for the future in order to maintain relatively
low beef prices.

251

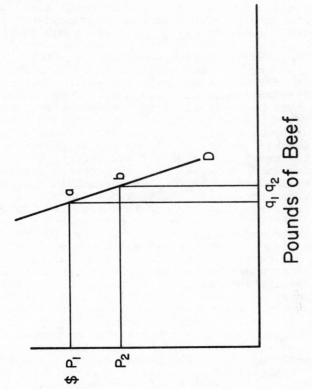

Figure 7.5: Consumer Demand for Beef

STRIKING A BALANCE BETWEEN EFFICIENCY AND EQUITY

Given the very large stake that consumers of recreation have in the western rangelands, and the potential conflict of interest between livestock producers and the recreating public, I must conclude that the rangelands should remain in public ownership. The right of access to a land where a portion of the forage is allocated to wildlife must be maintained. On the other hand, there is little reason why recreationists should not at least pay the average cost of recreation and wildlife development and management. If the public wishes to use the rangelands to develop public income, the marginal cost should be paid. In any case, recreation fees should be instituted and/or raised. Such a policy would increase both efficiency and equity. The public would be more responsive to costs, and equity would be served in the sense that recreational subsidies would be reduced or eliminated.

The basic advantages of private ownership of livestock ranches can be accomplished by guaranteed security of tenure. Ranchers traditionally have had reasonable security of tenure, as proven by the fact that grazing permits have acquired significant capitalized values. But the recent move toward more formalized security of tenure should be applauded. Ranchers basically have a private property right in their grazing permits and that right should continue.

It would be neither efficient nor equitable to increase annual grazing fees by any large amount -- especially not up to the full average value productivity of the forage resource. It would not be equitable since it would reduce the private capitalized value of the ranch, and would, in fact, be taking private property without compensation. A fee at the full average value productivity of the forage would reduce the ranch value almost to zero.⁹

Equity could be accomplished by compensating the rancher for his loss. But efficiency would not be served. The higher the annual rental fee and the lower the capitalized value of the permit, the closer the rancher is to being simply an annual renter. A pure renter clearly has no interest in the long-run value and productivity of a property.

In conclusion, I favor a management system for the western rangelands very much like the system that is in place today. The major change would be increased recreational fees to guarantee continued recreational access to a range of reasonable quality.

NOTES

1. The 1977 USDA and USDI grazing fee study estimates that only four to five percent of total U.S.
livestock feed comes from USFS and BLM lands in the
west. But because the lands are often intermingled
with state and private lands, and are crucial at
certain times of the year, I ascribe their importance
total beef production higher at about ten percent
(USDI-USDA, 1977, p. 3-5).

2. In Arizona, there are 1,755 ranch operations
with a make-up of rangeland partially or entirely
public land (Mayes and Archer, 1982). The number of
livestock ranches in the west is estimated at only
23,971 by the 1969 Census of Agriculture (USDI-USDA,
1977, p. C-25). The number clearly is low, but since
many public permits are for a very small number of
AUMs, it may not be much too low in terms of commercial operating units.

3. North Dakota was included because of extensive
federal mineral rights. Alaska was also included.
Thus, costs and returns attributable to the eleven
western states would be slightly less.

4. Obviously small parcels would be purchased for
real estate development. Recall, however, we are
discussing forty-one percent of all land area in the
west. Further, where lands are intermingled, one
could not expect a public sales policy that would
destroy the integrity of a ranch unit.

5. Ranchers who received their permitted use
free, upon passage of the Taylor Grazing Act, have
suffered an "opportunity cost" of holding land rather
than selling the capitalized value before now.
Further, this capitalized value has in many cases
become collateral to the banks.

6. I find it peculiar that Hanke (July 1982, p.
44) suggests that setting the sale price at the value
of the annual grazing fees capitalized at one percent.
Private individuals cannot borrow money at one percent
even if it is "the real long-term interest rate paid
by the U.S. Treasury." For every percentage point
higher than one percent the total sale value would
decline.

7. I am indebted to Scott Matulich (1982) for a
number of the insights on efficiency versus distribution covered in the preceding section.

8. Mathematically, marginal revenue declines
twice as fast as does average revenue (price).

9. I have equivocated by saying almost since I
believe that part of the ranch price is for
consumption rather than for production reasons. The
conclusion depends on how one interprets the "value of
the forage."

254

BIBLIOGRAPHY

Arizona Daily Star, "$110.7 Billion Federal Deficit Is
    Almost Double Last Year's." Tucson, Arizona,
    October 27, 1982.
Baden, John, and Richard Stroup, members of a panel
    discussion on "Privatizing Public Lands: The
    Ecological and Economic Case for Private Owner-
    ship of Federal Lands," Manhattan Report on
    Economic Policy, Manhattan Institute for Policy
    Research, Vol. II, No. 3, May 1982.
Gray, James R., Opportunities to Improve Rangelands:
    Economic Incentives, Costs and Benefits. Range-
    lands Policies for the Future, Forest Service
    GTR-WO-17, October 1979.
Gum, Russell L. and William E. Martin, "Problems and
    Solutions in Estimating the Demand for and Value
    of Rural Outdoor Recreation," American Journal of
    Agricultural Economics, Vol. 57, No. 4, November
    1975.
Gum, Russell L., William E. Martin, Arthur H. Smith
    and C. Duane Depping, Participation and Expendi-
    tures for Hunting, Fishing and General Rural Out-
    door Recreation in Arizona, Arizona Agricultural
    Experiment Station Research Report No. 270,
    August 1973.
Hanke, Steve H., "Pricing as a Conservation Tool: An
    Economist's Dream Come True?" in David Holtz and
    Scott Sebastion (eds.), Municipal Water Systems,
    Indiana University Press, Bloomington, pp. 221-
    239. 1978.
Hanke, Steve H., "Privatize Those Lands!", Reason,
    March 1982.
Hanke, Steve H., "Grazing for Dollars," Reason, July
    1982.
Martin, William E. and Gene L. Jefferies, "Relating
    Ranch Prices and Grazing Permit Values to Ranch
    Productivity," Journal of Farm Economics, Vol.
    48, No. 2, May 1966.
Martin, William E., "'Mitigating' The Economic Impacts
    of Agency Programs for Public Rangelands," pre-
    sented at the Workshop on Applying Socio-Economic
    Techniques to Range Management Decision-Making,
    sponsored by the National Academy of Science,
    Boise, Idaho, May 11-12, 1981.
Martin, William E., J. Craig Tinney, and Russell L.
    Gum, "A Welfare Economic Analysis of the
    Potential Competition Between Hunting and Cattle
    Ranching," Western Journal of Agricultural Eco-
    nomics, Vol. 3, No. 2, December 1978.
Matulich, Scott C., "The New Political Economy of
    Natural Resources: Discussion." American

Journal of Agricultural Economics, Vol. 65, No. 5, December 1982.

Mayes, Horace M., and Thomas F. Archer, Arizona Cattle Ranches on Public Land," Department of Agricultural Economics, College of Agriculture, University of Arizona, November 1982.

Nelson, Robert H., "An Analysis of 1978 Revenues and Costs of Public Land Management by the Interior Department in 13 Western States." Unpublished paper, Office of Policy Analysis, U.S. Department of the Interior, December 1979.

Nelson, Robert H., "The New Range Wars: Environmentalists versus Cattlemen for the Public Rangelands." Unpublished paper, Economics Staff, Office of Policy Analysis, U.S. Department of the Interior, 1980.

Nelson, Robert H., "Making Sense of the Sagebrush Rebellion: A Long Term Strategy for the Public Lands." Unpublished paper presented at the Third Annual Conference of the Association for Public Policy Analysis and Management, Washington, D.C., October 23-25, 1981.

Olson, Mancur, Jr., The Logic of Collective Action, Harvard University Press, Cambridge, Mass., 1965.

Richards, Merton, "Economic Measure of Non-consumptive Wildlife Values: Implications for Policy Analysis," Unpublished Ph.D. Dissertation, University of Arizona, September 1980.

Smith, Arthur H., and William E. Martin, "Socioeconomic Behavior of Cattle Ranchers, With Implications for Rural Community Development in the West," American Journal of Agricultural Economics, Vol. 54, No. 2, May 1972.

University of Nevada, Division of Agricultural and Resource Economics. Economic Impact of BLM Grazing Allotment Reductions on Humbolt County, Nevada. Report T27, February 1980.

U.S. Department of Commerce, Bureau of the Census, Statistical Abstract of the United States, 1980. U.S. Government Printing Office, Washington, D.C., 1981.

U.S. Departments of the Interior and of Agriculture, Study of Fees for Grazing Livestock on Public Lands. Washington, D.C., October 21, 1977.

U.S. Department of the Interior, Bureau of Land Management, Public Land Statistics, 1980. U.S. Government Printing Office, Washington, D.C., 1981.

U.S. Department of the Interior, Bureau of Land Management, Managing the Nation's Public Lands. January 1982.

U.S. Forest Service. An Assessment of the Forest and Rangeland Situation in the United States. FS-345, January 1980.

U.S. Forest Service, Range Management Staff, Annual
    Grazing Statistical Report; Use Summary 1980.
    Washington, D.C., September 1981.
Western Livestock Marketing Information Project, U.S.
    Cooperative Extension Service and U.S. Department
    of Agriculture, 1982.

Subsidization and Privatization
of Federal Rangeland:
A California Perspective

Bernard Shanks

The perspective from California is fairly interesting and fairly unique. It is often overlooked in the litany of complaints coming out of the west about the federal lands. California is a major public lands state. It has the third largest acreage of federal lands of any state, exceeded only in total acreage by the states of Alaska and Nevada. It also has twenty-four million people. There are two people in California for every person in the other ten western states. So California has twice the congressmen and twice the number of people as all the other western states combined. So the impacts on California's public lands are fairly significant.

I have some doubts about the importance of live-stock grazing on the public lands. For example, Martin used the figure of ten percent of the feeder calves produced on the western public lands. I've seen at different times a figure closer to one or two percent of the total beef production coming off public lands. There is a tendency among western agricultural economists in the land-grant schools to exaggerate the importance of public lands in the production of beef. I've always thought it would be interesting to determine whether completely eliminating beef production off the western lands would affect the price in the supermarket of a pound of hamburger. I have my doubts it would be very significant.

As to recreation receipts off the public lands, Martin's data show that the recreational receipts on BLM lands were quite low. That's true. However, the states capture much of the recreational benefits from hunting. Most of the western states Fish and Game

---

Bernard Shanks was assistant director for resources, State of California.

257

Departments are self-sufficient because hunting and fishing licenses pay for their operation. In that sense, hunters and fishermen tend to pay their own way. Among fish and game people in the west, there is great hostility toward a federal recreation fee.

The availability of water is the biggest issue in the arid west and it's been a major reason for almost a hundred years of concern for watershed. Many communities were severely impacted by overgrazing of sheep in the 1880s and 1890s. They prevailed upon the federal government to acquire private lands to protect the watershed. So the sense of the importance of land and watershed values is much more than an aesthetic sense.

Family ranchers in the west have earned a tremendous windfall profit from public land subsidies. From my political perspective to say that ranchers have a private property right in the grazing permits, and that such a right should continue, is incorrect.

I would like to emphasize that the sale of the arid rangelands would not return much. We're probably talking about a total value much less than one-tenth of one percent of what the public land energy resources are worth. I wonder if the recent concern over privatization isn't like the bomb going off in the village square as the bank is being robbed, because we see the largest transfer of public wealth, in terms of energy resources, to private hands during this administration than we ever have seen before. It is ironic that we have a far greater amount of public wealth going to the private sector now than in the 1870s and 1880s.

But, back to the point. Why not let the ranchers capitalize the rangeland subsidy into the value of the ranch? I have trouble with that. Why don't the public owners have the right to let the market work to their advantage?

Let the market work for the owners of the public lands. Let's end the subsidy of the commodity uses on the public lands. Everything that comes off the public lands that has a dollar value is subsidized to one extent or another - oil, gas, minerals, water, grass, and timber. If the market is going to work more efficiently, it seems only fair to get rid of some of those perversions. Take, for example, the incentive to overgraze on cheap public land instead of private land and the tendency to waste water when you're getting it for $2 an acre/foot out of the Sierra instead of paying its true price of something like $100 an acre/foot. So the market would encourage conservation, it would encourage better use, and it avoids a drastic solution that flies in the face of 100 years of conservation.

I'm astounded that no one here has mentioned that

we really tried privatization for 100 years. Congress
has passed several thousand public land laws. The
first public land law in 1789 was a privatization act.
I might give you a couple of examples from
California. On the California fish and game wildlife
refuges, they handle the livestock grazing in a fairly
simple manner. Late in the winter they hold an
auction. After public notice in the papers, ranchers
gather in a room, and the California Department of
Fish and Game auctions off grazing rights in the
wildlife refuges in that area. This year, even though
the federal grazing fees have gone down three years in
a row, grazing fees went up on the prime grazing land
in California. Some of them were from $25 - $30 an
acre per animal unit month (AUM); some were as high as
$32 an AUM. So I think it's an example of the state
public agency getting a fair market value. Since the
western states receive a share of the federal revenues
from leasing, they are beginning to see in this era of
tight budgets the opportunity for increased revenues
from the sale of resources off of the public lands.
    Another would be oil and gas leases. On state
lands (the first three miles of the tidelands),
California uses a competitive royalty bidding system.
By avoiding the bonus bidding up front that the
federal government has, this encourages the small
producers to get into the market. By using a flexible
royalty scale, instead of one fixed by legislation at
12 1/2 percent - 16 2/3 percent, the public gets a
much greater return. The average royalty on State of
California leases under this system is almost seventy
percent. Some of the bids that came in two and three
years ago were as high as ninety-two percent. That
is, for every dollar's worth of oil coming out of the
ground, ninety-two percent of it went back to the
public. And so it encourages competition, more small
producers, and lets the market work.
    The free market economists, the privateers, have
said that we have inefficiencies that must be corrected by very drastic solutions. On the public lands
in California, we've said they can be corrected in
part by letting the market work for the public. This
is a very practical and realistic solution that
doesn't require imposing an abstract theoretical
framework on a very complex political and cultural
world and a very complex ecological environment.
    I find it interesting that no major politician
has really latched on to the idea of the privatization
of public lands. The last public figure of any
stature to call for this was Herbert Hoover. He
called for it in his speech in Salt Lake City in 1928.
Until we get a major political figure advocating
privatization, I think we'll continue to look for
solutions like those we have turned to in California.

Part 5

Energy Resources Issues

8
Energy Resources, Revenues and the Public Lands

John J. Schanz, Jr.

Abstract: The author catalogs public land issues related to energy goals, alternative land uses, management of exploitation, land reclamation, government interaction, and public participation. Fossil fuel resources and royalties are discussed. Problems associated with "fair market value" and other aspects of energy leasing and management efficiency are also reviewed. Prescriptions for public land leasing adapted to the individual characteristics and institutions of each energy form conclude the paper.

Key words: management efficiency, revenue, energy leasing, fair market value, bidding process.

INTRODUCTION

To deal with the various value judgments held by diverse publics is largely a political decision. Somehow, we must decide incrementally how much public acreage is to be dedicated temporarily or permanently to various land uses which have value to these publics. This can be accomplished both by positive decisions and by default. An intriguing facet of this decision process is that the national publics we serve are both providers and users of these lands. Conflict emerges as the user public seeks to have its individual self-interests served, while the aggregate public ownership demands a mix of uses seeking some sort of societal optimum.

John J. Schanz Jr. is a senior specialist in energy resources, Congressional Research Service, Library of Congress. The views expressed are those of the author and not necessarily those of the Congressional Research Service.

Given this diversity of public values, the consistency of simultaneously serving a public that is
both provider and user, and the dissimilarities among
the possible uses of public land, it is most unlikely
that anybody's perception of the optimal use of the
public lands in the public interest will be perfectly
matched. Yet, we must not allow the futility of
searching for the optimum set of public land decisions
to immobilize us. Avoiding decisions serves the
public interest less well than venturing admittedly
imperfect moves that do achieve some -- if not optimal
-- net public gain. Moreover, whether optimal or not,
our elected and appointed leadership will continue to
face second-guessing of most public land decisions.

A TAXONOMY OF PUBLIC LAND MANAGEMENT DECISIONS

As we deal with such things as efficiency, market
value, or management strategy for the energy resources
located in the on-shore, public lands, the taxonomy of
public management decisions that are involved in the
process should be kept in mind.
1. Establishment of fundamental energy resource goals.
   a. Social objectives in general versus energy in
      particular.
   b. Public revenue objectives in energy resource
      development.
   c. National security considerations.
2. Resolution of the competition among land use alternatives.
   a. Non-exploitative use (preservation of natural
      environments) versus energy development.
   b. Exclusive dedication to energy development.
   c. Energy development versus other non-compatible,
      exploitative uses.
   d. Energy development concurrent or sequential with
      other compatible uses.
3. Provision for access.
   a. Pre-access determination of resource potential.
   b. Determination of criteria and conditions for
      access for exploration.
   c. Nature of, and control of, initial environmental
      impacts.
   d. Establishment of linkage between exploration and
      development rights.
4. Management of exploitation.
   a. Public participation in the development plan-
      ning.
   b. Land requirements in addition to those contain-
      ing the resource to be recovered.
   c. Establishing pace and diligence in development.

d. Continued control and regulation of environmental impact.
e. Resolution of conflicts among governmental agencies or between federal policies.
f. Regional socio-economic consequences.
5. Provision for post-exploration and post-exploitation land reclamation.
a. Establishment of goals and standards.
b. Implementation process.
c. Enforcement mechanisms.
6. Federal/state/local sharing of land management decisions.
a. Appropriate division of responsibility, authority and implementation.
b. Interaction of governmental groups.
c. Interrelationships of federal land management with the other fiscal and land use planning obligations of state and local jurisdictions.
7. Public participation in public land revenues.
a. The most effective level or stage at which the revenue sharing should occur.
b. Manner or form of revenue participation.
c. Achieving economic and operational efficiency in revenue sharing.
d. Equitable participation by developers and the public in the process.
e. Federal/state/local sharing of the revenue streams.
f. Determination of the time profile of revenue.
g. Adaptation of the revenue sharing strategy to economic, geologic, and technologic uncertainty and risk.
h. Adjustment to the speculative interests that may be involved.

Each of these concerns can generate conflict to be resolved by the political, administrative, or judicial process. Once we have decided that under specified circumstances it is socially desirable to exploit the energy found on the public lands, what is at stake and how do we deal with the revenues involved?

ENERGY RESOURCES

The future role of energy resources to be found on on-shore, public lands seems destined to be larger than in the past. Using various industrial and government estimates, my approximation of the proportion of on-shore fossil fuel resources located on the public lands looks something like this:

Energy Resource	On-Shore Government Lands (%)
Undiscovered Crude Oil	35
Undiscovered Natural Gas	30
Remaining Coal Resources	40
Recoverable Shale Oil	80

Unlike uranium, where the public land contribution to current production exceeds the public land proportion of estimated resources, current U.S. production of oil, gas, and coal remains skewed toward the private lands. In 1981, on-shore federally administered lands yielded six percent of U.S. crude production, six percent of natural gas, and fourteen percent of the coal produced annually, well below their resource potential.[1] Shale oil, of course, has no current production.

This picture has been changing gradually over the past twenty years for a variety of reasons. Unlike hard rock deposition of non-fuel minerals, oil and gas are quite frequently found entrapped below flat, accessible terrain in locations which have also attracted human occupation. In the United States, this meant that the readily found, more cheaply producible oil and gas frequently coincided with those lands which were or had become privately owned, although not always heavily populated. It has only been since the depletion and higher prices have been encountered that we have ventured into rugged mountainous terrain, Arctic reaches, or deep waters.

The coal situation is markedly different. Coal has never been readily transportable, so early industrial growth migrated toward regions providing nearby supplies of high BTU or coking quality coals. For many decades, our eastern coal fields provided a happy juxtaposition of people, markets, and coal. But the changing demographics of people and industry, the emergence of strip mining, the improving transportation ability of coal, and the quest for low sulfur coal has begun to change that pattern. As a consequence, the western coal fields, with roughly half of the U.S. coal resources, are emerging as major centers of future production.

Not surprisingly, the early history of public land leasing for gas and particularly coal, drew minimal attention both at the state or national level. More frequently, government had to try to attract and to facilitate the lease process. But the magnitude of current projections for future production, emerging concerns about local impacts, and an expanding flow of revenues have now changed this focus of attention. The increase in revenues has been dramatic in the last decade.

On-Shore Federal Lease Royalties -- 1970 v. 1981
(Millions of Current $s)

	1970	1981
Petroleum	73	605
Natural Gas	18	274
Coal	1	43

Source of Data: U.S. Department of the Interior
publications.

The recent oil and gas revenue increase has had
two components -- a markedly higher price and greater
production levels.   Coal prices were indirectly affected by OPEC actions, and the federal share (which
had been typically a few cents a ton) began to be
increased after amendments to the Coal Leasing Act in
1976.   Even more impressive than the royalty data is
the fact that the combined market value of oil, gas,
and coal sold from on-shore leases has now reached
$8.6 billion. These energy income and royalty shares
no longer are a minor consideration in the public
revenue scheme. Moreover, attention now must be paid
to the question of the kind of monetary return that
might be expected at the front-end of the leasing
process in addition to royalties from subsequent
production.
The larger market returns and royalty shares
have also called attention to another element of the
sharing process. Federal payments to states from oil,
gas, and coal revenues came to $51 million in 1970.
By 1980 this had climbed to $296 million. Now it is
projec̨ted that the total could reach $916 million by
1985.²   These monies have been moving on to counties,
to schools, and into impact assistance.
This revenue stream from the public lands to the
states is separate from that which they can generate
on their own from taxation. In 1980, state severance
taxes on federal land fossil fuel production amounted
to $202 million.   Those states fortunate enough to
have energy resources, particularly federally administered, now find the distributional effects of income
generation being scrutinized. Questions arise as to
whether energy consuming states are unfairly contrib-
uting to the internal fiscal burdens of the exporting
states? Are state revenues inhibiting domestic energy
production? Is the historical sharing of federal
energy revenues by the national community and the
regional community still an equitable arrangement?
What actions are both appropriate as well as feasible,
given the longstanding protection of states rights?

Internally, the federal government has a less
apparent but still real need to examine its management
efficiency. While increasing public land revenues may
appear as a windfall for the government, they are, of
course, not being obtained without cost. Departmental
expenditures by the Bureau of Land Management and the
Forest Service currently are over $2 billion. In
1981, the public land revenues of $1.077 billion were
distributed in this manner: $474 million to the
states, $443 million for costs, and $160 million as
the net federal gain. The fossil fuels provided $714
million, or seventy-three percent, of the total
revenue but only contributed twenty-seven percent of
the cost. This is in contrast to most of the other
public land activities where costs typically exceed
revenues.[3]
So it is apparent that among the many management
concerns about energy on public lands, revenue generation potential and the distribution of those revenues
is becoming an important item. One other dimension is
the determination of what portion of the income that
is derived from the production of energy on the public
lands should be retained by the producer and what
should be diverted to our "landowner" government?

THE FEDERAL PURPOSE

Are we capable of specifying a national goal,
thus providing some stable sense of federal purpose?
Historically, the federal establishment seemed to
expect little "up-front" money and was content to get
what had become the customary royalty payment, if and
when production would occur, plus subsequent tax
revenues. Should we, or are we, collecting royalties
and bonuses comparable to what private and public
landowners would currently expect to get if selling
comparable energy producing properties in an open
market? Or, as the largest single owners of most of
the remaining prime oil and gas targets, the bulk of
western coal, and most of the oil shale lands, is it
now in our overall public interest to slowly and
deliberately parcel out these lands with the intent of
maximizing revenues over time? This latter strategy
requires the federal manager to achieve a careful
balancing of more acreage leased and a lower return
per acre against less acreage and a higher return.
Even if we could settle upon a national public
land energy revenue strategy, we then encounter a
Pandora's box of conceptual, judgmental, and statistical problems. From resource economists, land managers, and legislative staff there is a flow of words --
"economic rent," "fair market value," "due diligence,"
"maximum resource recovery" -- all of which create an

aura of purity, precision, and prudence. Unfortunately as they surface in policies and legislation we are required to interpret their meaning as well as find a practical implementation of the intent.

These seemingly innocuous terms often can become a major hurdle in the way of expeditious development of smooth and efficient resource decision and federal land management. The mining law offers an example. While the intent seemed clear, the "prudent man" test concerning the validity of a claim ultimately had to be supplemented with additional measures, such as "marketability," to further clarify what is prudent.

Whenever legislative language involves quantification, the obstacles can become even more costly and difficult to overcome. The Federal Power Commission staff and many witnesses spent some ten years trying to cope with the determination of the cost of producing natural gas as a basis for price regulation. Eventually it was accepted that the allocation of costs to joint products is an arbitrary, judgmental exercise -- something that seemed apparent from the very beginning.

It appears we must face similar language and numerical disagreements in energy leasing. In a given circumstance it is conceivable that the federal government might attempt to capture as a revenue the difference between the price received for a naturally scarce commodity and what the producer would accept as a reasonably full recovery of his total costs. In theory, this will not alter his desire to acquire and produce these resources. But making such a determination does not hold for all properties or all operators. Moreover, any estimation can be challenged whenever there is no firm knowledge of the resources present or what the future recovery costs would be on a specific property.[4] Even with operating properties, the actual division of rents among landowner, operator, labor, management, and consumer is not certain. Thus, there is a wide chasm between the concept of "economic rent" and its use in practice.

Even if we assume that we can come close to estimating many of the parameters in well-explored parts of the public land, we still have not zeroed in on exactly what is the "economic rent." Within the difference between total revenue and the basic variable cost of production, are found such things as "rent-to-ability," "quasi-rent," "rent-due-to-supply-constraints," or "pure-rent." Beyond this, do we really know what operators require or should have as an adequate return? Have we adjusted for the government take from taxes or the cost of government requirements? Moreover, in an extreme case where a government intentionally or unintentionally captures

everything over and above the variable costs, it probably does so by stifling most future land acquisitions
and investments.⁵

It may be easier to draw back from the ill-de-
fined goal of capturing economic rents and pursue,
instead, "fair market value." What is the legislative
or administrative intent of the use of that term? Is
the emphasis on "market," suggesting a return resulting from some form of "competition?" Or is this
merely referring to the traditionally agreed-upon
price between a willing buyer and a willing seller who
have bargained at arms length about a specific site.
Some may even propose that it would be proper to view
this as a partnership in a joint venture rather than a
sale, with the public providing the land in return for
a share of the gross income. I find suggestions of
these and other meanings in the continuing debate
about energy leasing. Part of the difficulty stems
from the fact that there is no market for leases in
the same sense as there is for surface estate. If the
government is now moving toward playing a dominant
role on the supply side, altering by its own actions
the marginal revenue curve, then there can hardly be a
truly competitive marketplace at work. So it will
remain difficult to arrive at any scheme that will
perfectly match what may be visualized by those who
seek "fair market value."

But we are not done surmounting these semantic
hurdles. Once the lease is signed, our producer must
proceed with "diligence." Typical of landowners, the
government wants its revenues to flow in predictable
fashion and avoid the machinations of speculators.
Such concerns have a long standing with public and
private landowners, but how rigorous the conditions
and penalties imposed on the leases should be tends to
be answered on a "it-depends" basis. Should you not
determine, and allow for, a reasonable time to explore, evaluate, and get into production with adjustments for unanticipated delays? Should you perhaps
accommodate a need for timing in entering unstable
markets? Plus, you will have to identify what constitutes a bona fide production level.

We are not willing to tolerate wasteful practices
on the public lands, so we want assurances that the
operator is going to achieve "maximum resource recovery." That sounds fine. But does that mean mining
everything regardless of cost? Or can the operator
cut-off production when the marginal cost equals the
marginal revenue? Or should we deal in average costs?

Energy leasing on the public lands is a judgmental exercise. I am suggesting that there is no deter-
minable "right" or "best" bonus plus royalty payment
for a specific energy lease. Nor is there any bidding

process that will assure that "fair market value" has
been received. If I am correct, then the federal
government must do as owners have always done.
Prepare a pre-sale calculation of what is thought to
be a reasonable estimate of the worth of the public
land energy properties being leased, bolster these
numbers with comparative analysis, and then open the
door to bidders and be prepared to take the best price
offered so long as it exceeds the pre-sale estimate.
Obviously this process does produce occasional under-
estimation, but sometimes it will realize more return
than it should. Over sufficient transactions these
should average out, thus protecting the public interest.

If the government leasing process operates in
this fashion, then there exists a need to reach agreement on, and stick with, the agreed-upon, standard
pre-sale valuation methodology for minimum bid determination. It would also be prudent to make sure
enough have access to the sale. As for requiring
multiple bids per tract as a general rule, this seems
more critical if revenue maximization is the goal.

Whatever the procedure, it does seem in order to
execute the leasing transaction whenever the federal
pre-sale valuation is met or exceeded by the bid(s)
received. Unless there is evidence of incompetence or
actual miscalculation, or a lack of arms-length bar-
gaining, it is probably not productive to debate
interminably the size of the bids received or the
amount of acreage offered after the fact. In candor,
one has to recognize that legislators may be attracted
to this as providing evidence that they are alert to
protecting the public interest, lawyers delight in
their continual pursuit of process and equity, academ-
ics revel in exploring the finer points of the bidding
process, and those who would really want the lands to
be employed in some other fashion find that a leasing
decision built upon judgment and estimation provides a
soft spot to attack.

But even suggesting a straightforward evaluate-
bid-close procedures has its perils. There is the
problem of exactly how to arrive at the minimum bid.
Even if we have now avoided becoming entrapped by any
implicit determination of economic rent, and we have
finally agreed upon what procedure approximates fair
market value, we must enter into the quest for the
"discount rate." I call your attention to the ex-
tended half-century discourse about choosing discount
rates for cost benefit analysis of water projects.
More than likely, we must once again seek refuge in
arbitrary action. We must thrash our way out of the
thicket of private and public discounting, subdue our
concerns over what is the true social discount rate,

and finally tell our land managers what discount rate is to be used, and when and how to use it. Perhaps we may decide to change this in the future, and we can do that if we wish.

One final observation: public land leasing for energy needs to be adapted to match the individual characteristics and the established institutions for each energy form. The uncertainties facing the lease bidder are different for each energy form and need to be accommodated reasonably in deciding whether or not a bonus bid should be made, the form of the royalty, or how diligence standards are to be specified.

For oil, we must make provision for exploration and the lack of knowledge of the quantity of resources present. This can persist even after production has begun. Some change in tactics when leasing in the vicinity of known production versus rank wildcatting is appropriate. Institutionally, oil and gas operators are used to dealing with extensive expenditures in advance of actual discovery and bidding aggressively in "hot" territory. But in the royalties, established provision must be made for eventual recovery of losses experienced by the majority of operators in unsuccessful lease bids from the income they need to gain in those that are successful. Unfortunately, the low variable costs that accompany a big find invite government to behave as though this was the normal difference between costs and revenue.

In coal, a minimal geologic uncertainty frequently has been replaced by market instability and economic uncertainty. Historically coal markets were characterized by large purchasers manipulating small producers. Coal operators encountered modest capital needs but had to deal with a large variable labor cost. As a consequence, while coal mines were easy to open, a shut-down could be equivalent to abandonment. In an economic decline, mines would continue to run at minimal levels to help meet fixed costs while avoiding total shut-down. As a result, little up front money was paid by operators for coal rights, and land owners were offered a fixed sum per ton tied to production. The vast extent of virtually equivalent coal-bearing lands in the U.S. also minimized any leverage on the part of the land owner to get a better deal. While today's western coal mining has deviated from this pattern, some of the old conditions are still evident.

Oil shale leasing introduces another dimension. Like coal, the resource is large and fairly well defined. But there are also resemblances to oil -- with its customarily more stable market prices and volume requirement, and a large front-end capital commitment before getting into production. However, there is no established mining and processing technology with reasonably predictable costs. While bonus bidding is compatible with the experience of the petroleum firms doing the oil shale bidding, the appropriate size of that bonus is harder to estimate than for petroleum. In fact, the size of the bonus offered in the past federal leasing efforts seems to have been the inverse of the expertise of the company. As for oil shale royalties, there is little to be gained if they are initially set so high as to inadvertently trigger economic failure. Finally, there has been a unique need to determine where the royalty should be placed in the production process.

In closing, I think oil shale provides a fitting illustration of how puzzling energy leasing on the public lands can be. As of this moment the proved reserves of U.S. shale oil by definition are zero. The commercial viability over its lifetime of any plant now built without subsidy would seem to be right at or below margin. This suggests to me there may be no rent to capture at present. Nonetheless, if an oil shale tract were offered today I suspect some firm would offer a bonus bid, plus royalty. Some one would then argue that this bonus bid represents the capture by the government of the economic rent. Does it?

NOTES

1. U.S. Department of the Interior. Minerals Management Service, "Royalties: A Report on Federal and Indian Mineral Revenues for 1981." Government Printing Office, 1982.

2. Nelson, Robert H. "Past and Projected State Revenues From Energy and Other Natural Resources in 13 Western States," Office of Policy Analysis. U.S. Department of Interior, September 1981.

3. Nelson, R. H. and Joseph G. "An Analysis of Revenues and Costs of Public Land Management by the Interior Department in 13 Western States -- Update to 1981," Office of Policy Analysis, U.S. Department of Interior, September 1982.

4. In the OCS, where targets are chosen carefully, the USGS pre-drilling estimates of petroleum potential has an extremely poor correlation with petroleum discovered. The track record of the companies is not that impressive either. While the leases with higher bids are more likely to have petroleum, the correlation between the dollars bid and the size of the discovery is not very high.

5. For a detailed discussion of the difficulties in dealing with economic rent see: Tilton, J. E. "The Future of Nonfuel Minerals." Brookings Institution, 1977, pp. 34-39.

Explaining and Defending
the Existing Federal Lands
Energy Management System

Hope Babcock

My goal will be to defend the existing system of withdrawals, planning, leasing and permitting. I hope to do this by putting into perspective some of the assertions about whether or not to increase single purpose private access to public lands to develop their subsurface mineral wealth.

The federal government owns approximately one-third of the total land of the continental United States, about 738 million acres out of a total of 2.3 billion acres. (U.S. Department of the Interior, Bureau of Land Management {BLM, Public Land Statistics 1980. Washington, GPO, 1981, p. 10}).

These lands and their underlying mineral resources are administered under no less than seventy different statutes. These laws establish the manner, rate and cost of extracting the underlying mineral resource from public lands as well as the standards for protection of their surface resources. The vast majority of these laws are administered by the agencies of the Department of the Interior (i.e., the Bureau of Land Management (BLM), the U.S. Geological Survey (USGS), the Minerals Management Service, the National Park Service (NPS), and the Fish and Wildlife Service (FWS). Specifically, BLM administers 397.3 million acres; NPS sixty-eight million acres; and FWS 63.3 million acres.

If national forest lands are at issue, then the Forest Service (FS) of the Department of Agriculture has principal jurisdiction. The Forest Service manages 188 million acres consisting of 154 national forests and nineteen national grassland areas in forty-one states and Puerto Rico. (Office of the Federal

Hope Babcock is deputy counsel and director of NAS Public Lands, National Audubon Society.

Register.   U.S.   Government   Manual,   1981/1982, pp.
127-128)
     In 1980, the oil and gas resources underlying
these lands were valued at $4.88 billion, providing
royalties of $605 million to the federal government.
(U.S. Department of the Interior, USGS, Federal Lands
Coal, Phosphate, Potash, Sodium, and Other Mineral
Production, Royalty Income and Related Statistics,
1920-1980. Washington, GPO, June 1981, p. 20.) While
a return of $605 million dollars to the federal trea-
sury is not to be taken lightly, for the same time
period oil and gas from the Outer Continental Shelf
contributed over $2.14 billion royalties. (Ibid). In
fact, according to the current secretary of the interior, two-thirds of the United States' untapped oil
wealth lies underneath the Outer Continental Shelf.
In other words, the action with respect to developing
this country's oil and gas resources is off, not
onshore.
     A second important fact is that these onshore
lands offer more to the citizens of this country than
just their underlying mineral wealth. The many different laws that apply to these lands are illustrative. Some of these laws, like the Wilderness Act of
1964 (16 U.S.C. 1131), the National Forest Management
Act of 1976 (43 U.S.C. 1701), the Wild and Scenic
Rivers Act of 1968 (16 U.S.C. 1271-87), the National
Wildlife Refuge System Administration Act of 1966 (16
U.S.C. 668dd-668jj), and the various statutes establishing the national parks, actually withdraw lands
from mineral access in recognition of these other
values. Others of these laws establish stringent
management and operating regulations under   which
mineral development activities can occur on those
public lands which have not been withdrawn from mineral entry. This latter class of law recognizes the
need both to preserve the multiple use characteristics
of these lands and to minimize the adverse environmental effects associated with mineral development activities. These laws are implemented through the planning, leasing and permitting systems.
     Only a small fraction -- by our calculation less
than thirty percent -- of our public lands are actually closed to mineral entry; ten percent of those lands
are in the national park system, where the advisabili-
ty of withdrawal and protection of natural resources
is seldom disputed. (Data derived from Management of
Fuel and Nonfuel Minerals on Federal Lands, Office of
Technology Assessment, April, 1979; Draft   Policy
Options for the Cabinet Council on Natural Resources
and the Environment, Titled Availability of Federal
Lands for Exploration and Development of Strategic
Minerals, August, 1981; and Minerals and the Public

Lands, released by the National Audubon Society and other environmental organizations in October, 1981.) Significant portions of the nation's public lands are withdrawn from oil and gas development for non-environmental reasons. These include lands withdrawn for power sites, irrigation districts, military lands, native selections, rights-of-way, etc. These lands could, and should, be opened for mineral development before lands that have been set aside by Congress for protection of their natural resources.

Even on lands which have been withdrawn, some mineral development activities can take place. Discretionary leasing of oil and gas deposits under national parks and monuments is allowed when the deposit is being drained through directional drilling from outside the unit boundary. Most National Wildlife Refuge land is open to mineral leasing under the 1920 Mineral Leasing Act. While granting these leases in refuges is discretionary with the secretary of the interior, as of 1974, at least twelve National Wildlife Refuges had producing oil and gas wells. (U.S. Department of the Interior, Fish and Wildlife Service. Final Environmental Statement, Operation of the National Wildlife Refuge System. Washington, GPO, 1976, p. III-81).

With regard to the twenty million acres of national forest and BLM lands in the lower forty-eight states withdrawn from mineral entry under the Wilderness Act, there are specific additional facts to keep in mind.

Lands withdrawn for wilderness protection have been open to mineral entry and development for twenty years. Valid existing rights to the mineral resources underlying these lands established during this period or before are recognized and are not even subject to the non-impairment standard found in Section 603(c) of the Federal Land Planning and Management Act (FLPMA). All so-called RARE II lands (Roadless Area Review and Evaluation II), including 14.8 million acres (outside Alaska) recommended for further planning and wilderness designation, are open to mineral leasing, although subject to protective regulatory conditions.

BLM's twenty-four million acres of wilderness study areas (outside Alaska) are open to mineral exploration and development activities under the restriction found in Section 603 of FLPMA that these lands be protected from impairment until Congress acts on their designation.

In other words, almost all of the lands withdrawn for environmental reasons can be developed for their underlying oil and gas resources. However, I would be disingenuous if I did not note that every secretary of the interior, before the incumbent, pursued a policy of not allowing oil and gas development activities to take place on lands being studied for their wilderness potential or to a large extent on lands set aside for park or refuge purposes.

Most national park and wilderness area boundaries have been drawn in such a way as to accommodate mineral resource concerns. Examples of this can be found in the western overthrust belt (Lake Mountain Study Area, WY), and in Colorado (Dolores River Canyon Study Area), just to mention a few examples.

The resource simply is not there in sufficient quantities to justify entry into these unique and fragile areas. It has been estimated that less than 1.1 percent of the nation's oil and 1.2 percent of the natural gas can be found in lands withdrawn under the Wilderness Act, while less than 3.4 percent of the oil and 2.5 percent of the gas can be found in lands studied by BLM and the NFS for permanent wilderness protection under the same statute. (Leonard Fischman, Economic Associates research for TWS, 1981).

If energy conservation measures were adopted by this country, we could greatly decrease the need to exploit these fragile lands for their underlying mineral wealth. Specifically, use of energy conservation measures and renewable energy resources could meet twenty to thirty percent of U.S. energy needs by the year 2000 (Solar Energy Research Institute Report, (1981)). If the United States continues the momentum of its photovoltaic program of the past few years, by the year 2000 use of these devices could displace the equivalent of 330,000 barrels per day of oil (Solar Lobby, 1981).

If the debate over access to public lands for energy and minerals development is largely rhetorical in the lower forty-eight states, this cannot be said of Alaska. There the virgin nature of so much of that land from both a development and a preservation standpoint is a reality, and decisions have and will continue to be made for the next decade at least on the use of those public lands. Yet even in Alaska, the same facts which I have been discussing with respect to the lower forty-eight states apply.

Alaska has been and continues to be a focal point of the controversy over resource development and accessibility. Development of energy resources, in particular, was a hotly and very publicly debated issue throughout congressional deliberations on the Alaska Lands Act. Resource "lock-up" -- and particularly "lock-up" of oil and gas, or should I say potential oil and gas resources -- was the primary theme of opponents of that legislation.

But what, in fact, do we have in this law in the way of protection for resources and in the way of provision to assure that resource development may take place? The answer is that the Alaska Lands Act was truly compromise legislation. Boundaries were drawn and redrawn around parks and wildlife refuges and wilderness areas. The result, time and time again, was exclusion from the conservation system of units of areas which might have significant development potential. Mineral potential, for instance, was cause for boundary changes in both the Gates of the Arctic National Park and Southeast Alaska wilderness areas.

Not only were boundaries shaped with an eye to protecting future resource development options, but several mechanisms were spelled out in detail to assure flexibility for resource development in Alaska. (1) The Alaska Lands Act mandates an Interior Department study of oil and gas resources on all federal north slope lands outside of the National Petroleum Reserve-Alaska and the Arctic National Wildlife Refuge. A report on resource potential and impacts of development is due to Congress in 1988. (Sec. 1001) (2) For all other (non-north slope) federal lands in Alaska, the secretary of the interior was directed to establish an oil and gas leasing program, where allowed by law or on national wildlife refuges where deemed compatible with the purposes of the refuges. (Sec. 1008) (Not surprisingly the present administration has addressed themselves to this program with some vigor.) (3) The act also established guidance and a timetable for resource assessment and oil and gas exploration on the coastal plain for the Arctic National Wildlife Refuge. Based on regulations which are currently being finalized through the National Environmental Protection Act (NEPA) process, exploratory activity (both surface and seismic) will be permitted on the coastal plain. By 1986, the Interior Department will report to Congress the results of the assessment work. (Sec. 1002) (4) The statute also explicitly addresses the access issue. It sets up an approval mechanism for transportation systems across conservation system units. (Title XI) (Such systems include water transport systems {i.e., canals and pipes}, pipelines, slurry and emulsion systems, transmission systems for communications, improved rights-of-way for snow machines, air cushion vehicles and other ATVs {all-terrain vehicles}, roads, railways, tramways, airports and docks.) Granted, the approval process is to conform with existing law, but this is surely not unreasonable when we are talking about pristine wilderness and wildlife habitat in designated national parks and national wildlife refuges and national forest wilderness areas.

Because the Alaska Lands Act provides not only for resource protection, but also, very explicitly, for development mechanisms, it is important that we approach the law's implementation conservatively. Simply having the law on the books does not mean that any development, energy or otherwise, which can possibly take place within the framework of the act should be carried out. For instance, all the non-wilderness portions of the national wildlife refuge system in Alaska are open to oil and gas leasing, if it is determined to be compatible by the secretary of the interior. Although there is oil and gas activity on a number of refuges in the lower forty-eight states, I would suggest that compatibility of oil and gas development with the purposes of conserving "fish and wildlife populations and their habitats in natural diversity" (ANILCA, Title III) in the ecologically sensitive refuge ecosystems of Alaska seems very remote.

On the Arctic Wildlife Refuge, the Congress went even further. Despite concerns over the compatibility of oil and gas activity with the protection of arctic wilderness values and of the Porcupine caribou herd calving grounds and polar bear denning areas, Congress acceded to industry pressures to make the coastal plain of the Arctic refuge available for exploratory activity. The coastal plain was one of the very few areas included in a conservation system unit under the Alaska legislation which might possibly have significant potential for energy resources.

In Alaska, as in the lower forty-eight states, we are left then with a system of federally protected lands which, by and large, exclude areas of significant potential for energy development. The national parks (fifty million acres) and the wilderness areas (twenty-four million acres outside of the parks) in Alaska are closed to oil and gas activity. The approximately sixty million acres of non-wilderness wildlife refuges are closed subject to determination of compatibility. On the other hand, the State of Alaska and the Alaskan Native corporations have based much of their land selection on potential for resource development and are actively pursuing that course. Both industry and the federal government are actively developing Alaska's non-renewable mineral resources at present. The USGS annual report for 1982 mandated by the Alaska Lands Act notes the following: the federal lease sale of 1.5 million acres of National Petroleum Reserve-Alaska (NPR-A) earlier this year, BLM preparations for acceptance of lease applications on about 300,000 acres of federal land in central Alaska, new development in Prudhoe Bay in 1980 and 1981, significant discoveries along the Beaufort coast by Exxon, Conoco, Hamilton Brothers and Sohio. Elsewhere in the state, Chevron and Union were also active (unsuccessfully). USGS also completed thirteen exploratory wells and three development wells in NPR-A during 1980 and 1981. (1982 Annual Report on Alaska's Mineral Resources, Geological Survey Circular 884, just published, undated, USGS.)

If anything the Alaska Lands Act has opened the door for energy development activity in Alaska. It is important now to assure that the areas designated by the law for protection of their wilderness and wildlife values be, in fact, adequately protected. It is important that the integrity of the conservation system units in Alaska, as well as in the lower forty-eight states, not be jeopardized. Nor should we ignore the importance of environmental safeguards for energy development on BLM lands or, for that matter, state and native lands in Alaska. The sensitivity of the northern environment makes caution in development especially critical. The Alaska Lands Act establishes mechanisms for assessment of Alaska's mineral and energy resources. It establishes mechanisms for access which must be implemented judiciously and cautiously if we want to maintain a long-term balance between protection and development on Alaska'a public lands.

The principles discussed here are important not only to preserving and protecting our dwindling resources in the lower forty-eight states, but making intelligent decisions with respect to our much more abundant natural resources in Alaska. It is important to remember why lands have been set aside from mineral entry. It is important to remember that there are other alternatives to opening up these lands, whether in the form of reworking existing oil and gas fields, opening up lands withdrawn for other than environmental reasons, or by implementing and encouraging, at a national level, energy conservation policies to reduce demand. Finally, it is important to remember that these lands belong to all citizens, not just to the few who wish to exploit their underlying mineral wealth for private gain. Planning for the protection and environmentally sensitive development of these lands is part of the public trust that Congress and all of us have given to the executive branch of our government.

Oil Shale Problems and Issues

Mary Jane C. Due

Here is a brief chronology of events affecting oil shale in the last eighty-two years:

1900-1910   Congress decides U.S. vulnerable to oil and requirements and depletion of domestic sources. It establishes naval oil shale reserves; Interior classifies over four million acres of public lands valuable for petroleum and nitrogen for oil shale.

1910-1920   Public locate mining claims for oil shale under the 1872 Mining Law. Oil shale included in Mineral Lands Leasing Law no longer locatable.

1930   Texas oil field finds. Withdrawal of oil shale lands. Government contests mining claim locations.

1960   Studies of oil shale: Interior and Congress.

1970   Public Land Law Review recommendations:
(a)   legislation;
(b)   resolution of the claims situation;
(c)   experimental commercial development.

1971-1981   Environmental legislation.

Mary Jane C. Due is senior counsel, American Mining Congress.

1971   Oil embargo.
                Prototype leasing. Bid price: Tract
                c-a $210,305,600; c-b $117,780,000;
                u-a $75,596,000; u-b $45,107,200.

1980   Energy Security Act calls for 1.5
                million barrels a day from synthetic
                fuels by 1995; creates Synthetic Fuels
                Corporation; appropriates $17.552 bil-
                lion for synthetic fuels development.

1981   Economic slump begins.
                Sixteen oil shale projects ongoing with
                a projected capacity barrels per day of
                701,000.
                Oil glut.

1982   Three projects ongoing: Union, Geo-
                kinetics, White River Oil Shale.
                No legislation.
                Programmatic environmental impact
                statement.
                New prototype lease for multi-mineral
                purposes proposed by Interior.

I am accepting the congressional declaration in
Section 102 of the 1980 Energy Security Act that
energy security is essential to the United States and
that it can be accomplished through development of
synthetic fuels. The goal of reducing dependence on
foreign energy resources by 1995 with development of
1.5 million barrels per day of synthetic fuels is
unrealistic. But, the correctness of the congressional declaration that synthetic fuels must be developed
and that dependency reductions cannot be achieved
without a commitment of federal capital has been
reinforced by recent events. The prime example is the
Colony Project. Nevertheless, we need a synthetic
substitute for liquid crude for transportation and
petrochemical needs. We have gone from a situation
one year ago where there was active participation in
oil shale development to a situation today where only
three companies, Union Oil, Geokinetics and the White
River Project, remain on schedule.
    In addition to the general economic woes having
an effect on oil shale development, there are three
broad problem areas that require resolution. These
are: (1) financial, (2) legislative, and (3) regulatory.

FINANCIAL

The level of future international oil prices is obviously a factor and one of major uncertainties affecting the development of shale.

The Congress made a commitment of limited duration to provide financial assistance in conjunction with private sources of capital to facilitate the expeditious achievement of production from domestic resources.

The Synthetic Fuels Corporation wants to make a prudent distribution of some of that $15 billion that is available for "reasonable," "prudent" projects. In a speech before the American Mining Congress (AMC) meeting in Las Vegas in October, the chairman said, "We definitely see oil shale as an essential resource for synfuel development."

The Synthetic Fuels Corporation has said it is in business to help develop a domestic synthetic fuels industry, including oil shale. The risks to benefits ratio is clearly in the government's favor. Once the synfuels option is established, once the U.S. has the capability to produce liquids and gas from coal and oil shale, the country gains benefits whether or not there is extensive commercial production. For the industry sponsor, beyond production capability he must also be concerned with profit in a very uncertain energy marketplace.

The general economic climate is not conducive to the development of a high risk capital venture. And it is clear that companies are proceeding expeditiously but cautiously with preliminary work leading toward development.

LEGISLATIVE

The prototype leasing program has shown that there are significant problems with the legislative regime which must be resolved. Efforts to develop legislation during this session of the Congress has not been fruitful. AMC testified on the issues, stating:

> The national security and general welfare of the United States are dependent upon the continued ability of the mining industry to supply minerals in sufficient quantities at reasonable costs. It is in the national interest to develop, without delay, the nation's vast oil shale deposits under sound environmental safeguards. The American Mining Congress supports the

following positions on oil shale legislation as being necessary to achieve these
important goals.

1. Position on Economically Sized Lease
    Tracts

    Oil shale deposits can be so thin and
    lean, and capital requirements so
    intense, that more than 5120 acres
    may be required to constitute a
    resource which could support a pro-
    ject at an economic rate for an
    economically viable period. There-
    fore, it is our position that the
    size of an oil shale lease should be
    adjustable upwards from 5120 acres at
    the discretion of the Secretary if he
    finds an economic mining unit cannot
    be supported by only 5120 acres.

2. Positions on Per-Company Limitations
    on Number of Leases and By-Pass
    Leases

    The limitation on the number of
    federal oil shale leases a company
    may hold should be eliminated or
    increased to at least two per state
    and four nationwide. The current
    restriction of one lease per company
    is unnecessary, and it limits the use
    of experience gained from initial
    high risk operations on subsequent
    commercial projects. There should be
    no legislated specification of re-
    source characteristics that one lease
    must meet before additional leases
    may be awarded to a company.

    a. If a per-company limitation on
        the number of federal leases
        held is imposed, a company's
        share of ownership in a project
        operating under a federal lease
        should be counted as that frac-
        tion of a lease, without regard
        to the acreage encompassed by
        the lease.

    b. If a per-company limitation on
        the number of federal leases
        held is imposed, the limitation

should not apply to leases issued to avoid by-pass of small acreages of federal oil shale deposits. Such by-pass leases are necessary to permit economic mining on such small tracts, and should not be applied to company lease limitations because of their small size relative to regular lease tracts.

c. If a per-company limitation on the number of federal leases held is imposed, provision should be made to allow the holder of the maximum number of leases to acquire an additional lease if existing leases are in commercial production and at least one existing lease is nearing the point of exhausting its commercially recoverable reserves.

3. Position on Off-Tract Leases

The Secretary of the Interior should be granted authority to lease lands that may be required for operations necessary for the recovery of oil shale. These operations may include disposal of oil shale wastes and other materials removed from oil shale lands; location of plants, reduction works and other facilities connected with oil shale operations, but should not include the removal of any mineral deposits contained in the additional lands.

4. Position on Multi-Mineral Leasing Authority

The Secretary of the Interior should be authorized to issue leases allowing the mining, extraction and disposal of mineral deposits which may be leased under the Mineral Leasing Act of 1920, other than oil shale, and which are contained in the lands covered by oil shale leases.

The American Mining Congress believes that the
above four items are critical to the prompt and orderly development of an oil shale industry. We also
believe that this development will take place in an
environmentally responsible manner and will fully
satisfy the legitimate socioeconomic concerns of
affected states without additional legislative initia-
tives in these areas.

Secondly, technical data subsequently prepared by
one of AMC member companies has shown us that in order
to attract companies with the financial ability to
carry out these projects, reserves capable of supporting a 50,000 barrel per day operation for thirty years
are generally considered necessary. The limitation of
one lease to 5,210 acres is predicated on the fact
that Colorado oil shale deposits are rich and thick
enough to allow development within the 5,120 acre
limitation. The study to which I am referring supports the proposition that the acreage limitation of
5,120 is an unreasonable restriction on the development and that competitive economics alone will prevent
the development of these properties. Other member
companies confirm the correctness of this study.

REGULATORY

BLM is going ahead with its plan for setting up
the leasing regime, without waiting for the Congress
to pass needed legislation.

Prototype Leasing

BLM is under orders from the secretary of interior to offer additional tracts for leasing under the
prototype program which was established in 1973. BLM
is looking for multi-lease development of sodium
associated with oil shale.

As a result of the commencement of this action,
AMC and API in September 1982 advised BLM that they
found the supplemental Draft Environmental Impact
Statement for the prototype program seriously defi-
cient in three areas: air quality, hydrology and
socioeconomic. We have since been informed by BLM
that they are completely redoing the air model.

Programmatic Environmental Impact Statement

As a result of the scoping meetings in April
1982, the regional oil shale team state representatives outlined an alternative approach for the perma-

nent oil shale leasing program to that proposed by BLM. API and AMC supported that approach with certain exceptions: with regard to carrying capacity, we urged the department not to set rigid upper limits in the absence of valid data. We ask for time to comment on royalties, diligence, mine plan submissions, etc., before final decisions are made by the department.

This effort by AMC and API is probably the first time that industry and the environmentalists and the state representatives were in agreement on anything.

BLM advised us that they had taken our suggestions into consideration, and incorporated most of the elements proposed in the ROST alternative. According to a letter we received October 5, 1982, BLM desires to have a program in place by 1984 so that it can lease if, and only if, necessary. A draft programmatic environmental impact statement for oil shale leasing was sent to the Office of Management and Budget October 26.

Regional Management Plan (RMP)

Assuming the decision is made to implement an oil shale leasing program through the process known as a programmatic EIS, the bureau will then begin its land use planning process with the preparation of a resource management plan and associated EIS.

Piceance Basin RMP

The bureau has also initiated a Piceance Basin regional management plan, looking toward a February 28, 1984 date for completion.

Our Synthetic Fuels Committee identified the following significant issues in commenting on the proposed plan to the Bureau of Land Management.

o   The American Mining Congress recommends the plan include a recognition of the need for preferred areas for offsite waste disposal and for the location of other offsite surface operations including the building of plants, reduction works, and other facilities connected with oil shale operations. Such offsite locations will, in many cases, be required to enhanced a federal lessee's or private developer's ability to maximize the resource recovery and/or the efficiency of the operation. Consideration should be given to such factors as proximity to the leasehold and future mineral leasing of such offsite tracts.

o   The diverse and intermingled mineral and surface
     ownership patterns in the oil shale area will
     require a myriad of land use authorizations for
     access roads, pipelines, transmission lines,
     ancillary facilities (e.g., oil shale upgrader
     sites), water storage, and distribution systems,
     etc. for developers of both federal and nonfeder-
     al lands. BLM should focus its attention on
     streamlining regulations that implement sale,
     exchange, lease, special use permit and
     right-of-way provisions of the Federal Land
     Policy and Management Act in order to respond to
     land transaction applications.

o   The plan must identify federal land areas expect-
     ed to be needed in support of oil shale opera-
     tions on private or federal land including:
     - water storage areas
     - transportation corridors
     - utility corridors
     - product distribution corridors
     - worker living quarters
     - waste disposal areas

o   There must be an appropriate treatment and use of
     the concept of "carrying capacity" with recogni-
     tion that it should not be construed or applied
     as a rigid limitation on level of development.
     At the present time, there is no way of knowing
     precisely what level of growth the western slope
     communities can absorb. This concept of
     preestablishing a "carrying capacity" appears to
     be comparable to the recently abandoned "thresh-
     old" concept developed in the coal leasing pro-
     gram. The establishment of initial carrying
     capacities or acceptable levels of social, eco-
     nomic and environmental impact for a land use
     planning area essentially prevents the normal
     multiple use resource trade-offs. If a proposed
     action, for example oil shale leasing, is deemed
     to exceed a particular "carrying capacity," the
     proposed action would be automatically rejected
     without consideration of mineral resource value.

Free Markets, States' Rights, and Federal Coal

Dewitt John

Two specific issues are of special interest to me and perhaps to you. First, I will address how free market ideas might be applied to the leasing of federal coal. Second, I will advocate legislative or administrative repeal of the Ventura decision which threatens to limit the power of state and local governments to manage the socioeconomic impacts of energy and mineral development.

Those of you who have followed federal coal leasing issues over recent years may have a feeling of deja vu these days. In 1974-75, Secretary of Interior Rogers C. B. Morton proposed a leasing program for federal coal. The Natural Resources Defense Council (NRDC) sued and won. In 1982, Secretary Watt has proposed revisions of the federal coal leasing program, and once again NRDC has sued. The statutory context is different of course, but many of the substantive issues are the same.

NRDC is concerned that the land use plans will not be adequate before leases are issued. They are concerned that there is not adequate protection for surface owners. They feel that the requirements for diligent development of the federal leases are too lax. They want the Bureau of Land Management (BLM) to assess the environmental suitability of existing leases and preference rights to leases. And finally, they allege that the federal government has not complied adequately with the National Environmental Protection Act.

The first NRDC suit in 1976 helped provoke the Federal Coal Leasing Amendments Act. In addition, two other laws, passed in 1976 and 1977, had a tremendous

DeWitt John is assistant to the director, Colorado Department of Natural Resources.

impact on federal coal leasing: the Surface Mine
Reclamation Control Act (SMRCA) and the Federal Land
Policy and Management Act (FLPMA).

The second suit may also provoke legislation.
Environmentalists as well as other interests may seek
amendments to the Mineral Leasing Act to rectify what
they see as problems with Secretary Watt's proposed
leasing system.

There are, however, important differences between
the situation in 1976-77 and the situation today. One
difference is that in 1976-77 western governors were
not particularly vocal about federal leasing policies.
Now they are very vocal. The Carter administration
designed the mechanism to involve state governments in
federal coal leasing -- the Regional Coal Teams (RCT).
These teams meet regularly during the leasing process
and try to build a consensus, not only between the
federal government and the state government, but also
among industry, environmentalists, the public and
local governments. The new regulations reduce the
role of the RCTs. The governors have said many times
that they do not like this. (A week after these
remarks, Secretary Watt met with six western governors
and agreed to restore, fully, responsibilities of the
RCTs.)

The second important difference is the health of
the coal market. In 1976 and 1977, the coal market in
the west was growing, and there was a full-fledged
boom in the Powder River Basin. There were great
expectations about the future of western coal. In
1982, the situation is very different. The coal
industry is still growing, but much more slowly. The
hope -- or fears -- of a terrific boom in the 1980s
have largely receded.

One would think that a flat coal market would
decrease the demand for federal coal leases. But the
Interior Department is trying to increase the amount
of federal coal leasing. Why might this be so?

One explanation is that policies are lagging
behind economic reality. Industry criticized Secretary of Interior Cecil D. Andrus for not leasing
enough coal. Secretary Watt is now trying to lease
more coal, even though the market conditions have
changed dramatically. This perhaps cynically suggests
that federal policies about how much should be leased
are immune from events in the real world and are
determined solely by political fashion.

A second possible explanation for Interior's
efforts to lease large amounts of coal is suggested by
the Sierra Club, which has recently published a booklet entitled, The Great Giveaway. In this booklet the
Sierra Club alleges that the Interior Department is

simply leasing public resources at a cutrate price to
the detriment of the American taxpayer.
    The Interior Department has a third explanation.
They say that their new policy is an effort to allow
the free market to play a larger role in deciding what
coal is to be leased and produced.
    It is a great mistake not to take this free
market argument seriously. Even if you are comfortable as a progressive conservationist or environmentalist, you must recognize the appeal of libertarian
and free market ideas today. I'm not an apologist for
these ideas. My personal view is that libertarian
ideas play the same role in the 1980s as Marxism did
in the late 60s and early 70s. That is, libertarian-
ism -- like Marxism -- is fundamentally flawed, but it
does capture important and valid concerns of the public. It is excellent intellectual discipline to think
through the challenges that the libertarian is making
to settled ways of doing business. Libertarian and
free market thinkers are a source of new ideas that
one should not neglect.
    So let us take a closer look at the intellectual
undergirding for the new coal leasing policies of the
Interior Department. The rationale suggested publicly
by the administration, by some people in the coal
industry, and by a number of think tanks and consultants is as follows: First, the government's job is
not to plan the development of the coal industry, but
simply to make coal available. Industry can take it
from there. Second, there are no costs to overleasing
-- including no social costs. The regulatory system
that is in place will prevent environmental abuses.
    The arguments clearly do not hold water. There
are social costs to overleasing. For example, the
regulatory system looks at coal tracts one at a time.
Regulators are not prepared to handle cumulative
impacts very well. But there may be important social
problems and social costs connected with the development of a large number of coal tracts at the same
time. The time to weigh these costs is when coal is
leased.
    For another example, once a tract of federal coal
has been leased and once the company has spent money
on drilling and on preparing the permit application
for developing the lease, it is very difficult for a
state or a federal permitting agency to deny a permit.
It is possible to condition that permit to ask the
coal company to do things in a different way, but
denial is very difficult.
    These things must be obvious to people who know
the federal coal system well. The arguments suggested
in defense of the administration's policies are theoretical and really quite naive. So let us look

afield.   Let   us look at some free market economists
and see how their ideas might apply to coal leasing.

One idea that has been suggested by William
Niskanen, Gordon Tullock, and others is that, although
it may seem desirable to manage social costs, it is
often prohibitively expensive to do so. The costs   of
running a bureaucracy, and the strange decisions that
are sometimes made by bureaucrats, are a greater
burden than the social benefit of resolving the problems that the bureaucracy is supposed to cure.

So let us ask, is a policy of overleasing cheap?
Is it less expensive than a policy of restrained
leasing?

No, overleasing is more expensive.   The government must prepare additional studies, larger environmental statements, and increased numbers of lease
offerings.   Industry must respond to all these government studies, must do additional drilling on additional tracts and must prepare bids on a larger number of
tracts.   There also is the probability of increased
social conflict.   Increased leasing leads to heightened expectations of what may happen in a coal region.
This increases conflict and misunderstanding, which
may well result in litigation and delay.

There is another way in which overleasing is an
expensive policy.   It increases the cost of being in
the coal business.   Companies must buy more leases
simply to remain competitive.   They must bid on more
leases than will ever come to production.   In effect,
what a program of overleasing does is to levy a <u>tax</u> on
the coal industry.   Overleasing transfers money from
industry to the government, and the transfer is not a
productive expenditure.   Industry does gain access to
federal coal, but there is no increase in the amount
of coal that is produced.   In short, the arguments of
Niskanen and Tullock do not suggest that a policy of
unlimited leasing is a sound approach.

There is one plausible "free   market" rationale
for Interior's current policies.   Interior might be
trying to transfer control of federal coal to a large
number of private holders by one great market distortion.   Perhaps Interior's policy objective is to dump
the federal leases into private hands as fast as
possible.   Then there would be a relatively free
market among the lessees who could exchange leases
amongst themselves, as is allowed by current law and
regulation.

The disadvantages of this course are three:
First, there is the problem of the initial distortion
of the free market.   Second, policy probably would
cause increased opposition which would result in
delay.   And third, by transferring ownership into the

private sector, government would lose its power to
take social costs into account.
So let us try again. How would a free market in
federal coal leases work? Is it possible to achieve
some of the advantages of a free market system without
surrendering public control of coal lands?
If there were a free market, there would be a
large number of willing sellers and buyers. Also,
there would be good information about the goods that
are bought and sold in the market for coal leases.
(It is interesting to note that budgetary pressures
are forcing the federal government away from the free
market ideal of good information. The administration
has decreased drilling by the United States Geological
Survey on potential coal lease tracts. Interior has
even adopted a policy of offering tracts for lease
even if the government has not the faintest idea
whether there is any coal on a tract.)
The key element of the free market is a large
number of willing sellers and buyers. This is difficult to achieve because the federal government owns
about sixty percent of western coal and controls
another ten percent. One reason to want a large
number of willing sellers and buyers is to avoid
monopolistic behavior. To simulate the working of a
free market, the government should not act as a monop-
olist. It should not try to restrict its sales of
leases in order to maximize its revenue. On the other
hand, the government should not flood the market by
offering large quantities for lease and driving prices
down. Both the classical monopolistic approach of
restricting sales and suicidal monopolistic approach
of dumping everything are out of place in the smoothly
functioning free market.
In a free market, a stream of leases will come
onto the market as individual sellers offer leases and
make deals with individual buyers. The federal government could try to replicate this kind of situation. Interior could establish a program that would
offer a regular flow of lease offerings with opportunities for industry to purchase leases at a number of
points of time. In a free market you would expect
that when the demand for leases was greater more
leases would be offered, and when the demand for
leases was reduced fewer leases would be offered. Of
course, what is happening today is the demand for
leases has dropped, but the perverse policies of the
current administration are offering coal for lease.
In preparing for this discussion today, I read
several books and articles by free market economists
in my search for explanations of a policy of overleasing. One book was especially interesting and I
recommend it to you. It is by Gordon Bjork, entitled

Life, Liberty, and Property. Bjork is perhaps a different kind of free market thinker. He clearly takes environmental values very seriously, but he is against land use planning, zoning, and similar bureaucratic efforts to protect environmental values.

His book does not address coal leasing, for he is concerned primarily with land use planning and the question of urban sprawl. But Bjork does suggest a number of approaches which could be applied to federal coal leasing. He makes very clear that it is not necessary under a free market system to ignore social costs. His approach to the free market ideal is to suggest incentives which would encourage individuals to behave in a fashion which is socially desirable. Instead of regulating people by fiat, he suggests giving monetary incentives.

In the context of federal coal leasing, it would be possible to put prices, instead of prohibitions, on environmental values. Currently, the coal leasing system includes a number of unsuitability prohibitions, forbidding leases of coal where there are eagles' nests, alluvial valley floors, communities or other things which are protected by law or regulation. A free market approach would suggest eliminating these flat prohibitions and instead taxing "unsuitable" development or requiring extensive mitigation.

Free market ideas can also be applied to due diligence. Some months ago, the American Mining Congress (AMC) came to western states with proposals for the requirements that federal leases develop their coal diligently -- within certain time restrictions. Our immediate reaction was that we were strong supporters of diligence requirements, and therefore, we could not support the AMC proposals. But, when we thought about it, we changed our position. Instead of a flat requirement that one must surrender a lease if one is not producing after ten years, financial incentives could be written into law.

Free market theories might suggest a new approach to the question of how much money the government should receive for a coal lease. Currently the price of a coal lease must be equal to the "fair market value." Instead, Interior might want to ask that industry pay enough money to compensate society for the social costs of developing that lease. For example, the bonus should be big enough perhaps to cover the cost of building boom towns, for building salinity projects downstream, and for replacing habitat for wildlife.

These ideas do not constitute a new coal leasing system. They suggest a few ways that free market ideas can be applied to the leasing of federal coal -- ways that are environmentally sound and

environmentally responsible, but are very different
from the policies being advocated by Secretary Watt.
It is worthwhile noting, for example, that the administration is not proposing to replace an "unsuitability" with a more flexible system: it is simply
proposing to exempt certain kinds of leases from any
"unsuitability" requirements.

Let us ask a theoretical question: Suppose we
could design a free market approach to coal leasing
which was environmentally sound. Should we adopt such
a system? In response I will quote Milton Friedman,
though he has not answered the question directly, of
course. I will quote from his book, Capitalism and
Freedom, and suggest how his ideas might apply to
federal coal leasing. He wrote, "The existence of a
well specified and generally accepted definition of
property is far more important than just what that
definition is."

This could be applied to federal coal leasing.
The existence of a well specified and generally accepted definition of coal leasing is probably more
important than exactly what that definition is. A
system was in place and was working in 1980-81. I
would suggest that the system should have been left in
place with only careful incremental changes. Perhaps
in the late 80s, after we have tried the current
system and learned its weak points, we will be ready
to try a free market approach to leasing. But not
today.

The second issue I would like to discuss is the
Ventura decision. It is now generally accepted in the
west that boom towns need front-end funding. Construction workers come to town and need services
before there is a tax base to finance these services.
Federal money is hard to get, so developers of major
energy projects must provide a large part of the
financing. Negotiations about how much money the
developers should provide take place during the siting
process, when the developer applies for a permit under
state or local use legislation.

However, courts have recently ruled that mineral
lessees on federal land need not comply with local
land use regulations. The ruling was made in a specific circumstance in Ventura County, California.
Gulf drilled an oil well on lands zoned for open
space. These lands were part of a national forest.
Ventura County asked for an injunction, saying that
Gulf must apply for a variance to local land use
requirements. The district and appeals courts ruled
against Ventura County, and the Supreme Court upheld
their decisions without writing its own opinion.

The argument advanced by the lower courts was as
follows: The Mineral Leasing Act declared Congress'

intent to develop minerals. The act explicitly allows
the state certain powers, including the right to tax
and to regulate employment practices and regulate the
conservation of resources. But it does not mention
land use legislation. Therefore, local land use legislation is pre-empted and lessees are exempt from
such regulation.

I will not argue the legal questions, and will
only address the practical effects of this ruling.
The land use permit is the only permit that can be
conditioned on socioeconomic impacts. If there is no
local land use permit (or if there is no state siting
permit in states where there is a state siting system), there is no legal mechanism for the state or the
county to require front-end funding for the costs of
public facilities and boom towns.

Projects do need other permits. They may need
permits to run trucks overweight on a highway, or they
may need public health permits. They must comply with
local buildings codes. But none of these permits are
adequate to address broad socioeconomic problems.

The consistency provision of FLPMA is no help
either. Under FLPMA, federal leases must be in con-
formity with federal land use plans, federal land use
plans must generally be consistent with local land use
plans. But most counties in the west do not have land
use plans and few states have land use plans.

Even if these local land use plans did exist, it
is unrealistic to expect such plans to address socioeconomic impacts adequately. A town of 2,000 people
cannot plan ahead for all the mitigation that would be
required by a project that would bring 800 construction workers and 500 permanent employees into town.
What the local community must do is to establish
standards and procedures, wait until a company comes,
and negotiate with the company in the circumstances of
a particular subject.

We in Colorado have tried voluntary methods of
negotiating agreements with energy developers. The
Joint Review Process (JRP) is one means: it is a
voluntary process for bringing the developer together
with all permitting agencies at the same time. In the
JRP meetings, there is opportunity to discuss the need
for front-end funding. If good will is present,
something acceptable can often be worked out.

We have also organized the Cumulative Impacts
Task Force, which is a voluntary state-local-industry
effort to agree on a methodology for assessing the
need for front-end funding. But the JRP cannot include all major projects, and some companies may well
dig in their heels and refuse to provide adequate
front-end funding.

If there is no clear legal mechanism to address
socioeconomic impact -- which the courts have taken
away from the states -- there will be political confrontation. This will often result in delay and in
arbitrary results.

There are several possible solutions. The BLM
might stipulate, as part of its leases, that lessees
must comply with state and local use regulations.
Alternatively Congress might clarify the Mineral
Leasing Act. If sweeping language is not acceptable
-- then a more limited version might be adopted.

For example, Congress might require compliance
with all "nondiscriminatory" state and local laws or
only with state and local land use legislation.
Another possibility, which would be much less workable, would be to require lessees to comply with all
"reasonable" state and local land use laws. Who would
determine whether a local requirement was reasonable?
Another possibility would be for the federal land
manager to develop specific requirements for frontend
financing. But this is impractical, because the
amount of financing needed depends on how local government facilities are managed and financed.

Whichever approach is taken, there must be a way
to reverse or modify the Ventura decision. It is
intolerable that when a major coal mine or other large
project is proposed on federal land, no state or local
permitting agency has the capability and the legal
right to review socioeconomic impacts. We understand
that the federal government is sovereign on its land.
But is very difficult to accept that the federal
lessee is sovereign as well.

Index

301

304

308

Safe Minimum Standards,
154
Sagebrush Rebellion, 88,
117-119, 121, 124,
134, 230
San Juan National Forest,
40, 122
Santini, James, 42
Save-the-Redwoods League,
51
Scaled sales. See Timber
Scarcity,
of resources, 30-31,
81. See also.
Efficiency
Schelling, Thomas,
in The Public
Interest, 69
Schmitt, Harrison, 42
Scientists' Institute for
Public Information
(SIPI), 224
Sierra Club, 44, 46, 292
Simon, Julian, 30-31, 41
The Ultimate Resource,
30
SIPI. See Scientists'
Institute for Public
Information
SMCRA. See Surface Mining
Control and Re-
clamation Act
Smith, Adam, 37, 44, 240-
241
SNG. See Synthetic natural
gas
Spillovers. See Exter-
nalities
Sporhase V. Nebraska, 113
Social interests. See
Interests
Social value. See values
Soviet Union, 199
State Government, 84-
85, 88, 92, 292-299
Strauss, Simon, 211
Study on Federal
Regulation, 97
Subsidies,
and pricing of federal
resources, 91,
178, 237, 257-259
of timber, 118, 121

Supreme Court, 86, 110,
113. See also
individual cases
Surface Mining Control
and Reclamation Act
(SMCRA), 92, 106, 109,
112, 292
Sustained yield, 87, 92,
122, 160, 173
Synfuels, 34-35
Synthetic Fuels
Corporation, 41, 285
Synthetic natural gas
(SNG), 32

Taxes, 119, 125(n6), 166
Timber, 121-123, 149(table)
contract specifications,
163-164
cost accounting, 143,
164-165
demand for, 137-140,
153(figure), 185
harvest levels, 151
management of 140-148,
151-165, 173-
175, 178-180
prices, 145, 146(table),
147(table), 174-175,
179
product demany theory,
134-136
product supply theory,
136-137, 148
roads, 145, 156-158,
175
sales, 157, 158-163
Tragedy of the commons.
See common property
Treasury, 119, 123-124,
152-155. See also
Federal Government
Tribe, Laurence, 16
Trueblood, Ted,
in Field and Stream, 47
Trust for the Public Lands,
80
Tucker, William, 73
Turnage, William, 47
TWS. See The Wilderness
Society

The Ultimate Resource, 30